WOMEN'S IMPRISONMENT AND THE CASE FOR ABOLITION

In 2007, the Corston Report recommended a far-reaching, radical, 'women-centred' approach to women's imprisonment in England and Wales. It suggested a 'fundamental re-thinking' about how services to support women in conflict with the law are delivered in custody and in the community, recommending the development and implementation of a decarceration strategy. This argued for appropriate treatment programmes in the community, reserving prison for only those women who commit serious and violent offences. Ten years on, what progress has been made? What is the relationship between Corston's vision and a more radical abolitionist agenda?

Drawing on a range of international scholarship, this book contributes to the critical discourse on the penal system, human rights, and social injustice, revealing the consequences of imprisonment on the lives of women and their families. A decade on from Corston's publication, it critically reviews her report, revealing the slow progress in meeting the reforms it proposed. Identifying the significant barriers to change, it questions the failure to reverse the unrelenting growth of the women's prison population or to transform state responses to women's offending. Reflecting the global expansion of women's imprisonment, particularly marked in advanced democratic societies, the chapters include comparative contributions from jurisdictions where Corston's recommendations have relevance. It concludes with a critical appraisal of reformism and the case for penal abolition.

Essential for applied and theory courses on prisons, punishment, and penology; social justice and the criminology of human rights; gender and crime; and feminist criminology.

Linda Moore is Senior Lecturer in Criminology in the School of Applied Social and Policy Sciences at Ulster University, UK.

Phil Scraton is Professor of Criminology in the School of Law, Queen's University Belfast, UK.

Azrini Wahidin is Professor of Criminology and Criminology Justice and Associate Dean for Research and Innovation in the School of Social Sciences, Humanities and Law, Teesside University, UK.

WOMEN'S IMPRISONMENT AND THE CASE FOR ABOLITION

Critical Reflections on Corston Ten Years On

Edited by Linda Moore, Phil Scraton and Azrini Wahidin

Routledge
Taylor & Francis Group

LONDON AND NEW YORK

First published 2018
by Routledge
2 Park Square, Milton Park, Abingdon, Oxon OX14 4RN

and by Routledge
711 Third Avenue, New York, NY 10017

Routledge is an imprint of the Taylor & Francis Group, an informa business

British Library Cataloguing in Publication Data
A catalogue record for this book is available from the British Library

Library of Congress Cataloging in Publication Data
Names: Moore, Linda, 1961– editor. | Scraton, Phil,
editor. | Wahidin, Azrini, 1972– editor.
Title: Women's imprisonment and the case for abolition: critical
reflections on Corston ten years on / edited by Linda Moore,
Phil Scraton and Azrini Wahidin.
Description: Abingdon, Oxon; New York, NY: Routledge, 2018. |
Includes bibliographical references and index.
Identifiers: LCCN 2017036414 | ISBN 9781138700253 (hardback) |
ISBN 9781138700260 (pbk.) | ISBN 9781315204819 (ebook)
Subjects: LCSH: Women prisoners—Government policy—
Great Britain. | Female offenders—Effect of imprisonment on—Great
Britain. | Alternatives to imprisonment—Great Britain. | Criminal
justice, Administration of—Great Britain.
Classification: LCC HV9647 .W665 2018 | DDC 364.6082/0941—dc23
LC record available at https://lccn.loc.gov/2017036414

ISBN: 978-1-138-70025-3 (hbk)
ISBN: 978-1-138-70026-0 (pbk)
ISBN: 978-1-315-20481-9 (ebk)

Typeset in Bembo
by codeMantra

MIX
Paper from
responsible sources
FSC
www.fsc.org
FSC™ C013985

Printed in the United Kingdom
by Henry Ling Limited

CONTENTS

List of Contributors   *vii*

Acknowledgements   *ix*

Introduction   1
Linda Moore, Phil Scraton and Azrini Wahidin

1 The post-Corston women's penal 'crisis' in England and
  Wales: Exploring the failure of reform   10
  Linda Moore and Azrini Wahidin

2 After Corston: Community, change, and challenges   32
  Loraine Gelsthorpe

3 From 'troubled' women to failing institutions: The
  necessary narrative shift for the decarceration of women
  post-Corston   51
  Becky Clarke and Kathryn Chadwick

4 The imprisonment of women in Scotland: Restructure,
  reform or abolish?   71
  Margaret Malloch

5 Post-Corston reflections on remanded women's experiences
  in Northern Ireland   88
  Gillian McNaull

6 Corston principles in Canada: Creating the carceral Other
  and moving beyond women in prison   109
  Vicki Chartrand and Jennifer M. Kilty

7 In pursuit of fundamental change within the Australian
  penal landscape: Taking inspiration from the Corston Report   129
  Julie Stubbs and Eileen Baldry

8 'Ukhohliwe': A South African perspective on the Corston
  Report   150
  Lillian Artz

9 Beyond Corston: The politics of decarceration and
  abolition in a punitive climate   172
  Phil Scraton and Bree Carlton

Index   195

LIST OF CONTRIBUTORS

Linda Moore is Senior Lecturer in Criminology in the School of Applied Social and Policy Sciences at Ulster University, UK.

Phil Scraton is Professor of Criminology in the School of Law at Queen's University Belfast, UK.

Azrini Wahidin is Professor of Criminology and Criminology Justice and Associate Dean for Research and Innovation in the School of Social Sciences, Humanities and Law, Teesside University, UK.

Loraine Gelsthorpe is Professor of Criminology and Criminal Justice at the Institute of Criminology at the University of Cambridge, UK.

Becky Clarke is Senior Lecturer in the Department of Sociology at Manchester Metropolitan University, UK.

Kathryn Chadwick is Principal Lecturer in the Department of Sociology at Manchester Metropolitan University, UK.

Margaret Malloch is a Reader in Criminology with the Scottish Centre for Crime and Justice Research at the University of Stirling, UK.

Gillian McNaull is a Research Fellow and PhD researcher in the School of Law at Queen's University Belfast, UK.

Vicki Chartrand is Associate Professor in the Sociology Department at Bishop's University, Québec, Canada.

Jennifer M. Kilty is Associate Professor in the Department of Criminology, University of Ottawa, Canada.

Julie Stubbs is Professor in the Faculty of Law at the University of New South Wales, Australia.

Eileen Baldry is Professor of Criminology in the School of Social Sciences at the University of New South Wales, Australia.

Lillian Artz is Associate Professor in the Gender, Health & Justice Research Unit at the University of Cape Town, South Africa.

Bree Carlton is Senior Lecturer in Criminology in the School of Social Sciences at Monash University, Australia.

ACKNOWLEDGEMENTS

Linda would like to thank her co-editors Phil and Azrini who are great colleagues and dear friends. Thank you to Thomas Sutton at Routledge for your support for the idea of the book and to Hannah Catterall for support in seeing the project through. Many thanks also to Francesca Monaco and Erin Arata and the team at codeMantra for your expert support and your patience. Thank you also to all of our co-authors. It had been a privilege to work with such wonderful scholars and activists. I hope to work with you all again. The Criminology team at Ulster University are fantastic colleagues – thank you to Jonny Byrne, Una Convery, Michael Davidson, Ruth McAlister, Rachel Monaghan and Brian Payne. I am grateful for continuing support from my previous and current Heads of School, Ruth Fee and Kris Lasslett. Thanks to Olivia Barnes, Deena Haydon, Ann Jemphrey, Agnieszka Martynowicz and Conor Murray for helpful discussions on imprisonment and criminalisation which have furthered my understanding of these processes. Higher education and academic freedom are under threat from marketisation and I pay tribute to my friends at UCU at Ulster University and UCU regional office for defending the public university. Thanks to my family including Tim, Paloma, Conor and Amaia, Sam and Ying Ying, Mal, Helen, Andy and Ada. My parents Alec and Libby Moore have been an amazing support as always. Huge thanks to Henry, Alex and Annie – you mean the world to me.

Phil thanks co-editors, Azrini and Linda – working together challenges the isolation of working alone. Thanks to all the production team whose support always has been prompt and helpful. My first and most important acknowledgement is to all prisoners down the years who have put their trust in those of us who seek to bring their experiences to a wider audience as a challenge to ever-increasingly punitive measures that diminish their lives. In various ways, from the conception of the project through to its realisation, my good friends have been incredibly supportive. Profound thanks to Kathryn Chadwick, Janet Johnstone, Karen Lee, Barry Goldson, Sara Boyce, Edel Quinn, Gillian McNaull, Raju Bhatt, Anne-Marie McAlinden, Bree Carlton, Scott Poynting, Lizzy Stanley, Rebecca Scott-Bray, Eileen Baldry, Tony Platt, Paddy Hillyard, Margaret Ward, Fran Gale, Michael Dudley. To my colleagues in the Department of Sociology, University of Auckland, thank you for hosting a supportive fellowship that supported the development of this collection. Special mention of the remarkable work of INQUEST and its indefatigable Director, Deb Coles. The authors who have contributed to this fine collection were prompt in delivering their chapters, always responsive to our suggestions. It has been a privilege to work with you all. The support of fellow researchers in the European Group for the Study of Deviance and Social Control remains invaluable. Its annual conference continues to be a place where critical scholarship is sustained and flourishes. Finally, to my partner Deena Haydon, to Paul, Katrin and Lotte, to Sean, Ailis and Cillian – your love and support carries me through.

Azrini thanks co-editors, Linda and Phil – who have been great co-authors and good friends. My first acknowledgement goes to the prisoners who have shared their experiences with me over the years and to the book's contributors.

Thanks to Georgios Antonopoulos, Dot Newbury-Birch, Sarah Cardew, Paul Crawshaw, Simon Hodgson, Cindy Hunter, Annabelle James, Dave Morland, Andrea Outen, Jane Turner and Georgios Papanicolaou at Teesside University. My thanks goes to Yvonne Barnett, Michelle Burman, Maureen Cain, Pat Carlen, Malcolm Cowburn, Pam Davies, Loraine Gelsthorpe, Gail Heath, Paddy Hillyard, Helen Jones, Margaret Malloch, Gill McIvor, Norbani Mohamed Nazeri, Judith Phillips, Mary Rogan, Nickolas Rose, Hafizah Selamat, Joe Sim, Alex Sporidou and Shirley Tate, for their intellectual input.

Finally, my thanks goes to Che Mah Wahidin and Wan – Nita Wahidin for their continued support.

INTRODUCTION

Linda Moore, Phil Scraton and Azrini Wahidin

In 2007, Baroness Jean Corston[1] was commissioned by the United Kingdom (UK) government to investigate the treatment of 'vulnerable' women in the criminal justice system in England and Wales. The context for her review was a steep increase in women's imprisonment. More specifically, the review was triggered by the deaths of six women in Styal Prison in Cheshire, England. Within a 12-month period, 2002–2003, Julie Walsh, Nissa Ann Smith, Anna Baker, Sarah Campbell, Jolene Willis and Hayley Williams died soon after entering the prison. Each woman's story reflected her personal struggles and profound sadness. Typical of so many incarcerated women, they had faced a combination of addictions, mental health difficulties, homelessness, bereavement and trauma, together with numerous other debilitating challenges. As had happened in similar circumstances in the 1980s, following several deaths at Cornton Vale women's prison in Scotland, for a brief time, the deaths in Styal, and in other women's prisons, raised public awareness. This included important questions regarding the impact on the women's families and serious concern regarding proportionality and effectiveness in the state's response to offending. Concluding his report on the Styal deaths, the then Prisons and Probation Ombudsman condemned contemporary women's imprisonment as 'disproportionate, ineffective and unkind', stating that 'virtually everyone' agreed with this conclusion, including 'staff, prisoners, relatives, outside interests' (Shaw 2005: 60).

In addition to the profound public concern regarding Styal and the growing awareness of self-harm and suicide in women's prisons, Corston's review was also commissioned in the context of significant national and global expansion of prison populations, particularly the rapid and unprecedented increase in women's imprisonment. From the 1990s, this increase was exponential. In England and Wales, the number of women held in prison peaked at 4,467 in 2005 (Allen and Watson 2017: 5). A growing body of evidence identified significant gender differences in offending, particularly in offences involving the use of violence, which were rare among women. Analysis of offending behaviour showed that women's imprisonment was unconnected to crime rates but was linked to increasingly punitive legislation, tougher policies and harsh sentences. This included the so-called war on drugs; the criminalisation of migration; growing inequality, particularly as a consequence of economic austerity; and cuts in community mental health provision (Sudbury 2005). Building on Pat Carlen's groundbreaking 1983 study of women's imprisonment at Cornton Vale, Scotland, critical and feminist research highlighted women's gendered experiences of the pains of imprisonment.

This body of research revealed that women's 'pathways' into and through the criminal justice system are laid by poverty, mental ill health and experiences of trauma, violence and coercion. Further, it demonstrated the gender-specificity of women's carceral experiences: how women are infantilised, oppressed and debilitated by prison regimes. For many, this included enforced separation from their children; for others, during pregnancy, through childbirth and during the postnatal period. The continuum of violence more generally associated with incarceration impacts women differentially, ranging from gendered verbal abuse, the emotional distress of isolation, oppressive monitoring and surveillance through to unsanctioned − and sanctioned − use of force, including strip-searches and physical restraint (Scraton and McCulloch 2009).

In recognising the devastating consequences of imprisonment for women and their children, institutional gender-specific initiatives have developed internationally, ostensibly in response to campaigns demanding recognition of women's complex needs (Covington and Bloom 2006). The *United Nations Bangkok Rules for the Treatment of Women Prisoners* (2010) provides a universal foundation for gender-specific prison regimes and community-based alternatives to custody. Critics, however, have noted the potential for net widening with support mechanisms woven into existing, punitive criminal justice processes. These critics fear the extension of punishment and surveillance within seemingly progressive community intervention programmes and warn that the involvement of criminal justice agencies and supervision processes threatens the independence of community-based, statutory and voluntary organisations. In this vein, Pat Carlen (2002) had already identified the dangers of 'carceral clawback' through which seemingly positive initiatives become incorporated and neutralised within the penal system. This process encourages those delivering sentences to believe that custody offers a 'rehabilitation' opportunity to women made vulnerable by their circumstances. What is striking, and confirms Carlen's position, is that the increase in women's imprisonment has 'occurred *alongside* the increasing investment in gender-responsive reforms' (Carlton and Segrave 2013: 5).

Against this backdrop, Corston's (2007) review acknowledged that excessive numbers of women are held in custody for non-violent crimes, often as a direct consequence of oppressive relationships with male partners. She recognised that many women prisoners are themselves victims/survivors of circumstance and that poverty, homelessness, abuse, mental illness and addictions underpin their offending. Corston highlighted the damaging impact of imprisonment and the onerous challenges for women (re)settling in communities following release. Consequently, her recommendations focused on decarceration while improving prison conditions for the small number of women whose crimes, in her view, required a custodial sentence. Corston (2007: cover page) advocated a 'distinct, radically different, visibly-led, strategic, proportionate, holistic, woman-centred, integrated approach'. She was clear that only those women who commit violent and serious offences and whose actions constitute a danger to the public should be imprisoned, concluding that jail was 'not the right place for many damaged and disadvantaged women' (Corston 2007: 69). She was critical particularly of the widespread use of strip-searching, recommending that its practice should be reduced significantly. Her report emphasised the importance of meeting women's needs by providing a network of independent women's centres and through statutory-voluntary sector partnerships; bespoke services should be instituted nationally to meet the particular needs of Black and Minority Ethnic (BME) and Foreign National women. Keen to ensure that her review was not simply a paper-exercise, Corston provided a blueprint for implementation, with plans for an independent Commission for women 'who offend or are at risk of offending' to deliver significant reform.

Most of Corston's 43 recommendations were agreed and accepted in principle by the government. A reduction in the use of strip-searching was achieved, bringing a positive response from Corston (HoCJC 2013: 11). However, her crucial recommendation, the dismantling of the existing women's prison estate and the replacement of large institutions by small, locally based centres, was rejected explicitly and without explanation. Five years after her review, witnesses to a parliamentary inquiry agreed that 'despite initial "flurries of activity"', progress on her other recommendations 'appeared to have stalled' (HoCJC 2013: 13). In practice, there has been minimal implementation of her initially welcomed recommendations (WIP 2017).

Ultimately, there has been no transformation in women's imprisonment in England and Wales. A decade after the review, the number of women receiving prison sentences has reduced only slightly, and they continue to be remanded routinely into custody. Prison deaths are higher than at the time the review was published. Many independent women's centres, the spine of Corston's strategy, have closed due to financial cutbacks, their work, which delivers essential services, threatened by competition from the private sector. The election of successive Conservative-Liberal and then Conservative governments had a negative impact on the political will to address women's imprisonment, with increased emphasis on making 'value for money' punishment more 'effective'.

Limited progress post-Corston has led campaigners to 'ask ourselves to what extent there has been fundamental systems change for women affected by the criminal justice system and what major barriers still impede its implementation?' (WIP 2017: 3). Women in Prison[2] (2017: 3) conclude,

> In order to achieve true systems change for women affected by the criminal justice system, it is vital for policy makers to recognise that criminal justice solutions alone are not sufficient to deal with offending [...] What is required is a joined-up approach that takes into account the root causes of women's offending. This approach must encompass an understanding of the compelling opportunities for change that appropriate housing, mental health support and gender-specific women's community support services can offer.

Similarly, Annison et al. (2015: 249) argue for an approach that 'opens the door to exploring what women's needs are and what might "work" in a holistic way to ameliorate problems and thus help reduce women's offending'.

The commitment underpinning this book derives from a quite different perspective. It is argued that rather than focusing on women's offending, the starting point should be challenging the criminalisation of women and the material circumstances in which it occurs. Based on their primary research in Scotland, Margaret Malloch and Gill McIvor (2013: 7) state that 'criminalised women are usually disadvantaged and victimised women who have been let down by the state, with increased penalisation of the welfare state having had a particular and pronounced impact on women'. Therefore, viewing experiences of poverty, disadvantage, mental ill health and gendered harm as 'pathways' to offending holds women responsible as individuals for situations derived in structural inequalities. This further compounds the injustices of marginalisation through the infliction of criminalisation. More appropriately, as Carlen (2013: xv) proposes, 'the critical penal gaze might be reinvigorated by turning towards the spheres of economics, politics and more radical conceptions of social justice'.

This collection is intended as an antidote to the liberal reformist agenda. It roots the criminalisation and subsequent incarceration of women within the context of economic, political and social determinants in a range of jurisdictions. It is argued that through her focus on individual women and the circumstances surrounding their offences, Corston reinforced the responsibilisation of marginalised women, deflecting attention from the need to challenge broader social and economic injustice. The following chapters offer a critical understanding of the impact of imprisonment on the lives of women, their families and their communities. They explore the significant disjuncture between penal policy and practice, examining policy intentions and the realities of implementation.

It is argued that the gender-specific reform of women's incarceration has failed because in form, content and delivery, it cannot succeed. Commitment to penal reform dates back to Elizabeth Fry's nineteenth-century endeavours to create regimes appropriate for women's rehabilitation. Ultimately, prisons are punitive, oppressive institutions; however, they are reformulated and whatever dubious claims are made in their defence. Like its predecessors, the twenty-first-century prison 'grinds down the poor and the powerless' (Carlen 2013: xiv), while the criminal justice system rarely operates to police and prosecute corporate or state crime. Amid the despair produced by the global penal crisis, however, there are positive developments. In England, a strong campaign has developed to reclaim the site of the now-closed Holloway Prison for affordable social housing and services rather than for private development. In May 2017, Sisters Uncut occupied the site, aiming to 'translate the victimisation of women into an expression of political power, giving political agency back to women and non-binary people' (Archer 2017). It would be an appropriate and powerful legacy on a site of desolation and so much suffering.

The chapters

The collection brings together authors who have researched women's punishment and imprisonment in depth, providing a critical assessment of the post-Corston penal landscape. It focuses on UK jurisdictions, with chapters on England and Wales, Scotland and Northern Ireland, alongside a strong international dimension, reviewing states in which gender-specific responses have been, or are being, considered. They include contributions from Canada, Australia and South Africa. Together, the chapters provide evidence of the continued harm caused by the violence of incarceration, including self-harm and deaths in custody as well as institutionally harmful processes, particularly the use of strip-searches, isolation cells, physical restraint and the inadequate provision of gender-specific services within male-focused systems. These chapters have been written at a time of austerity when significantly less expensive but more effective community 'alternatives' have been rejected in favour of imprisonment. Despite some notable strengths and positive intentions, Corston's reproduction of administrative criminological frames of reference, through the discourse of 'criminogenic needs' and 'pathways to offending', was a fundamental weakness. The authors explore the limitations of reformism, arguing for narratives and practices informed by decarceration and abolitionism inspired by movements for social justice and equality.

The first three chapters focus primarily on the situation in England and Wales. In Chapter 1, Linda Moore and Azrini Wahidin open the discussion with an analysis of the impact of Corston on women's imprisonment in England and Wales. As noted above, Corston's review was commissioned due to concerns about women's deaths in custody. Yet, a decade later, deaths in custody reached a record high. Moore and Wahidin outline Corston's findings and recommendations, and review their implementation or lack of implementation under successive governments: (New) Labour, the Conservative-Liberal Democrat Coalition and the current Conservative Government. They identify the shift away from Corston's ideals towards a more punitive approach that responsibilises individuals for their offending within a climate of privatisation and 'payment-by-results'. Reflecting on the recurrent nature of penal 'crises' in the face of persistent attempts at reform, the authors support Carlen's (2002) thesis of 'carceral clawback', within which the prison system has adopted the mantle of gender-specificity in policymaking without meaningful change in regimes for women prisoners. Moore and Wahidin argue that despite the obvious merits of her review, Corston accepted a narrative that portrays inequality and injustice as 'pathways to offending', thus requiring individual women to change their behaviour. Alternatively, Moore and Wahidin propose a social justice approach, breaking down unequal, discriminatory social structures. This necessitates the abolition of a damaging and destructive penal system that fails to address social harm and increasingly marginalises and damages those that it processes.

In Chapter 2, Loraine Gelsthorpe explores post-Corston developments regarding community sentencing in England and Wales, focusing on the establishment and functioning of community centres for women. She analyses the landscape of provision for women in the community following the Offender Rehabilitation Act 2014, examining the relationship between community rehabilitation companies and centres for women. She raises concerns that Corston's positive impact on community-based independent services for women is now threatened by the rehabilitation revolution, with the effectiveness of contracted-out supervision based on payment-by-results. She questions whether real progress has been achieved in advancing the treatment of women in conflict with the law. Finally, Gelsthorpe recommends that budgets should be ring-fenced to enable the National Probation Service to commission appropriate services for women.

In Chapter 3, Rebecca Clarke and Kathryn Chadwick focus on the criminalisation of women, critiquing narratives that prioritise individual choice and responsibilisation. While acknowledging the strengths and positive intentions within Corston, the authors argue that her liberal penal reform agenda fails to engage with the class-based, racialised and gendered structural realities for criminalised women. They urge a shift in emphasis from individualising women's 'offending behaviour' to establishing interventions that tackle structural injustice and inequality. They conclude that it is essential to develop a radical agenda derived in fresh narratives, including advancing the case for penal abolition.

The use of imprisonment and noncustodial alternatives for women in Scotland has remained a priority throughout the decade since the publication of the Corston Report. In Chapter 4, Margaret Malloch maps this progress. Events in Scotland have been influenced significantly by the Commission on Women Offenders, whose final report was published in 2012. The Commission recommended the closure of Scotland's women's prison, HMP and YOI Cornton Vale. It also focused considerable attention on the structural organisation of the prison system and its impact on women, committing to new forms of custody and a more effective use of 'punishment in the community'. However, the 'fragmented landscape' of community provisions remains a focus of concern for penal reformers, and, as this chapter argues, the potential for radical change in Scotland – as in England and Wales – requires a more comprehensive critical analysis of 'justice' for women.

The strength of the articles published in this collection is their derivation in empirical research. Based on primary empirical research with women prisoners in Northern Ireland, a society in transition from thirty years of civil war, following which much of recent research has focused on politically affiliated prisoners, in Chapter 5, Gillian McNaull explores the 'liminal space' (Baldry 2010) occupied by women remanded to custody. This includes reflections on their experiences prior to and during their incarceration. Despite recommendations that imprisonment should be limited to the few women who pose a demonstrable risk to the public (Corston 2007), women 'at the margins' – as a consequence of 'race', poverty, mental ill health and multiple vulnerabilities – continue to experience custodial remand regardless of the severity of their crimes. A significant proportion of remanded women serving time in prison are found 'not guilty' or do not receive a custodial sentence, yet the impact of prison on their lives is often overlooked. In this chapter, McNaull considers the impact and implications of remand on these women's lives.

Corston heralded an international revival of women-specific correctional reform agendas throughout many Anglophone jurisdictions. In Canada, there has been recognition that the most significant theme arising from Corston is the need for integrated, holistic and gender-sensitive responses to criminalised women. As in Britain, numerous reports document the problems and abuses of women's imprisonment, each of which advocates systemic change. Yet 25 years after the groundbreaking Creating Choices report calling for women-centred corrections in Canada, more women than ever are behind bars, with women's imprisonment increasing four times faster than the rate for men. In Chapter 6, Vicki Chartrand and Jennifer Kilty reflect on the history of women's imprisonment in Canada, tracing the key shifts in discourse and policy. They analyse therapeutic initiatives in Canadian federal prisons, particularly individualised responses that fail to address structural disadvantage. As they observe, when therapeutic responses fail, self-harming and suicidal women prisoners are subjected to disciplinary segregation, causing significant further physical and psychological damage. As in other jurisdictions, women in Canadian prisons are exposed to the violence of incarceration through strip-searching, the use of force, isolation and even transfer to male prisons. In this context, the authors emphasise the criminalisation and punishment of indigenous women. In conclusion, they argue that abolitionist perspectives offer significant alternative possibilities, challenging the idea that disadvantaged women are in need of regulation or containment.

In Australian states and territories, the Corston Report generated renewed pressure by advocates, anti-discrimination campaigners and correctional officials to transform women's prison facilities, regimes and programmes, to prioritise the needs of women prisoners and to address structural issues leading to their criminalisation. The criminalisation and incarceration of Aboriginal and Torres Islander women continues to raise particular concerns regarding institutionalised racism. Focusing comparatively on criminal justice in Victoria and New South Wales, and women-specific policies and programmes introduced since 2005, in Chapter 7, Eileen Baldry and Julie Stubbs consider contrasting initiatives to reduce criminalisation. This chapter analyses the transformative value of penal reforms targeting gender discrimination and the provision of effective alternatives to deliver justice for criminalised women.

In Chapter 8, Lillian Artz considers the relevance of Corston to the incarceration of women in South Africa. Her practice-based research provides a rare insight into the cultural specificities that contextualise women's criminalisation and punishment. This includes prosecutions and sentences for 'offences' derived in gendered determining contexts of sexual morality, including sex outside of marriage, same-sex relationships and the procurement of abortions. Conditions for imprisoned women in South Africa are dire. As more women suffering structural, gendered inequality and poverty are sentenced for longer periods, jails have become severely overcrowded with harsh, unsafe regimes, resulting in high mortality rates. Despite this, in the context of high levels of abuse and violence experienced by most women prisoners prior to their incarceration, Artz notes that for some women, prison offers a place of relative safety. Noting that the transformation envisioned by Corston would be difficult to achieve in South Africa, she argues for more pragmatic and less ambitious women-sensitive penal reform based on the women's lived realities.

In the final chapter, Phil Scraton and Bree Carlton present the case for decarceration in the short term as a precursor to the eventual abolition of prisons. Noting the inexorable rise of women's imprisonment in many advanced capitalist societies within a relentlessly punitive political and ideological climate, the chapter revisits recent carceral history. It considers the theoretical imperatives that inform penology and exposes the deficits of penal reformism. Drawing on the emergence and consolidation of the United States as the exemplar of harsh punishment and ever-expanding incarceration, particularly targeting those that live at the political and economic margins, the chapter considers the full impact of penal incapacitation. It demonstrates the broader significance of harsh and discriminatory punishment in a brief excursion into the institutionalised racism within Australian prisons. Finally, it notes that prison abolition has a long tradition that, in its contemporary manifestation, offers realistic alternatives to the painful, damaging violence of incarceration. Ending the prison industrial complex and the pipeline from marginalised communities to jail, however, requires a profound and lasting shift in the structural, material inequalities that blight the lives of so many; a shift that runs through all political and economic institutions, delivered through necessary investment in housing, neighbourhood, community, schooling, health, welfare and social support.

Notes

1 Baroness Jean Corston is a Labour Party peer in the United Kingdom, House of Lords.
2 Women in Prison is a London-based non-governmental organisation which campaigns for a 'recognition and response to the distinct needs of women affected by the criminal justice system' (WIP n.d.).

References

Allen, G. and Watson, C. (2017) *UK Prison Population Statistics*, London: MOJ.

Annison, J., Brayford, J. and Deering, J. (2015) 'Conclusions', in J. Annison, J. Brayford and J. Deering, *Women and Criminal Justice: From the Corston Report to Transforming Rehabilitation*', Bristol: Policy Press.

Archer, N. (2017) 'We at Sisters Uncut have occupied Holloway prison. Why? Domestic violence', *The Guardian* 1 June 2017. At: www.theguardian.com/commentisfree/2017/jun/01/domestic-violence-services-occupying-holloway-prison-sisters-uncut-cuts-women. Accessed 4 June 2017.

Baldry, E. (2010) 'Women in Transition: From Prison to…' *Current Issues in Criminal Justice* 22(2) 253–267.

Carlen, P. (1983) *Women's Imprisonment: A Study in Social Control*, London: Routledge.

Carlen, P. (2002) *Women and Punishment: The Struggle for Justice*, London and New York: Routledge.

Carlen, P. (2013) 'Preface', B. Carlton and M. Segrave eds., *Women Exiting Prison: Critical Essays on Gender, Post-release Support and Survival*, London: Routledge, pp. xiii–xv.

Carlton, B. and Segrave, M., eds. (2013) *Women Exiting Prison: Critical Essays on Gender, Post-release Support and Survival*, London: Routledge.

Corston, J. (2007) *The Corston Report: A Review of Women with Particular Vulnerabilities in the Criminal Justice System*, London: Home Office.

Covington, S. and Bloom, B. (2006) *Gender-Responsive Treatment and Services in Correctional Settings*. At: http://stephaniecovington.com/assets/files/FINALC.pdf. Accessed 24 August 2017.

House of Commons Justice Committee (2013) *Women Offenders: After the Corston Report, Second Report of Session 2013–14*, London: Stationery Office.

Malloch, M. and McIvor, G. (eds.) (2013) *Women, Punishment and Social Justice: Human Rights and Penal Practices*, London: Routledge.

Scraton, P. and McCulloch, J. (2009) *The Violence of Incarceration*, London: Routledge.

Shaw, S. (2005) *The Death in Custody of a Woman and the Series of Deaths in HMP/YOI Styal August 2002 – August 2003*, London: Home Office.

Sudbury, J. (2005) *Global Lockdown: Race, Gender and the Prison-Industrial Complex*, New York, London: Routledge.

United Nations (2010) *United Nations Rules for the Treatment of Women Prisoners and Non-custodial Measures for Women Offenders* (Bangkok Rules). At: www.un.org/en/ecosoc/docs/2010/res%202010-16.pdf. Accessed 20 August 2017.

Women in Prison (2017) *Corston+10: The Corston Report 10 Years On*, London: WIP.

Women in Prison (n.d.) 'What we do'. At: www.womeninprison.org.uk/about/what-we-do.php. Accessed 24 August 2017.

1

THE POST-CORSTON WOMEN'S PENAL 'CRISIS' IN ENGLAND AND WALES

Exploring the failure of reform

Linda Moore and Azrini Wahidin

Introduction

> I want to ensure that fewer women die in custody.
>
> *(Corston 2007: 15)*

> The number of suicides, assaults and cases of self-harm in prisons in England and Wales has reached record levels. Figures from the Ministry of Justice show 119 prisoners killed themselves in 2016, 29 more than the previous year. The number of incidents of self-harm reached almost 38,000. Frances Crook of the Howard League for Penal Reform says it's a national scandal … The Justice Secretary Liz Truss stressed that the government was taking action to tackle the problem.
>
> *(BBC Radio 4 News Bulletin 26 January 2017)*

In her 2007 review of 'vulnerable' women in the criminal justice system in England and Wales (E&W), Baroness Jean Corston[1] expressed hope that the 'radical changes' she proposed would result in a reduction in women's suffering, self-harm and deaths in custody. The review was commissioned by the (then) Labour Government in the context of an explosive rise in women's incarceration at the close of the twentieth century and the deaths of six women between August 2002 and August 2003 in Her Majesty's Prison (HMP) Styal in Cheshire, England. The deaths by hanging of Nissa Ann Smith, Anna Baker, Jolene Willis and Hayley Williams and the deaths by substance overdose of Julie Walsh and Sarah Campbell (INQUEST 2005) were considered the nadir of a system in 'crisis', providing tragic evidence of the need for an alternative response to women with mental health difficulties and addictions. Individual inquests into the deaths delivered highly critical verdicts. An investigation by the Prison's Ombudsman (2005: viii) found 'serious inadequacies' in 'regimes, facilities and procedures' at Styal. Within this context, Corston was tasked with reviewing the treatment of 'vulnerable' women within the criminal justice system.

Based on observations and consultations with women prisoners and prison staff, the scenario depicted by Corston was grim. The women she encountered were mothers, pregnant, in poor physical health, mentally ill and addicted to drugs and alcohol. They had histories of poverty, abuse, trauma, self-harm and su-icide attempts and included an over-representation of Black and Minority Ethnic (BME) and Foreign National women. Many women's prisons were overcrowded, unhygienic, vermin-infested and lacking in privacy and decency, with minimal access to fresh air or healthy food. There were 'toilets, often without lids, in cells and dormitories, sometimes screened by just a curtain, sometimes not screened at all' (Corston 2007: 4). Corston (2007: 4) considered it 'humiliating for women to have to use these facilities in the presence of others, most particularly during menstruation'. Enduring the degrading practice of strip-searching and 'cramped' circumstances with 'limited autonomy' and 'often, no other person to talk to', women were 'distressed and sometimes frightened of spending long hours locked alone into single cells' (p. 26). While noting the commitment shown by many staff and managers, Corston portrayed a system that was fundamentally unsafe and disrespectful, further undermined by inadequate services to meet a tangible high level of need. Yet she was optimistic that the time was right to 'adopt a new approach to women in the criminal justice system' (p. 13). Accordingly, her 43 recommendations were aimed at achieving decarceration by providing commu-nity 'alternatives' coupled with gender-specific prison reform. Most, but signifi-cantly not all, of her recommendations were accepted by the government (MOJ 2007), and her vision was widely welcomed as being 'thoughtful and realistic' and a 'blueprint for reform' (House of Commons Justice Committee 2013a: 9).

Corston influenced official policies in United Kingdom (UK) jurisdictions (e.g. DOJ (NI) 2010) and beyond (e.g., Joint Probation Service – Irish Prison Service Strategy 2014). Ten years later, however, her optimism seems misplaced. The 'crisis' in the prison system (male and female) remains firmly entrenched, with persistently high population figures, overcrowding, poor conditions, staff-ing problems, lengthy lockups and unsafe and non-rehabilitative regimes (PRT 2016). Prison deaths (male and female) reached a tragic high in 2016, including the deaths of 22 women, at least 12 of which were self-inflicted (three await classification in March 2017) (INQUEST website). Moreover, the deaths in 2015 and 2016 of Vicky Thompson, Joanne Latham and Jenny Swift highlighted the degrading and dangerous practice of placing transgender women in male prisons.

In this chapter, we analyse the impact of Corston, asking why her strong review failed to ignite a transformation of women's imprisonment in E&W. The chapter opens with a reference to the prison's historical role in regulating and punishing women and the episodic attempts to reform women's penal regimes from the nineteenth century onwards. The late twentieth-century influence of feminist and critical criminology is acknowledged in highlighting women's experiences of imprisonment and generating arguments for gender-specific reform. Corston's vision and official responses to her recommendations are explored, identifying the perspectives adopted by successive Labour, Coalition and Conservative UK governments. The authors then consider the post-Corston, continued 'crisis' in imprisonment, touching on how intersectionalities shape women's experiences. Given this evidence, it is argued that Corston failed to acknowledge that 'crises' are not exceptional but inherent within the political and material conditions of penal punishment. Further, she underestimated the potential within the system to 'claw back' and subvert positive reforms (Carlen 2002). In conclusion, we propose that the failure of Corston's programme for reform suggests the need to develop and progress abolitionist strategies.

Contextualising women's imprisonment

Playing the key role in the punishment and containment of women, the prison system has historically experienced recurrent states of 'crises' and attempts to reform. Prior to the development of the modern prison system, houses of correction and bridewells were used to detain women for behaviours associated with immorality, such as prostitution or adultery. John Howard's damning reports on eighteenth-century jail conditions included concerns that mixed-sex environments encouraged depravity. His work inspired the development of a model prison at Gloucester with separate sections for men and women (McConville 2015). The nineteenth-century reformer Elizabeth Fry campaigned for separate facilities where women would be supervised by female wardens and treated with 'gentleness and sympathy so that they would submit cheerfully to the rules and cooperate willingly in their own reform' (cited in Zedner 1998: 301). By the end of the nineteenth century, separate female institutions began to emerge in the UK, Canada, the United States of America (USA) and Australia. Progress, however, was inconsistent, with women often confined in units within larger male institutions. The reformatory movement, particularly prominent in the USA, aimed to provide 'softer' regimes for women, but in practice, surveillance in reformatories was 'much more intense than that experienced by male prisoners housed in larger and far more anonymous cellblocks' (Dodge 2017: 101). Reflecting institutional racism, reformatories were reserved primarily for white women, while Black women continued to be held in harsher prison environments (Rafter 1985).

A persistent theme has been the formal and informal categorisation of deviant women as 'bad' or 'mad' (Edwards 1986). The development of nineteenth-century psychiatry increased the emphasis on medicalisation, as illustrated by the creation of a separate section for those classified as 'criminal lunatics' in London's Bethlem Hospital and by the opening of Broadmoor Criminal Lunatic Asylum. In 1907, Aylesbury Convict Prison for Women became the first in the UK to segregate 'feeble-minded' prisoners (Zedner 1998: 320). The predominant view throughout the twentieth century was of the 'fundamental pathology of female prisoners' (Carlen 1998: 16), clearly illustrated by the history of Holloway Prison. Built in 1852 as a mixed-sex prison, in 1903, Holloway became England's first officially designated women's prison, soon notorious for the detention and force-feeding of suffragettes and as a site of execution until the 1950s. The belief that most women were potential mental health patients led to the decision in 1968 to redevelop Holloway as a secure hospital based upon therapeutic principles (Carlen 1998). However, by the completion of rebuilding in 1984, political ideology had shifted in a more punitive direction towards 'retribution, incapacitation, and the management of risk' (Garland 2001: 8). Operationally, Holloway reflected this approach (Rock 1996), an inspection finding overcrowded, filthy conditions and high levels of mental ill health, self-harm and violence (Home Office 1985 cited in Scott and Codd 2010). In 1995, inspectors walked out in protest about conditions (Ramsbotham 2005).

A central feature of the women's prison 'crisis' has been population growth, yet women's incarceration remained relatively stable for much of the twentieth century. During the 1960s, women averaged just 2.5 per cent of the total prison population in E&W, leading the Home Office (1970, cited in Carlen 1983: 23) to predict that by the end of the century, 'penological progress' might mean 'ever fewer or no women at all being given prison sentences'. Such optimism was misplaced, and the population of women in prison doubled between 1995 and 2010, from under 2,000 to over 4,000 (PRT 2017). In 2015, over 700,000 women were imprisoned globally, the population rise having affected all five continents, with particularly high increases in Central and South America, and Southeast Asia (Walmsley 2015). Yet evidence suggests that the rise in women's imprisonment has not been driven by any corresponding rise in offending (McIvor and Burman 2011). Rather, within the context of neoliberalism and neocolonialism, the 'poorest, most marginalised, least powerful and most vulnerable people' are disproportionately imprisoned within societies riven by discrimination (Scraton and McCulloch 2009: 15). Sudbury (2010: 12) identifies four contributory factors: a 'war on the poor', including criminalisation of 'women's survival strategies'; criminalisation of addictions through the 'war on drugs'; criminalisation of migration; and consolidation of the prison industrial complex as a profit-making enterprise. Law (2009: 165) likewise attributes the increase to punitive drug laws and welfare policies, which combine 'to push poor women, particularly women of color, closer to prison'.

Awareness has grown of women's gendered needs and experiences and different routes into the criminal justice system (HMCIP 1997). Research on what have been termed 'pathways into criminality' indicates that women's offending is overwhelmingly non-violent, most often occurring within contexts of abuse and poverty (Bloom et al. 2003). Women are more likely than men to be first-time defendants in court, to have mitigating factors for their offending and to receive short sentences. They are also more likely to be on welfare benefits and in poor mental health and to have self-harmed, attempted suicide, lived in the care system, experienced violence and abuse in the home, and to have offended due to coercive relationships (MOJ 2016a). Thus, women find themselves 'trapped in a vicious cycle of victimisation and criminal activity', a situation 'worsened by poverty, substance dependency or poor mental health' (PRT 2017: 3). BME women are more likely to experience social exclusion and mental ill health and to have stigmatising, discriminatory encounters with the criminal justice system; they are over-represented in custody (Chigwada-Bailey 2003).

Research has also highlighted the gendered nature of women's prison experiences (Carlen 1983, 2002; Wahidin 2004; Moore and Scraton 2014; Crewe et al. 2017). Carlen's (1983) seminal research on Scotland's only women's prison, HMP Cornton Vale, broke new ground in revealing women's experiences of stigma in the context of repressive, infantalising regimes. Subsequent research confirms that women's needs in prison are distinctive, as are their carceral experiences. As a relatively small prison population, there are fewer female prisons, with many women incarcerated long distances from home. Women tend to have more restricted access to services than men, including education, training, 'rehabilitative' programmes, leisure and healthcare (Moore and Scraton 2014). Security processes are gendered, with strip-searching experienced as distressing and degrading, especially during menstruation (McCulloch and George 2009; Moore and Scraton 2014). Pregnancy and motherhood cause particular pains of imprisonment. Pregnant women and new mothers experience significant anxiety, fearing separation from their babies if space in a Mother and Baby unit is not available or placement is considered inappropriate (Abbott 2015). More than two-thirds of women in prison are mothers of children under 18 years of age. Often separation from children is experienced as 'physical, deep pain', accompanied by a strong sense of guilt, with women feeling they have failed both through their offending and as mothers (Baldwin 2015: 161).

Clearly, women in prison have specific needs regarding reproductive health, menstruation, ante- and postnatal care and menopause. Their 'overwhelming experience' is that 'their health needs are not consistently dealt with in a respectful and appropriate way' (Carlen and Worrall 2004: 61). Being pregnant in prison is 'by definition stressful and something which may exacerbate pre-existing mental health issues' (Abbott 2015: 189). The shackling of pregnant women during labour provoked a media and public outcry in E&W and the USA, leading to anti-shackling bills in several American states (Law 2015). In general, prisons neither identify nor respond to the needs of older prisoners (HMIP 2004). Older women regularly fail to receive adequate healthcare, inadequacies including denial of access to nutritional supplements, appropriate physical examinations, vision screenings and mammograms (Wahidin 2004). Older women may be discouraged from seeking vital medical services, for example, by having to climb stairs to reach facilities or being labelled as 'hypochondriacs' for requesting treatment (Wahidin 2004).

Hawton et al. (2014) note that women's self-harm in E&W's prisons is 10 times higher than that for men, with 20–24 per cent of women and girls self-harming each year and suicides 20 times higher than for women in wider society. Despite the appointment of suicide prevention coordinators and the development of strategies, deaths remain a 'permanent and enduring feature of prison life', with lengthy lockups, separation from family, bullying, inadequate healthcare, insufficient staff training and poor communications each contributing to women's deaths (INQUEST 2013: para 10). The situation is exacerbated for Foreign National women who are 'more likely to feel isolated in custody, less likely to seek help and face additional language and cultural barriers' to accessing support (Smee and Moosa 2010: 6).

Following release, prison-associated trauma is a persistent barrier to resettlement as women ex-prisoners experience isolation, boredom and disappointment (Carlton and Segrave 2011). With their needs unmet, they are 'highly vulnerable to the "revolving door syndrome" of relapse, crime and imprisonment' (Plugge et al. 2006: 62). Women who have become institutionalised into prison routines often experience difficulties adapting, even to mundane tasks (Eaton 1993).

In response to spiralling rates of imprisonment and compelling evidence of the harms of incarceration, gender-specific initiatives have developed across jurisdictions (Malloch and McIvor 2013). These are founded on the premise that interventions should take into account the specific context of women's lives and be 'more informal, less structured and supportive of needs other than offending behaviour' (Barry and McIvor 2008: 6). Reflecting these principles, in 2010, the *United Nations Rules for the Treatment of Women Prisoners and Non-custodial Measures for Women Offenders* (Bangkok Rules) established international standards consistent with the provision of gender-sensitive treatment in custody, alongside a commitment by states to provide effective alternatives to imprisonment. Building on this recently developed body of research, Corston's (2007) findings and recommendations aimed to transform policies and practices contextualising women's incarceration, seeking alternatives while responding to the identifiable needs of those sentenced.

While there is considerable consensus regarding the positive potential for gender-specific reform, scholars and campaigners have expressed concerns. Player (2013: 2) queries the possibility of progressing a rights-based approach within a system 'dominated by the management of risk' and the 'concept of less eligibility'. Although intentionally positive, community 'alternatives' do not necessarily alter sentencing practices and have resulted in 'net-widening' (Hedderman 2012: 4) in practice, often reinforcing discipline and punishment (Pollack 2008). Moreover, such 'alternatives' use the 'explicit threat of incarceration' as punishment for non-compliance (Carlen 2002: 115). Carlen (2002) warns that official discourse often appropriates and neutralises critique, convincing sentencers and reformers to have faith in the rehabilitative potential of imprisonment. Thus, well-intentioned, gender-specific reform may in practice represent a flawed attempt to reinvent the punitive core of the prison (Hannah-Moffat 2001).

Corston's vision: decarceration and penal reform

> There are some crimes for which custody is the only resort in the interests of justice and public protection, but I was dismayed to see so many women frequently sentenced for short periods of time for very minor offences, causing chaos and disruption to their lives and families, without any realistic chance of addressing the causes of their criminality.
>
> *(Corston 2007: i)*

Corston recognised that women's incarceration is often 'disproportionate and inappropriate', particularly given the relatively minor, non-violent nature of their offences and their perilous vulnerability. Consequently, she proposed 'a radical new approach, treating women both holistically and individually – a women-centred approach' requiring a 'fundamental re-thinking' about custodial and community services (p. 2). Advocating a twin-track approach, she proposed significant decarceration, coupled with prison reform. Referring to a 'shocking level of need' (p. 16), she noted that most women prisoners are socially and economically marginalised, have high levels of mental illness, addictions and prior experiences of abuse, violence and trauma. Thus, frequently they are 'victims as well as offenders' (p. 3), 'more "troubled" than "troublesome"' (p. 16).

Corston resisted the narrow focus of the Review's Terms of Reference on 'particularly vulnerable' women whose 'risk factors could lead them to harm themselves in prison' (p. 90), focusing on 'all those women whom I consider to be inappropriately located in prison' (p. 15). She recognised that imprisonment exacerbates women's existing problems, causing separation from children, loss of accommodation, shame and worsening mental ill health. She considered that custodial remands and short sentences do particular harm, disrupting lives yet providing little rehabilitation. The prison system, she stated, was designed for a male population and thus consistently neglects women's needs. The relatively small population of women prisoners were generally held further away from home. Service provision, specifically healthcare, education, training, employment and leisure, was frequently inferior to that in men's prisons. Regimes were developed with male prisoners in mind, thus exposing women to inappropriate levels of security, including routine strip-searching. Echoing Sykes (1958), Corston (p. 23) stated that men's imprisonment means 'an interruption in their lives, a loss of freedom and of personal autonomy, deprivation of goods, services and heterosexual relationships', whereas prison separates women from their children, sometimes permanently. She noted that Those constituting 'minorities within a minority', including BME, Foreign National, lesbian and transgender women, faced higher levels of criminalisation and less access to appropriate services, necessitating 'additional support and interventions' based on 'individual needs' (p. 27).

Corston (p. 21) concluded that 'tweaking' the system would not resolve its institutionalised deficiencies. Rather, wholesale change was required. Accordingly, she made 43 recommendations. Encouraging decarceration, she recommended: that custodial sentences be restricted to 'serious and violent offenders who pose a threat to the public'; that community sentences for non-violent offences 'should be the norm'; custodial remand only when there was a likelihood of a custodial sentence; and prioritising the needs of dependent children when deciding on remand (p. 9). For women with serious mental health difficulties, 'prison is not the right place': they need 'help and caring, therapeutic environments to assist them rebuild their lives' (p. 34). Self-harming women who had committed more serious offences should be cared for 'either in an NHS resource or shared multi-disciplinary care in prison' (p. 76). To enhance accountability, Corston endorsed a call from INQUEST[2] for public funding for bereaved families to be adequately represented at inquests. Core to her strategy was a network of 'one-stop-shop' women's centres to deliver 'wrap-around', holistic services, including services appropriate for minority-group women. By diverting women from criminal justice processes, these would deliver a 'real alternative to prison' (although curiously, this chapter of Corston's report is entitled: 'Prison without Walls' (p. 10)).

Despite her concerns regarding its harms, Corston argued that imprisonment is appropriate for certain offences to protect the public and facilitate justice. Reminiscent of Elizabeth Fry's nineteenth-century campaign, Corston sought 'clean and hygienic' institutions. Most strip-searching was considered unnecessary: 'humiliating, degrading and undignified and a dreadful invasion of privacy' (p. 5). Thus, its use should be reduced to the absolute minimum. Corston sought a 'clear strategy to replace existing women's prisons with suitable, geographically dispersed, small, multi-functional cstodial centres within 10 years' (p. 5). In due course, such units, each holding 20–30 women, 'should be removed from the Prison Service and run by specialists in working with women, under the direction of the Commission for Women who offend or are at risk of offending' (p. 86). The suggestion that the units would '(over time) replace prisons' (p. 79) was the closest Corston came to advocating abolitionism.

Corston was optimistic that government and criminal justice practitioners were enthusiastic for change. She argued that the 'aspirational' would become reality (p. ii), aided by 'reasoned' and 'enlightened' public debate (p. 11). To achieve this, every criminal justice agency must 'prioritise and accelerate preparations to implement the gender equality duty and radically transform the way they deliver services for women' (p. 25). To accomplish change, she recommended the establishment of a cross-departmental 'commission for women who offend or are at risk of offending' (p. 81). Significantly, she did not propose improvements only for women, stating that her recommendations should be piloted for other groups as well, specifically young men (p. 69).

Implementing Corston: political responses

Corston (2007) was significant in giving formal status to campaigns for reform of women's imprisonment. Responding to the importance of her analysis, the

House of Commons Justice Committee (HOCJC 2013a: 10) stated that there was 'general agreement that the majority of women offenders pose little risk to public safety', that imprisonment is 'frequently an ineffective response' and it is 'not permissible for women offenders to be dealt with in the same way as men'. Despite this early influence, however, the Committee noted that subsequent reforms do not meet the expectations of Corston's vision, raising profound concerns that an opportunity has been lost, and positive developments 'may not be sustainable' (p. 14). Since Corston, successive governments, including [New] Labour (1997–2010), Coalition (Conservative-Liberal Democrat) (2010–2015) and Conservative (in office at the time of writing), have adopted distinctive criminal justice policies. Yet all presume that imprisonment has a positive role to play in the delivery of justice.[3] Further, justice policy remains delivered within a context of financial cutbacks to public and community services.

Prior to commissioning Corston, the 'New' Labour Government, elected in 1997, had already taken initiatives on women and criminal justice. Notably, this included the 2004 Women's Offending Reduction Programme, a cross-departmental strategy aimed at providing community support for women 'at risk of offending' and reducing the women's prison population. Having commissioned Corston in December 2007, the Labour Government accepted 40 of her recommendations fully or partially, committing to a 'more sophisticated, intelligent, visibly led and better co-ordinated approach to address the issues for women' (MOJ 2007: 5). Government Minister Maria Eagle was appointed Champion for Women in the Criminal Justice System, and a Criminal Justice Women's Strategy Group was established within the Ministry of Justice (MOJ) to promote Corston's implementation. Yet no additional budget for service development was provided (Radcliffe and Hunter with Vass 2013). Following persistent lobbying, in February 2009, the government announced £15.6 million funding over two years to extend the capacity of women's centres and enhance bail support services (Radcliffe and Hunter with Vass 2013). A network of 46 women's projects was developed, delivering a range of services, including training and employability, healthcare, support for drug and alcohol addictions and welfare advice (WIP 2017: 18). However, these were vulnerable to insecure funding within the climate of austerity that followed the banking crisis of 2008.

Corston's analysis influenced the development of Gender Specific Standards for Women Prisoners (annexed to Prison Service Order 4800), requiring provisions appropriate to the discrete needs of women prisoners and their resettlement, regarding conditions, regimes and services and with specific provision for younger, older and BME women (HMPS 2008). Claiming that 'most of these standards are "best practice" already in many establishments', the Prison Service warned that it would 'not be possible to implement all standards immediately because of resource pressures' (p. 1). Some standards were limited in ambition, for example, in allowing shared transport with male prisoners, although this was recognised as potentially exposing women to verbal abuse (HMPS 2008). Instructions on strip-searching were also published, advising that women 'must not be full-searched as a matter of routine' and that this process must only be used on 'intelligence or reasonable suspicion that an item is being concealed on the person which may be revealed by the search' (MOJ 2011: 11).

Corston's important recommendation that existing prisons be replaced by small, geographically dispersed custodial units was not accepted immediately. Instead, an MOJ study was established to report on the future of the women's custodial estate. In June 2008, Minister Eagle announced to parliament that it had concluded that small units were 'neither feasible nor desirable' because of restrictions on access to services and women's fears of bullying. Instead, the study recommended the development of smaller units within larger prisons, intended within HMP Bronzefield (a purpose-built women's prison that opened in 2004 in Middlesex, England) (Samuel 2008). Money saved from any reduction in women's prison numbers would be reinvested into the estate but only 'if necessary, and if resources allow' (Samuel 2008). In 2009, a 'short study on women offenders' concluded that women should be 'punished appropriately', but efforts must be made to 'tackle the underlying causes of crime' and 'break cycles of disadvantage' (MOJ and Cabinet Office 2009: 3). This was a vision more in line with Tony Blair's (1995) mantra to be 'tough on crime, tough on the causes of crime' rather than Corston's approach, which recognised that many women who offend are also victims, and which emphasised support rather than punishment.

Three years after Corston reported, a thematic inspection of women's imprisonment (HMIP 2010) found that an increased number of women were being held further away from home, thus creating a significant barrier to family contact. While noting improvements in most female prisons, serious concerns remained. Relationships between prisoners and staff were reported as mainly positive, but some prisons had an over-representation of male staff. Despite examples of purpose-built accommodation, some women prisoners lived in cramped dormitories, and most regimes failed the expectation of ten hours per day out-of-cell. One third of women reported being depressed or suicidal on reception to prison; however, there was generally insufficient access to Listener support. Inspectors were concerned about the impact of segregation, strip conditions and force and restraint on self-harming and suicidal women. Support for substance users had improved, but some prisons failed to provide prescribed medication on induction, and too few prison staff were experienced in dealing with the dual-diagnosis of mental ill health and addictions. Resettlement support was often inadequate, with minimal effective links to community-based training and employment services. Chief Inspector Anne Owers noted that female prison numbers remained 'obstinately static', concluding that work was 'certainly needed to improve the prisons we inspect' and, further, to 'create and properly use viable and more appropriate alternatives to prison' (HMCIP 2010: 6).

The 2010 formation of the Conservative-Liberal Coalition Government halted progress and a parliamentary review soon lamented 'a hiatus' in implementing Corston's recommendations (HOCJC 2013a: 3). The Coalition's *Programme for Government* (2010: 23) committed to a sentencing policy based on deterrence and punishment, alongside a 'rehabilitation revolution' with funding for private providers to conduct supervision in the community. In an early speech, Justice Minister Ken Clarke stated that imprisonment was too often 'a costly and ineffectual approach that fails to turn criminals into law-abiding citizens', with short sentences being particularly ineffective (BBC 30 June 2010). It was a statement warmly greeted by reformers (see Clinks 2010). For Clarke, 'banging up more and more people for longer without actively seeking to change them is what you would expect of Victorian England' (Woodcock and Bogustawski 2010). Based on Clarke's ideas, a Green Paper, *Breaking the Cycle*, proposed that prisons should become 'places of hard work and industry'. There should be an increased role for the private sector and reform of community sentences to make prisons more 'credible' and 'rigorous', with 'payment-by-results' for service providers (MOJ 2010: 14, 17, 38). The prison population would be reduced through sentencing reform, including diversion for people with mental illness and deportation or 'administrative removal' (p. 65) of some Foreign National prisoners. Reduced to a brief section on women, a few of Corston's key themes were restated, specifically acknowledgement of women's different offending patterns and complex needs and of the importance of community provision.

In July 2011, an All Party Parliamentary Group on women in the penal system was established, chaired by Corston (Howard League for Penal Reform 2011). In her foreword to the group's report, Corston stated that 'while a great deal has been achieved, there is more to be done' (p. 2). The report welcomed the publication of Gender Specific Standards and Gender Equality Schemes under the 2007 Gender Equality Duty, the reduction in strip-searching, gender-specific staff training and investment in community alternatives. It expressed concern, however, that significant Corston recommendations had not been progressed, concluding that the 'scale of the problem' remained 'significant' (p. 9).

By summer 2011, the Coalition Government had begun to withdraw support for prison reduction in response to media allegations of their being 'soft' on crime (Garside and Ford 2015). In 2012, Clarke's replacement as Justice Secretary by the less liberal Chris Grayling confirmed the shift. Meanwhile, Chief Inspector of Prisons Nick Hardwick (2012) opened a university lecture by bleakly declaring, 'we can't go on like this'. Referring to an inspection of Styal prison, he stated that despite some improvements, inspectors found conditions in the Keller Unit 'shocking and distressing', with officers frequently using force to remove ligatures from self-harming women (p. 1). Hardwick concluded that conditions for some of the 'most disturbed women' were 'simply unacceptable' and predicted that 'we will look back on how we treated these women in years to come, aghast and ashamed' (p. 2). He placed responsibility for the lack of progress firmly on the government.

Responding to the ongoing problems, the independent sector continued to lobby for reform. The Prison Reform Trust (2012) published a three-year strategy for women's imprisonment in the UK. A coalition of non-governmental organisations (NGOs) and service providers produced a strategy (Third Sector

Advisory Group 2012: 25), apparently endorsing aspects of Coalition policy by advocating payment-by-results pilots for women to 'ensure that the implications of new funding models were considered from a gendered point of view'.

In its *Strategic Objectives for Female Offenders*, the MOJ (2013: 4) established four priorities: 'credible, robust sentencing options in the community'; gender-specific services to meet identifiable needs; custodial rehabilitation while simulta-neously punishing women and protecting the public; and promotion of 'better life management by female offenders'. To realise these objectives, an Advisory Board for Female Offenders was established. A review of the women's custodial estate, commissioned by the National Offender Management Service (NOMS), recom-mended closure of both women's open prisons and their reconstitution as open units within 'strategic prison hubs' (Robinson 2013: 3). The review recommended that women in Wales, which has no female prisons, be accommodated in HMP Eastwood Park and HMP Styal in England. Regarding Corston's key recom-mendation of local custodial units, the review determined that it might prove too difficult to provide adequate services, including healthcare, on such a small scale.

Criticising the loss of momentum in implementing Corston's recommenda-tions, the House of Commons Justice Committee (HOCJC 2013a) stated that the 'Transforming Rehabilitation' proposals were male-oriented, and women's organisations might have difficulty evidencing their impact, given the smaller numbers of women in the criminal justice system. The committee recommended a 'gradual reconfiguration' of the women's custodial estate, an increased use of residential alternatives to custody and maintenance of the network of women's centres (p. 4).

The May 2015 election of a Conservative government brought further changes to prison policy. In November 2015, Justice Secretary Michael Gove announced the closure of the 'inadequate and antiquated' Holloway Prison so that women could 'serve their sentences in more humane surroundings better designed to keep them out of crime'. Holloway closed in July 2016, with women being dis-persed to Bronzefield and Downview prisons (Surrey, England). Via the Queen's Speech in May 2016, the government announced that its forthcoming Prisons Bill would create six 'reform prisons' and increase the autonomy of prison gov-ernors (UK Government 2016). Following the referendum on UK membership of the European Union, Gove was replaced by Liz Truss who announced plans to create five new 'community prisons' to accommodate women prior to release (MOJ 2016b). Some reform campaigners welcomed this development, caution-ing, however, that these must replace, not add to, existing prisons (see WIP 2016). In discussing her intentions for the Prisons and Courts Bill, Truss (2017) was clear that she would not use sentencing reform to cut prison numbers but in-stead would prioritise prison-based rehabilitation. In June 2017, a 'snap election' returned a Conservative government to power, with a reduced majority and an increased Labour opposition under Jeremy Corbyn's leadership. The subsequent Queen's Speech made no mention of prison reform, thus criticised by the current Chief Inspector of Prisons Peter Clarke as a 'missed opportunity' (Bulman 2017).

From 'crisis' to 'clawback': the limitations of reform

Traditional explanations identify factors central to the 'prison crisis' as increased numbers, overcrowding, poor conditions, a 'toxic mix' of prisoners, under-staffing, staff unrest, security problems and prison disturbances (Cavadino et al. 2013). Referring to previous critical research, Cavadino et al. (2013) add further factors of legitimacy (particularly regarding high rates of recidivism); penolog-ical resources (including those within communities); and visibility (previously regarding secrecy, more recently responding to public concerns about deaths in custody, as exposed by official reports and campaigning organisations). Crisis factors are each experienced in gendered ways.

The persistence of the 'numbers crisis' (Cavadino et al. 2013) is the most visible and quantifiable barrier to achieving Corston's recommendations to-wards significant decarceration. Without substantial law reform, the women's penal population was never likely to experience a sustained reduction. Despite the stated high-level commitment to reducing women's prison numbers, 3,978 women were in prison at the end of March 2017, a slight rise from 12 months be-fore (MOJ 2017a) and over 2,300 more than in 1993 (PRT 2016). While the male remand population fell by 15 per cent in 2016, women on remand rose (MOJ 2017b: 2). Between 2014 and 2016, women recalled to prison while under super-vision in the community rose by over 80 per cent (PRT 2016). This situation is negatively affected by the crisis of penological resources in a period of austerity, which now has seen women's centres, a central plank underpinning Corston's approach, threatened by severe cuts (Howard League 2016). Corston identified accommodation as crucial to women's resettlement, but the crisis in housing has become 'even more desperate' since the publication of her report (WIP 2017). Ironically, insufficient addiction service results in some women offending simply to access services in prison (WIP 2017).

Contributing to the rise in prison numbers is the ageing prison population. While this is a universal phenomenon, prisoners over 60 years of age have be-come the fastest growing group in the UK (HOCJC 2013b). In March 2017, there were over 513 women prisoners aged 50 years and over (ONS 2017). This ageing demographic places additional strains on the system. Older prisoners ex-perience higher rates of disability and illness, including dementia. Moreover, an increasingly ageing prison population results in more people dying in prisons (HOCJC 2013b).

The growth in Foreign National women prisoners has also been dispropor-tionately high. This group now comprises 11 per cent of the women's prison population, almost one-third imprisoned for drugs offences, often committed under coercion. Further, penal expansionism has also included a growth in different forms of incarceration, such as immigration removal centres. Many Foreign National women are held in prison beyond their sentence while await-ing deportation (WIP 2017: 7). A 2017 inspection of immigration removal to Jamaica evidenced the level of force involved in this process. Many detainees 'did not know what would happen to them on arrival and those who had very few or no prior links with anyone in Jamaica did not know what resources would be available for them' (p. 7). The report described a 57-year-old woman 'forced into compliance by use of a rigid handcuff applied purely to inflict pain, then fitted with a waist restraint belt' (HMCIP 2017a: 5).

High levels of self-harm and suicide persist among women prisoners, and the 'initial downward trend' in self-harm has reversed (HMCIP 2016: 55). A decade after Corston, almost half of women surveyed told inspectors that they had felt unsafe while in prison (HMCIP 2016). The death of 32-year-old Sarah Reed in Holloway in January 2016 attracted media attention, not least because CCTV evidence was available online of a Metropolitan Police officer brutally assaulting Sarah following her arrest for alleged shoplifting in 2012.[4] Sarah had mental health issues related to her baby's death in 2003. She and her baby's father had experienced the trauma of being given their daughter's body wrapped in a sheet, to transport to the undertakers by taxi. Following the 2012 police assault, Sarah was sectioned under mental health legislation, more recently treated at home within a 'care in the community' scheme. Charged with Grievous Bodily Harm while sectioned, Sarah was on bail but was unexpectedly remanded to custody in autumn 2015. Complaining she was not receiving appropriate mental healthcare, Sarah wrote in a Christmas card, 'Mum, this is just to say Merry Xmas... PS. Get me out of jail'. Days later, she was found dead in her cell (Gentleman and Gayle 2016).

The deaths of four transgender women within a period of 14 months between 2015 and 2016 also demonstrates the significant risks of harm of imprisonment, particularly when individuals' acquired/affirmed gender is not recognised and supported (House of Commons, Women and Equalities Committee 2016). The Ministry of Justice (2016c) recently published initial official statistics indicating that in March/April there were 70 transgender prisoners in 33 (of 123) prisons in E&W. Policy guidelines (Prison Service Instruction 17/2016) state that transgender prisoners 'must be allowed to express the gender with which they identify'. Yet any decision to locate a person in a prison not in accordance with their legal gender must be referred to the local Transgender Case Board for which applicants must provide evidence of their living as the gender with which they identify. Jenny Swift's death in a Doncaster Prison in December 2016 demonstrates the damage caused by this flawed policy. Remanded to a male prison, Jenny was allegedly refused the female hormones she had been taking to assist with her transition, and media reports stated she had complained about being called 'mister' by prison staff and about taunting by other prisoners (Halliday 2017).

Following Corston, initiatives aimed at supporting prisoners with mental illness appeared to have some impact. However, safeguarding strategies leave intact structural issues of inequality and injustice that underpin women's self-harming and deaths (INQUEST 2013). Moreover, suicide prevention measures do not remove the deep pains of confinement (Sykes 1958). On the contrary, such techniques often contribute to the violence of incarceration: for example, through the use of physical restraint to remove objects of concern or isolation and surveillance of suicidal prisoners (Moore and Scraton 2014). A culture of official denial persists, evident in the claim by Truss (2017 quoted above) that government is 'taking action to tackle the problem' of prison deaths. This displays the common political tactic of neutralising protest by insisting that fundamental change is imminent. In September 2011, the Corporate Manslaughter and Corporate Homicide Act (2007) was extended to include deaths in custody. The Act has particular significance as inquest findings and inspection recommendations are often ignored (Tombs 2016). As Steve Tombs (2016) argues, a successful prosecution would deliver a 'powerful, symbolic message that the routine, systematic deaths of those to whom the state and the prison service has a duty of care cannot continue without legal accountability'.

Ten years after Corston, Women in Prison (2017) confirmed implementation of only two of her recommendations, one of which was only implemented in part. Regrettably, Corston's advocacy of state-led reform of the criminal justice and prison systems was flawed. It overestimated the commitment to promote change by political and prison leaders and underestimated the degree to which 'carceral clawback' (Carlen 2002) would undermine and halt advances in decarceration. Evidence of the system's expansionist tendencies are evident in the establishment of small units outside Styal and Drake Hall women's prisons – integrated into, rather than replacing, existing prisons (WIP 2017). The 2016 closure of HMP Holloway, while apparently reflecting Corston's recommendations, in practice created significant inhibitions on women prisoners from the Greater London area and their families. Moreover, the dispersal of Holloway prisoners created further pressures on the receiving prisons (HMCIP 2017b). Meanwhile, the two open women's prisons scheduled for closure following the 2013 review (Robinson 2013) remained open three years later (HMCIP 2016: 54).

Conclusion: arguments for abolition

The Corston review was conceived out of 'crisis', yet despite her recommendations, women's imprisonment has not been transformed. Noting that as long ago as 1895, the Gladstone Committee had reported on prison overcrowding, mental ill health and high levels of reoffending, Cavadino et al. (2013: 9) ask, 'how long can a crisis last while remaining a crisis rather than business as usual?' Given the cycles of 'crisis', each of which fails to be resolved, they characterise the system as suffering from a 'deep malaise' (Cavadino et al. 2013: 9). This term, while accurate regarding the enduring problems associated with imprisonment, does not adequately reflect the distressing and dangerous personal crises experienced by women prisoners, regularly with fatal consequences.

Responding to the failure of reform, campaigners have called for the abolition of women's imprisonment as a first step to wider abolition (Scott and Codd 2010). Five years before the publication of Corston, Carlen (1990: 121 cited in Ryan and Sim 2016: 728) stated that to reduce prison numbers, 'we must first reduce the number of prisons; to reduce the number of prisons we must first abolish certain categories of imprisonment. Women's imprisonment is, for several reasons, a prime candidate for abolition'. Carlen proposed that for an 'experimental' five years, women's imprisonment be restricted to a maximum of 100 places for those convicted or remanded for 'abnormally serious crimes'.

More recently, Howard League's Chief Executive Francis Crook (2014) summarised the key arguments for abolishing women's imprisonment as 'a much easier' first step before doing 'pretty much the same thing for men'. Her arguments are that women's offending is different, that women are more often primary carers and that women respond differently to imprisonment. While any reduction in imprisonment would be welcome, framing arguments for decarceration around women's lesser offending and vulnerability risks exceptionalism. Such an approach allows the proposition that for *some* offences, in *some* circumstances, prison *is* necessary. Yet, as Crewe et al. (2017: 18) found, female life and long-term prisoners, those who would still receive custodial sentences under a reductionist scenario, experience particularly acute 'deprivations and debasements'.

Despite her critique, Corston underestimated the degree to which the prison is 'counter-productive, difficult to control and itself a major social problem' (de Haan 1990: 53). Without question, she recognised imprisonment as damaging and largely ineffectual but, through her advocacy of gender-specific reform, Corston bolstered attempts to reposition the prison as 'an imaginary place for the healing of the social and economically marginalised' (Sim 2011: 139). To suggest that prison can resolve the significant problems that women experience - prior to, during and after imprisonment - is to downplay its punitive function, and to underestimate the pain and deprivation which lies at the heart of the incarceration process (Sykes 1958; Scraton and McCulloch 2009). As expressed by Deborah Drake and David Scott (2017):

> Prisons constrain the human identity and foster feelings of fear, anger, alienation and social and emotional isolation. For many prisoners, prisons offer only a lonely, isolating and brutalising experience. At best, prison environments are dull and monotonous living and working routines depriving prisoners of basic human needs. At worst, they are places of violence, suffering and physical and psychological pain.

Corston proposed that women in the justice system should have improved access to appropriate services – for example, housing, mental health care, community support – however she was less forthright in identifying and challenging the structural inequalities underpinning and reproducing their plight. Casualised, insecure employment, criminalisation of poverty and punitive welfare and penal powers and practices are characteristic of contemporary neoliberal society (Wacquant 2008). Rather than focusing on individual 'pathways to offending', and thereby holding women responsible for the circumstances surrounding their imprisonment, there is a need to challenge the institutional and structural issues which result in the criminalisation of women, as argued by Becky Clarke and Kathryn Chadwick (Chapter 3 of this collection).

In conclusion, there is a need for strategies to be developed and progressed to abolish the damaging and violent institution of the prison. Such strategies could include a moratorium on prison-building, which must be accompanied by significant decarceration to ensure that women (and men) do not continue to be confined within institutions in poor physical condition and with inappropriate environments. As stated in an open letter to the press from a coalition of individuals and organisations (Guardian 26 January 2017):

> Rather than investing £1.3bn in building new prisons, the government should be prioritising policies that radically reduce the number of people in prison. This could include meaningful jobs, social housing, healthcare, education, transport – for all.

A campaign to reclaim the disused site at Holloway prison for collective good, rather than luxury housing, highlights the connection between decarceration and social justice (Archer 2017). Abolitionism, therefore, is about more than prison closure, crucial though this is. It is also about tackling the structural injustices and punitive practices that underpin women's criminalisation and imprisonment.

Notes

1 Jean Corston is a Labour Party peer, having taken her seat in the House of Lords (upper house of United Kingdom Parliament) in June 2005.
2 INQUEST is a campaign-based organisation committed to the monitoring of all custodial forms regarding custodial deaths.
3 Responsibility for criminal justice in Scotland was devolved following the re-establishment of the Scottish Parliament in 1999. Devolution of Criminal Justice in Northern Ireland occurred after the signing of the multiparty Hillsborough Agreement (2010).
4 Metropolitan Police Constable James Kiddie was dismissed from the service and given 150 hours of community service for this attack (Gentleman and Gayle 2016).

References

Abbott, L. (2015) 'A pregnant pause: expecting in the prison estate', in Baldwin, L. (ed.) *Mothering Justice: Working with Mothers in Criminal and Social Justice Settings*, Hampshire: Waterside Press.

Archer, N. (2017) 'Why the old Holloway Prison in North London should become a new women's building', *Open Democracy*, 12 April 2017, www.opendemocracy.net/5050/nandini-archer/why-old-holloway-prison-in-north-london-should-become-new-womens-building/feed. Accessed 20 April 2017.

Baldwin, L. (2015) *Mothering Justice: Working with Mothers in Criminal and Social Justice Settings,* Hampshire: Waterside Press.

Barry, M. and McIvor, G. (2008) *Chaotic Lives: A Profile of Women Offenders in the Criminal Justice System in Lothian and Borders*, Peebles: Lothian & Borders Justice Authority.

Blair, T. (1995) *Leader's Speech, Labour Party Conference, Brighton,* reproduced at www.britishpoliticalspeech.org/speech-archive.htm?speech=201. Accessed 5 April 2017.

Bloom, B., Owen, B. and Covington, S. (2003) *Gender-Responsive Strategies: Research, Practice and Guiding Principles for Women Offenders,* Washington, DC: US Department of Justice: National Institute for Corrections.

Bulman, M. (2017) 'Queen's speech: chief inspector of prisons expresses fury after penal reform dropped from agenda', *The Independent,* 21 June 2017.

Carlen, P. (1983) *Women's Imprisonment: A Study in Social Control,* London: Routledge and Kegan Paul.

Carlen, P. (1988) *Sledgehammer: Women's Imprisonment at the Millennium,* Basingstoke: Macmillan.

Carlen, P. (2002) *Women and Punishment: The Struggle for Justice,* London and New York: Routledge.

Carlen, P. and Worrell, A. (2004) *Analysing Women's Imprisonment,* Cullompton: Willan.

Carlton, B. and Segrave, M. (2011) 'Women's survival post-imprisonment: connecting imprisonment with pains past and present', *Punishment and Society* 13(5): 551–570.

Cavadino, M., Dignan, J. and Mair, G. (2013) *The Penal System: An Introduction,* London: Sage.

Chigwada-Bailey, R. (2003) *Black Women's Experiences of Criminal Justice: Race, Gender and Class, a Discourse on Disadvantage,* Hampshire: Waterside Press.

Clinks (2010) 'Ken Clarke's Keynote Speech on 30th June 2010: "What does it mean for the Community and Voluntary Sector"', www.clinks.org/sites/default/files/Members%20Briefing%20-%20Ken%20Clarke%27s%20Speech%20June%202010.pdf. Accessed 3 April 2017.

Corston, J. (2007) *The Corston Report: A Report by Baroness Jean Corston of a Review of Women with Particular Vulnerabilities in the Criminal Justice System,* London: Home Office.

Crewe, B., Hulley, S. and Wright, S. (2017) 'The gendered pains of life imprisonment', *British Journal of Criminology.* doi:10.17863/CAM.7437.

Crook, F. (2014) 'I would give up women's imprisonment', www.crimeandjustice.org.uk/resources/i-would-give-womens-imprisonment. Accessed 10 May 2017.

De Haan, W. (1990) *The Politics of Redress: Crime, Punishment and Penal Abolition,* London: Unwin Hyman.

Department of Justice (Northern Ireland) (2010) *Women's Offending Behaviour in Northern Ireland: A Strategy to Manage Women Offenders and Those Vulnerable to Offending Behaviour 2010–2013,* Belfast: DOJ.

Dodge, L. M. (2017) 'Discipline, resistance and social control at the Illinois state reformatory for women, 1930–1962', in E. Rhodes Hayden and T. Jach (eds.) *Incarcerated Women: A History of Struggles, Oppression and Resistance in American Prisons,* Lanham, MD: Lexington Books.

Drake, D. and Scott, D. (2017) 'Build communities not prisons', 29 June 2017, *Reclaim Justice Network.* At: https://reclaimjusticenetwork.org.uk/2017/06/29/build-communities-not-prisons/. Accessed 25 August 2017.

Eaton, M. (1993) *Women after Prison,* Buckingham: Open University Press.

Edwards, S. (1986) 'Neither bad nor mad: the female violent offender reassessed', *Women's Studies International Forum* 9(1): 79–87.

Garland, D. (2001) *The Culture of Control: Crime and Social Order in Contemporary Society,* Oxford: Oxford University Press.

Garside, R. and Ford, M. (2015) *Criminal Justice in the United Kingdom: 2010–2015,* London: Centre for Crime and Justice Studies.

Gentleman, A. and Gayle, D. (2016) 'Sarah Reed's mother: my daughter was failed by many and I was ignored', *The Guardian* 17 February 2016.

Gove, M. (2015) 'Written statement to Parliament: Prisons announcement' 25 November 2015. www.gov.uk/government/speeches/prisons-announcement. Accessed 5 April 2017.

Guardian newspaper, letters page, 26 January 2017. https://www.theguardian.com/society/2017/jan/26/building-more-prisons-is-not-the-answer. Accessed 20 August 2017.

Halliday, J. (2017) 'Transgender woman found dead in cell at Doncaster Prison', *The Guardian* 5 January 2017. https://www.theguardian.com/society/2017/jan/05/transgender-woman-jenny-swift-found-dead-at-doncaster-prison. Accessed 20 August 2017.

Hannah-Moffatt, K. (2001) *Punishment in Disguise: Penal Governance and Federal Imprisonment of Women in Canada*, Toronto: University of Toronto Press.

Hardwick, N. (2012) *Women in Prison: Corston Five Years On*, Lecture delivered at University of Sussex. www.justiceinspectorates.gov.uk/prisons/wp-content/uploads/sites/4/2014/02/women-in-prison.pdf. Accessed 8 May 2017.

Hawton, K., Linsell, L., Adeniji, T., Sariaslan, A. and Fazel, S. (2014) 'Self-harm in prisons in England and Wales: an epidemiological study of prevalence, risk factors, clustering, and subsequent suicide', *The Lancet* 383(9923): 1147–1154. doi: 10.1016/S0140-6736(13)62118-2. Epub 2013 December 2016.

Hedderman, C. (2012) *Empty Cells or Empty Words? Government Policy on Reducing the Number of Women Going to Prison*, London: Criminal Justice Alliance.

Her Majesty's Chief Inspector of Prisons (1997) *Women in Prison: A Thematic Review*, London: Home Office.

Her Majesty's Chief Inspector of Prisons (2004) *No Problems – Old and Quiet: Older Prisoners in England and Wales – A Thematic Review*, London: HMIP.

Her Majesty's Chief Inspector of Prisons (2010) *Women in Prison: A Short Thematic Review*, London: HMIP.

Her Majesty's Chief Inspector of Prisons (2016) *Annual Report 2015–2016*, London: HMIP.

Her Majesty's Chief Inspector of Prisons (2017a) *Detainees under Escort: Inspection of Escort and Removals to Jamaica, 7–8 March 2017*, London: HMIP.

Her Majesty's Chief Inspector of Prisons (2017b) *Annual Report 2016–2017*, London: HMIP.

Her Majesty's Prison Service (England and Wales) (2008) *Gender Specific Standards for Women Prisoners*, London: Ministry of Justice.

House of Commons Justice Committee (2013a) *Women Offenders: After the Corston Report, Second Report of Session 2013–14*, London: Stationery Office.

House of Commons Justice Committee (2013b) *Older Prisoners*, London: Stationery Office.

House of Commons, Women and Equalities Committee (2016), *Transgender Equality HC 390 2016-16, 14 January 2016*. London: House of Commons.

Howard League for Penal Reform (2011) *All Party Parliamentary Group on Women in the Penal System: Women in the Penal System: Second Report on Women with Particular Vulnerabilities in the Criminal Justice System*, London: Howard League for Penal Reform.

Howard League, *Ten Years after the Corston Report, Is This the End of Successful Women's Centres?* 8 November 2016. http://howardleague.org/news/isthistheendofwomenscentres/. Accessed 14 December 2016.

INQUEST (2005) 'Verdict in Sarah Campbell Inquest – 18-year-old woman who died in HMP Styal', Press Release Monday January 24th, 2005, http://inquest.org.uk/pdf/2005/Sarah%20Campbell%20Inquest%20verdict%202005.pdf. Accessed 8 May 2017.

INQUEST (2013) *Preventing the Deaths of Women in Prison,* London: INQUEST.

INQUEST website. *Deaths of Women in Prison,* www.inquest.org.uk/statistics/deaths-of-women-in-prison. Accessed 30 March 2017.

Joint Probation Service – Irish Prison Service Strategy (2014) *An Effective Response to Women who Offend,* Dublin and Longford: Probation Service and IPS.

Law, V. (2009) *Resistance behind Bars: The Struggles of Incarcerated Women,* Oakland, CA: PM Press.

Law, V. (2015) 'Giving birth while shackled may be illegal, but mothers still have to endure it', *Guardian,* 13 February 2015. https://www.theguardian.com/us-news/2015/feb/13/mothers-prison-illegal-shackled-while-giving-birth. Accessed 20 August 2017.

McConville, S. (2015) *A History of English Prison Administration,* Oxon: Routledge.

McCulloch, J. and George, A. (2009) 'Naked power: strip searching in women's prisons' in P. Scraton and J. McCulloch (eds.) *The Violence of Incarceration,* Oxon: Taylor & Francis, pp. 107–123.

McIvor, G. and Burman, M. (2011) *Understanding the Drivers of Female Imprisonment in Scotland,* Glasgow: Scottish Centre for Crime and Justice Research.

Malloch, M. and McIvor, G. (eds.) (2013) *Women, Punishment and Social Justice: Human Rights and Penal Practices,* London: Routledge.

Ministry of Justice (2007) *The Government's Response to the Report by Baroness Corston of a Review of Women with Particular Vulnerabilities in the Criminal Justice System,* London: MOJ.

Ministry of Justice (2010) *Breaking the Cycle: Effective Punishment, Rehabilitation, and Sentencing of Offenders,* London: MOJ.

Ministry of Justice (National Offender Management Service) (2011) *National Security Framework: Searching of the Person,* London: MOJ.

Ministry of Justice (2013) *Strategic Objectives for Female Offenders,* London: MOJ.

Ministry of Justice (2016a) *Statistics on Women in the Criminal Justice System 2015,* published 24 November 2016, London: MOJ.

Ministry of Justice (2016b) *Prison Safety and Reform,* London: MOJ.

Ministry of Justice (2016c) *Prisoner Transgender Statistics: March to April 2016,* 9 November 2016, London: MOJ.

Ministry of Justice (2017a) *Weekly Population Bulletin 31 March 2017,* London: MOJ.

Ministry of Justice (2017b) *Offender Management Statistics Quarterly, England and Wales, July to September 2016 (with Prison Population as at 31 December 2016),* London: MOJ.

Ministry of Justice and Cabinet Office Social Exclusion Task Force (2009) *Short Study on Women Offenders,* London: MOJ.

Moore, L. and Scraton, P. (2014) *The Incarceration of Women: Punishing Bodies, Breaking Spirits,* Basingstoke: Palgrave Macmillan.

Player, E. (2013) 'Women in the criminal justice system: the triumph of inertia', *Criminology and Criminal Justice,* 14(3): 276–297.

Plugge, E., Douglas, N. and Fitzpatrick, R. (2006) *The Health of Women in Prison: Study Findings,* Oxford: Oxford University.

Pollack, S. (2008) *Locked In and Locked Out: Imprisoning Women in the Shrinking and Punitive Welfare State,* Waterloo: Wilfred Laurier University.

Prisons and Probation Ombudsman (E&W) (2005) *The Styal Report: The Death of a Woman in Custody and the Series of Deaths in HMP/YOI Styal August 2002–August 2003,* London: P&PO.

Prison Reform Trust (2012) *Women in Prison,* London: Prison Reform Trust.

Prison Reform Trust (2016) *Prison: The Facts, Bromley Briefings Autumn 2016,* London: PRT.

Prison Reform Trust (2017) *Why Focus on Reducing Women's Imprisonment? Prison Reform Trust Briefing February 2017*, London: PRT.

Queens Speech (18 May 2016) www.gov.uk/government/speeches/queens-speech-2016. Accessed 5 April 2017.

Radcliffe, P. and Hunter, G. with Vass, R. (2013) *The Development and Impact of Community Services for Women Offenders: An Evaluation*, London: Institute for Criminal Policy Research, Birkbeck College.

Rafter, N. (1985) *Partial Justice: Women in State Prisons 1800–1935*, Boston, MA: Northeastern University Press.

Ramsbotham, D. (2005) *Prisongate: The Shocking State of Britain's Prisons & The Need For Visionary Change,* London: Simon and Schuster.

Robinson, C. (2013) *Women's Custodial Estate Review*, London: NOMS.

Rock, P. (1996) *Reconstituting a Women's Prison: The Holloway Redevelopment Project 1968–88*, Oxford: Clarendon Press.

Ryan, M. and Sim, J. (2016) 'Campaigning for and campaigning against prisons', in Y. Jewkes, Bennett, J. and Crewe, B. (eds.) *Handbook on Prisons* (2nd edition), London: Routledge, pp. 712–733.

Samuel, M. (2008) 'Ministry of Justice rejects small custodial units for women', *Community Care*, June 26th, www.communitycare.co.uk/2008/06/26/ministry-of-justice-rejects-small-custodial-units-for-women/. Accessed 2 April 2017.

Scott, D. and Codd, H. (2010) *Controversial Issues in Prisons*, Maidenhead: Open University Press.

Scraton, P. and McCulloch, J. (eds.) (2009) *The Violence of Incarceration*, Oxon: Taylor & Francis.

Sim, J. (2011) 'Pain and Punishment: the real and the imaginary in penal institutions', in P. Carlen, (ed.) *Imagined Penalities* (2nd edition), Oxon: Routledge, pp. 135–156.

Smee, S. and Moosa, Z. (2010) *Realising Rights: Increasing Ethnic Minority Women's Access to Justice*, London: Fawcett Society.

Sudbury, J. (2010) *Unpacking the Crisis: Women of Color, Globalization and the Prison-Industrial Complex*, Berkeley, CA: University of California Press.

Sykes, G. (1958) *Society of Captives: A Study of a Maximum Security Prison*, Princeton, NJ: Princeton University Press.

The Coalition Government (2010) *Our Programme for Government*, London: HM Government.

Third Sector Advisory Group (2012) *Reducing Reoffending Third Sector Advisory Group (RR3): A Report of the Task & Finish Group: Breaking the Cycle of Women's Offending: A System Re-design: Executive Summary*, London: TSAG.

Tombs, S. (2016) 'Prison deaths: a case of corporate manslaughter', *The Independent*, 2 December 2016.

Truss, E. (2017) 'Elizabeth Truss outlines her views on sentencing and the size of the prison population at The Centre for Social Justice' 14 February 2017, www.elizabethtruss.com/news/elizabeth-truss-outlines-her-views-sentencing-and-size-prison-population-centre-social-justice. Accessed 6 April 2017.

United Kingdom Government (2016) 'Biggest shake-up of prison system announced as part of Queen's Speech', Press Release 18 May 2016, www.gov.uk/government/news/biggest-shake-up-of-prison-system-announced-as-part-of-queens-speech. Accessed 20 April 2017.

United Nations (2010) *United Nations Rules for the Treatment of Women Prisoners and Non-custodial Measures for Women Offenders* (Bangkok Rules). http://www.un.org/en/ecosoc/docs/2010/res%202010-16.pdf. Accessed 20 August 2017.

Wacquant, L. (2008) *Punishing the Poor*, Durham, NC: Duke University Press.

Wahidin, A. (2004) *Older Women and the Criminal Justice System: Running Out of Time*, London: Jessica Kingsley.

Walmsley, R. (2015) *World Female Imprisonment List* (3rd Edition), London: Birkbeck University Institute for Criminal Policy Research.

Women in Prison (2016) *Women in Prison's Response to the Secretary of State for Justice Liz Truss' Announcement on Women's Imprisonment and the Creation of Five 'New Community Prisons for Women' Built on Adjacent Land to Existing Sites as Published in the Prison Safety and Reform White Pape*r (Press Release), www.womeninprison.org.uk/news-and-campaigns.php?s=2016-11-04-justice-secretary-statement. Accessed 1 June 2017.

Women in Prison (2017) *Corston+10: the Corston Report 10 Years On*, London: WIP.

Woodcock, A. and Bogustawski, L. (2010) 'Ken Clarke plans radical reform of the prison system', *The Independent*, 20 June 2010.

Zedner, L. (1998) 'Wayward sisters: the prison for women' in N. Morris and D. Rothman (eds.) *The Oxford History of the Prison: The Practice on Punishment in Western Society*, Oxford: Oxford University Press.

2

AFTER CORSTON

Community, change, and challenges

Loraine Gelsthorpe

Introduction

This chapter explores post-Corston developments regarding community sentencing, particularly the establishment and functioning of community centres for women. There has been some progression following the Corston Report (2007) regarding the treatment of women in the criminal justice system, but arguably, this has regressed. The storyline regarding Baroness Jean Corston's review sometimes skates over earlier developments that paved the way for her report. It is important to consider those key developments here, not least because they allowed Corston to build on pre-existing scaffolding. In the conclusion, concerns about the landscape of provision for women in the community following the Offender Rehabilitation Act 2014 are outlined, focusing on the relationship between the Community Rehabilitation Companies and centres for women. The question is raised whether this is another compromise in the history of the treatment of women.

Early developments

After two decades of important research in the United Kingdom (UK), beginning in the 1970s and including seminal contributions from Carol Smart (1976), Pat Carlen (1983, 1987 (with Worrall), 1990), Frances Heidensohn (1985), Dobash et al. (1986), and Ann Worrall (1990, 1997), amongst others, together with organisations such as the Howard League for Penal Reform and the Prison Reform Trust, powerful arguments challenging the overuse of imprisonment for women were constructed. Carlen (1990) in particular raised concern about the increasing number of women being sent to prison each year, arguing that little was known about alternatives to custody or community support for ex-offenders. She reviewed existing provision, identified innovative projects in other jurisdictions, and outlined the impediments (ideological and political) to reducing women's imprisonment. Carlen (1990) produced a blueprint for abolishing women's custody, arguing for a specialist legal service for women prisoners (with particular focus on medical treatment and child custody issues), the creation of halfway houses for imprisoned addicts and their babies, the provision of a 'welcoming' visitors' centre in all women's prisons, and the need for a 'feminist jurisprudence' and a 'women-wise penology' – both recognising women's needs in a system so clearly designed for men. A central proposition was that realistic alternatives to custody could be used for women.

Consequently, there was sufficient information and concern to persuade the then Conservative Government that women commit less crime than men, that women's crimes are less serious, and that women have shorter criminal careers. Thus, the treatment of women in the criminal justice system should receive close examination to avoid 'discriminating against any persons on the ground of race and sex or any other improper ground'. The Conservative Government's addition of Section 95 to the Criminal Justice Act 1991, making explicit this requirement, was hard fought for by pressure groups. The result – a requirement to collect statistical information on women and separately on race – was an important symbolic victory. In 1992, the Home Office published the first Section 95 report on women. From 1999, new editions have been published regularly, the most recent having been published in 2015 (Ministry of Justice [MOJ] 2016).

The Labour years

When the Labour Government came to power in 1997 with a large majority, the expectation was that progressive ideas would become practice. Labour's Manifesto commitment to being 'tough on crime and on the causes of crime' (New Labour 1997), however, was immediately translated into uneven interest in these two strands of thinking, with particular emphasis on being 'tough on crime' (new offences were created, along with 50 criminal justice bills, between 1997 and 2008) (Open University 2008–9). Yet there were discernible differences between the Labour Government and its predecessor. There was an interest in 'what works', a recognition of 'social' dimensions of pathways into crime as well as 'individual' pathways, and an acknowledgement of the need to consider research evidence in dealing with offenders. Thus, the 'prison-centricity' that had dominated Conservative Government thinking in earlier years, reflected in the claim that 'Prison Works', was not shifted. New ideas developed, emphasising that imprisonment had to be made more effective, but there was no avowed interest in decarceration. Hope was placed in the Labour Government's Social Exclusion Report (SEU 2002), *Reducing Re-Offending by Ex-Prisoners*. In the Foreword to the Report, Prime Minister Tony Blair explained that it was not that imprisonment was excessive but that there had been 'a failure to capitalise on the opportunity prison provides to stop people offending for good' (SEU 2002: 3). The

Report, however, acknowledged that women's needs often were greater than men's but were often overlooked, or not prioritised, in a system designed for male offenders (SEU 2002). There was also recognition that the women's prison population was growing at a greater rate than that of men with no evidence that women were committing more crimes or more serious crimes (see Gelsthorpe and Morris 2002). The Report outlined the prospect of the Women's Offending Reduction Programme (WORP):

> The Programme's plan of action, to be formally launched later in 2002, will provide a framework for building on existing good practice to reduce women's offending. It will also enhance the growing recognition across the criminal justice system that there needs to be a distinct response to the particular needs of women.
>
> *(SEU 2002: 142)*

The WORP Action Plan materialised in 2004, stating boldly,

> Statistics show that the courts have been using custody more frequently for women over the last few years, even though the nature and seriousness of their offending has not, on the whole, been getting worse [...] The evidence suggests that courts are imposing more severe sentences on women for less serious offences.
>
> *(Home Office 2004: 3)*

The Action Plan aims were welcomed by well-aware academics and practitioners:

> Its purpose is to reduce women's offending and the number of women in custody, by providing a better tailored and more appropriate response to the particular factors which have an impact on why women offend. The intention is not to give women offenders preferential treatment but to achieve equality of treatment and access to provision.
>
> *(Home Office 2004: 5)*

No new funding materialised; rather, the aim was to embed a consideration of women's needs in existing systems and approaches. The Sentencing Guidelines Council[1] was invited to produce guidance and instructions on how the new sentencing powers established by the Criminal Justice Act 2003 might impact women differently. The Women's Policy Team (2006) set up a cross-departmental liaison group, encouraged the development of guidance concerning services for women on probation, and lent support to existing initiatives to improve community-based responses to women's mental health needs. The Policy Team negotiated £9.15 million to build on best practice developed by small-scale initiatives, such as the 218 Centre in Scotland

(Loucks et al. 2006) and the Asha Centre in England and Wales (Rumgay 2004). It supported a demonstration project, *Together Women*, that sought to provide holistic support for women who were former or current offenders or whose social exclusion needs were thought to put them at risk of offending (Hedderman et al. 2008).

Cumulative evidence suggested that something needed to be done regarding the treatment of women in the criminal justice system. There were two immediate prompts. The first related to the very high increase in the number of women in prison. This was linked to a simultaneous change in women's social and economic marginalisation and to legislative reform that encouraged a 'punitive turn' (Gelsthorpe and Morris 2002). It was also suggested that women's offending had become more serious and persistent, for instance, in relation to burglary (Deakin and Spencer 2003). A further explanation related to the harsher sentencing climate fuelled by media demands for the courts to use custody (Hedderman 2004). There was also the idea that following improvements in prison regimes, women's prisons had become modern day 'social services', so to speak (Carlen and Worrall 2004). Yet women continued to commit less serious crimes than men and were less likely to persist in offending. There was, therefore, little evidence to support the increased use of custody.

The most immediate prompt for action was the deaths of six women in Styal prison. This exposed the high number of women in custody and the negative consequences, as evidenced by specific studies of health. Douglas et al. (2009) reported that the initial shock of imprisonment, separation from families, and enforced living with women suffering drug withdrawal and serious mental ill health impacted the wider community of women in prison. Women prisoners themselves have testified that detention in unhygienic facilities and disempowering regimes, withdrawing the most basic of decision-making and the poor quality of food, militate against any respite from lives characterised by poverty, substance misuse, and domestic violence (Douglas et al. 2009). Notwithstanding differences in detention practice, this is a picture found in women's imprisonment across Europe. Women prisoners consistently report higher rates of victimisation from violence and ill health on a range of physical and mental health indicators, and there is huge worry about their families (Quaker Council for European Affairs 2007; Panayotopoulos-Cassiotou 2008).

The women's deaths prompted the government to commission Corston to review women 'with particular vulnerabilities' in the criminal justice system. She interpreted her brief broadly, seeing most women in prison as 'vulnerable':

> There are many women in prison, either on remand or serving sentences for minor, non-violent offences, for whom prison is both disproportionate and inappropriate. Many of them suffer poor physical and mental health or substance abuse or had chaotic childhoods. Many have been in care.
>
> *(Corston 2007: i)*

Contextual developments

A further prompt came from the new legislation concerning equality. Central to the Equality Act 2006 was the 'gender duty', bringing equality concerning women in line with other public sector duties. In particular, the legislation promoted the introduction of Gender Impact Statements (GIAs). This highlighted the need to address what works for women in sentencing, bearing in mind that equality of treatment should not be equated with the same treatment, a point developed by Corston in her review.

Second, a report commissioned by the Fawcett Society, and authored by Loraine Gelsthorpe, Gilly Sharpe, and Jenny Roberts (2007), included a survey of key findings from the research literature concerning women, noting unmet needs regarding physical and mental health, housing and income and training and employment. It was also recognised that women's sexual and violent victimisation can contribute to the onset and persistence of offending and that there might be high rates of substance misuse, especially opiates, among women offenders. The research literature indicated that women's offending often is associated with poverty and financial difficulties and that financial difficulties are exacerbated by having sole responsibility for dependent children. The survey of research evidence on desistance and resettlement highlighted the pains of imprisonment for women and the extent to which it disrupts both their lives and the lives of their children, indicating that women are less resistant than men to accepting community supervision and resettlement. Service providers were also consulted. They noted the need for suitable accommodation for women and the need to attend to practical needs, including mental health. Scoping possible alternatives to imprisonment in the community, a national survey of community-based provision for women identified 120 projects or services, 24 of which were contacted directly. Eighteen site visits were made, ranging from the much-vaunted 218 Centre in Glasgow as a 'one-stop-shop' for women, including a residential unit (Loucks et al. 2006), to the Cambridge Women's Resources Centre. The latter was not knowingly working with women offenders at the time but was open to the idea. The researchers effected an introduction between workers at the Centre, the local probation office, and the Asha Women's Centre in Worcester[2] (Gelsthorpe et al. 2007). As a result of the survey, an extensive review of the literature on what might 'work' with women, detailed case studies of four projects or centres, and 'nine lessons' for the creation of further provision in the community were produced. The researchers concluded that such provision should:

1. Be women-only, fostering safety and a sense of community and enabling staff to develop expertise in working with women;
2. Integrate offenders and non-offenders, thus normalising women offenders' experiences and facilitating a supportive environment for learning;
3. Foster women's empowerment to ensure sufficient self-esteem to engage in personal problem-solving and to motivate them to seek appropriate employment;

4. Utilise what is known about effective learning styles with women, specifically collaborative learning;
5. Take a holistic, practical approach to helping women address social problems that may be linked to their offending;
6. Facilitate links with mainstream agencies, especially health, debt advice, and counselling;
7. Have capacity and flexibility, enabling women to return for 'top ups' or continued support and development;
8. Ensure that women have a supportive milieu or mentor to whom they can turn when they have completed offender-related programmes as personal care is important in addressing offending behaviour;
9. Provide women with practical help with transport and childcare to maintain their involvement in the programme.

These 'lessons' were transformed into 'nine questions' for commissioners of services to actively explore what might be available, adaptable, and convertible into specialist provision for women in the community (Gelsthorpe et al. 2007). Thus, the prospects of specialist provision for women had never seemed stronger.

Moving forward with optimism

Corston's presentation of concerns and endeavours, including existing initiatives, played a positive role in bringing these to politicians' attention. The government accepted 25 of her 43 recommendations in full and a further 14 in part or in principle (MOJ 2007; see also Chapter 1). Her vision included the expansion of community penalties, stating, 'It seems to me that it is essential to do more to address issues connected with women's offending before imprisonment becomes a serious option' (Corston 2007: Foreword, i). She then presented a blueprint for a 'radically different, visibly-led, strategic, proportionate, holistic, woman-centred, integrated approach' (p. 79). Most forcibly, Corston added two new 're-ducing reoffending pathways' to those seven already indicated by the MOJ in its strategy to reduce reoffending (accommodation; skills and employment; health; drugs and alcohol; finance, benefits and debt; children, families and relationships; attitudes, thinking and behaviour). These were 'supporting women who have been abused, raped or experienced domestic abuse' and 'supporting women who are or have been involved in prostitution' (p. 46).

Subsequent developments, including further funding for community-based programmes to address women's specific needs, suggested real progress. Carol Hedderman commented,

> There is no question that in the last few years of its administration, the Labour government made important progress in supporting and fostering the development of community-based programmes for women offenders; and that support was not just rhetorical but financial. While £26 million is not

a huge sum compared to £3 billion spent on prisons each year, it bought a significant amount of support for some of the most socially disadvantaged women in England and Wales.

(2010: 495)

Indeed, with renewed momentum inspired by the Corston Report, the MOJ committed significant funding to voluntary organisations to take the lead in working with statutory agencies to provide additional and enhanced community support for women at risk of offending or reoffending. The Government Equalities Office organised regional events, bringing together statutory and voluntary service (third sector) agencies to consider how best to work together to divert women away from both crime and custody. The effectiveness of the MOJ's strategy for women offenders and those at risk of offending was encapsulated in *A Distinct Approach: A Guide for Working with Women Offenders* (NOMS 2012). This was important in reflecting an accumulation of research findings and establishing important precepts. It outlined the extent of the problem in terms of the number of women offenders, acknowledged the needs of different groups of women, and provided a useful explanation of the Equality Duty (with a reminder that equality does not mean sameness). The document outlined two key issues affecting women: violence and self-harm. It did not, however, have impact beyond the criminal justice system. While it was clear that the government recognised that policy and practice must be guided by research findings, it became evident that there were implementation difficulties.

The MOJ's analysis of community services for women offenders and those at risk of offending, introduced between late 2006 and early 2007 through the 'Together Women' (TW) project, recognised a number of positive features (Hedderman et al. 2008). First, TW was considered by local stakeholders to fill an important gap in provision (although concerns remained about the supply of suitable accommodation, access to counselling, and mental health outreach services). Individual care plans were important, and most women interviewed early on were optimistic about their chances of avoiding further offending. However, later interviews introduced a note of caution as women recognised that progress would not be linear. Significantly, there was acknowledgement that women who were struggling most, because of addictions and associated difficulties, could turn to TW long after other agencies, family, and friends had given up on them. Regarding holistic support, it became clear that whilst a wide range of agencies were described as 'willing and enthusiastic participants', a number of stakeholders and staff noted that accessing appropriate representatives from local health services had been slow and difficult, reflecting the complexity of local health arrangements rather than a lack of commitment (Hedderman et al. 2008: 16). Notwithstanding the difficulties in measuring the effectiveness of TW regarding diversion from crime and from custody, the overall impression of the services was positive. Service users who had sustained contact with TW in its first year of operation highly valued the assistance provided and the facilitated access to other agencies. Such positive findings are recorded in the evaluation, establishing 'what women want' (Hedderman et al. 2011).

Positive feedback from women's centres is aplenty. Building on *Unlocking Value*, published in 2008, the new economics foundation strongly suggested that communities benefit from investing in alternatives to prison for women offenders. The authors concluded that using women's centre provision as an alternative to custody could deliver £14 of social value for every £1 invested. Later research from the New Economics Foundation (Nicholles and Whitehead 2012), funded by the MOJ, the Corston Independent Funders Coalition, and the Women's Diversionary Fund, investigated the impact of the 'Women's Centres' on women offenders across five sites, suggesting positive outcomes in relation to women's optimism, autonomic- and self-efficacy, and securing supportive relationships. As Nicholles and Whitehead indicate,

> Women's community services can significantly improve the well-being of vulnerable women, and in doing so help them achieve long-term changes in their lives. The services offer women the key tools they need to begin to make changes – a feeling of being more in control of their lives, supportive relationships, a sense that their lives have meaning, and hope for the future.
>
> *(2012: 2)*

Evaluation of the Liverpool Women's Turnaround Project (McCoy et al. 2013) measured women's progress against the nine reducing reoffending pathways as set out in the Corston Report. The median number of needs identified for a cohort of women using the centre in the first quarter of 2012 was three (with a range of one to eight needs). Positive progress was identified for 64.4 per cent of the women, and 75 per cent achieved positive progress on 50 per cent or more of their identified needs. Interviews with 26 women revealed positive experiences of non-judgemental support and improvements in the use of alcohol as well as physical health, mental health, relationships, offending, and social skills.

The Inspire project at Brighton Women's Centre noted that for the year 2014/15, Inspire engaged with 351 women of whom 90 per cent successfully completed their community orders. Furthermore, in 2012, a sampled cohort of women offenders demonstrated that a year after engagement with Inspire, offending levels had reduced by 87.5 per cent (Inspire 2017). In addition to these outcomes, there is arguably a strong financial case behind this work: A woman offender supported by Inspire costs £997 per year. The cost of a prison place is £56,415 (PRT 2016; Inspire 2017).

The Inspire Women's Project in Northern Ireland, established in October 2008, aimed 'to develop and deliver in the community a new, enhanced range of women-specific services which directly contribute to reducing women's offending through targeted community based interventions' (DOJ 2010). The evaluation of this service involved analysis of a cohort of women (mostly between 20 and 49 years of age), referred to Inspire between October 2008 and July 2010, with 89 per cent on community sentences (Easton and Matthews 2011). Most were compliant with their community sentences (72 per cent) and were positive about available provision in relation to the quality of supervision and the variety of support options. Women were positive regarding women-only provision and physical space, the non-judgemental attitude of probation officers, and the flexible, yet boundaried, approach. They also mentioned 'the opportunity for support from their peers; the support provided around specific issues such as debt, housing, attending court'; the links they made in the community; and the range of meaningful activities and interventions provided (Easton and Matthews 2011: 5). Interviews indicated that 78 per cent had not committed a further offence since engaging with Inspire.

These are snapshots of the achievements of the centres. Undoubtedly, there is similar feedback from the 58 organisations currently registered as members of Women's Breakout, a national network of service providers across England and Wales.[3]

Realities on the ground

Yet policy and practice can be in tension, particularly in relation to the aspirations for the treatment of women. In regard to the Women's Specific Conditional Caution (WSCC),[4] for instance, there was some evidence to suggest that whereas previously, the police referred women to women's centres informally, they now referred them formally (via a WSCC) (Easton et al. 2010), bringing concerns about net-widening. Further, the evaluation of pilot schemes across three sites linked to the Together Women initiative revealed inconsistencies regarding the number and type of conditions used in conjunction with the WSCC. Women generally welcomed the WSCC as a positive disposal that addressed their needs and offered them a lifeline, but there was confusion about the requirements, services, and support available at centres. There was a reduction in offending, with all but one of the 21 women interviewed as part of the evaluation reporting that they had not reoffended since receiving a WSCC (Easton et al. 2010). However, information exchange protocols did not always facilitate voluntary agency/ community work liaison with probation staff in regard to risks and concerns about women. Further, it was established that there was insufficient bail accommodation available for women. While it was suggested that women should be screened for mental ill health, mental health liaison schemes were under considerable strain, and women were not always referred to the specialist services they required. There were inadequate dual diagnosis resources (e.g. drug misuse and mental health), and the approach of commissioning meant that services competed rather than providing a holistic service (Page 2013; Grace et al. 2016). Given competition in commissioning, there was scope for integrated commissioning to reflect women's complex difficulties and pathways into crime.

There have also been concerns about TW. It was not clear that magistrates fully understood the use of women's centre services as a sentencing resource, and they did not appear to understand that placing women offenders with others who endure challenging circumstances not necessarily involving crime can be beneficial (Hedderman and Gunby 2013). Moreover, the analysis of reoffending following TW (Jolliffe et al. 2011) highlighted a lack of standardised measures and systems for recording data and inconsistencies in how service users were defined alongside contrasting support provided. TW was designed to be locally planned and delivered while functioning as a national demonstration project. Despite initial concerns about evaluation and monitoring recorded by the early stage action research, in 2008, there were no substantive improvements, limiting quantitative analysis of patterns of reoffending as a measure of outcomes. Yet TW offered offenders and non-offenders a range of services, and it is questionable whether such a service can be evaluated appropriately using only official measures of proven reoffending. Comparing a group of women in the TW group with a 'broadly matched' group who had simply commenced probation supervision, 35.3 per cent of the TW women had reoffended within 12 months, compared to 35 per cent of the non-TW group. In sum, TW did not appear to reduce the prevalence or frequency of proven reoffending for those referred to TW with a recent criminal record when compared to those commencing supervision. More encouraging, Data Lab analysis (MOJ 2017a) regarding reoffending behaviour after participation in the Brighton Women's Centre Inspire Programme showed that those who received support had a lower frequency of reoffending than those who did not.

There are broader critical points regarding the locally developed community services for women. Some lack a theoretical basis (in terms of what might motivate change). Non-reconviction benefits are difficult to measure, and different centres have developed different approaches. Unfortunately, because there is no consistency between projects in how outcomes are measured, there is no reliable evidence to argue that other existing measures should be used in place of, or alongside, reconviction, although there is positive work towards the creation of interim outcome measures. It is important to note that when women are supported because their social problems may put them at risk of offending, but they have no history of offending, it is not possible to estimate the impact this might have on future offending because there is no 'counterfactual'. There is no way of estimating what would have happened in the absence of intervention. These problems aside, and achievements far outweighing these problems, what specific problems do community centres for women face under the Transforming Rehabilitation agenda?

The challenges of the Offender Rehabilitation Act 2014

The argument that the public sector should not have a monopoly on the provision of public services is made clearly in discussion papers published a quarter of a century ago by the Conservative Government (Home Office 1990a,b, 1992). The most significant impact of these was on the relationship between the probation service and the voluntary sector. It noted that each local probation service was required to allocate a proportion of its budget to partnership schemes, almost entirely with voluntary sector organisations. The Association of Chief Officers of Probation gave a muted welcome to this more formal approach to working with other agencies (ACOP 1993). Yet the 1997 Labour Government simply fuelled the push for privatisation. It also continued with policies to enable the voluntary sector, often referred to as the third sector, to take a greater role in the delivery of reformed public services (Alcock 2010). The 2003 Correctional Services Review was charged with recommending changes to the prison and probation services in order to reduce crime, maintain public confidence, and control expenditure. It advocated greater use of the private sector as a provider of correctional services (Carter 2003). Without supporting evidence, the review argued that privatisation had resulted in improvements in the prison service and that marketisation could only improve service delivery and cost effectiveness to other offender management interventions.

The 2010 Coalition Government announced a 'rehabilitation revolution' to reduce reoffending, reduce the size of the prison population, and reduce over-reliance on centrally set targets at the expense of outcome-orientated innovation (MOJ 2010). Ironically, reoffending rates for those on probation were lower than for those leaving prison, but this significant fact escaped the notice of the government (MOJ 2012a). Future proposals were contextualised by economic austerity and the need for the MOJ to make financial cuts. A Competition Strategy for Offender Services (MOJ 2011) restated the government's commitment to competition for probation services to improve outcomes and secure value for money.

An unanticipated element of the consultation document *Punishment and Reform: Effective Probation Services* was a split between areas of work that would remain the business of public sector probation trusts and other work that would be opened up to competition (MOJ 2012b). Advice to courts, decisions about risk assessment and enforcement action for all offenders – except those on stand-alone curfew requirements – and the supervision of those assessed as high risk would remain with probation trusts, who would then commission other services, including the management and supervision of low- and medium-risk offenders, thus establishing a new market of providers.

The proposals to divide probation caseloads on the basis of risk and outsource the management of low- and medium-risk cases to private providers survived the consultation period. However, a decision paper (MOJ 2013) indicated that the 35 probation trusts were to be abolished and replaced by a new public sector National Probation Service (NPS), which would operate in conjunction with private or voluntary sector organisations to be called Community Rehabilitation Companies (CRCs). These CRCs would be commissioned by the National Offender Management Service (NOMS) to work in 21 'contract package areas'. The Transforming Rehabilitation proposals maintained a commitment to payment-by-results as the means of ensuring that services successfully reduced reoffending. The proposals also extended statutory post-release supervision to short-sentence prisoners serving less than 12 months in custody. The successful bidders for the CRCs (MOJ 2014) were, with one exception,[5] consortia led by private sector companies working with voluntary agencies, including new agencies formed by staff from probation trusts. Three big winners were Sodexo Justice Services (working with the large voluntary sector organisation Nacro), Purple Futures (led by the company Interserve, working with voluntary sector organisations including Shelter, Addaction,[6] and P3) and MTCnovo (a joint venture between a US-based private company, MTC, and a consortium of private, public, and voluntary sector providers). Sodexo and MTC operate private prisons; Interserve has previous involvement in prison-building.

Unsurprisingly, the abolition of probation trusts led to considerable uncertainty and insecurity (Burke and Collett 2015; Robinson et al. 2016). It raised questions about the future of professional practice, workloads, employment status, employment security, pay, benefits, and redundancy. There were particular concerns about women, given that probation staff had been central in driving forwards the need to attend to women's specific needs (Worrall and Gelsthorpe 2009).

Alongside these major organisational changes, the ORA 2014 introduced an extension of post-custody statutory monitoring and supervision to offenders serving short-term custodial sentences for a mandatory period of up to 12 months. It also amended license conditions for those serving sentences of 12–24 months to ensure that they do not receive shorter periods of supervision than those serving sentences of less than one year.

Crucially, do these changes impact provision for women in the community? ORA 2014 (implemented 1 February 2015) states (in section 10) that

> in providing supervision or rehabilitation the Secretary of State must comply with the public sector equality duty under the Equality Act 2010 as it relates to female offenders and must also identify anything in the arrangements that is intended to meet the particular needs of this group.

The organisational changes introduced the incentivisation of different providers to engage in the delivery of supervision and support, based on payment-by-results.[7] Fox and Albertson (2012) noted four main benefits which have been claimed for an approach based on outcomes achievement rather than on 'inputs' (e.g. number of staff) or 'outputs' delivered (e.g. referrals to drug services). These were greater efficiency, greater innovation, reduced costs, and a broader range of services as new suppliers are attracted into the 'market', although they expressed serious doubts about these being achieved (see also, Dominey 2012; Dominey and Gelsthorpe 2017). From the outset, there were concerns that women's services would not benefit from this organisational change. As Gelsthorpe and Hedderman (2012) observed, the number of women involved was likely to be small, thus proving that impact to a statistically significant level in reducing reoffending would be difficult. Women in the criminal justice system have significant and complex needs, even if their risks of reoffending are lower than those for men, thus there may be limited attraction for new suppliers in working with this group. Further, the NOMS publications *Effective Interventions for Women Offenders: A Rapid Evidence Assessment* (Stewart and Gobeil 2015) aimed at assisting in the design of an evidence-based commissioning approach, and *Better Outcomes for Women Offenders* (NOMS 2015) arguably came too late to be absorbed by CRCs when developing their bids.

In 2013, Clinks[8] published an interim study, *Run Ragged*, of the experiences of initiatives and centres providing community support to women offenders. There was a follow-up study in 2014: *Who Cares? Where Next for Women Offender Services?* This study found that 89 per cent of projects considered their service to be 'less secure' or 'as insecure' as 12 months previously. Probation trust funding stopped at the end of January 2015 when the CRCs assumed responsibility. *Changing Lives*, the women's centre in Cardiff, for example, was informed that its contract would not be renewed despite its having been named by Working Links as a subcontractor in the original bid submitted to NOMS. It has now closed, with the loss of experienced staff, although the CRC retained the city centre premises as a women's hub. Thames Valley CRC withdrew funding for work delivered by Alana House, an award-winning centre in Reading that had worked for several years with probation services to deliver a quality service to women offenders. Provision for women in other areas has been similarly affected (Prison Reform Trust 2015). Some contracts were extended, some became part of complicated supply chains with uncertain funding, and some centres for women closed as a consequence of the new probation landscape.

The House of Commons Justice Committee's follow-up on women offenders (2015: paras 3 and 4) noted,

> We are concerned that funding appears to be a recurring problem for women's centres and that future funding arrangements have not been put on a sounds basis as we recommended...we reiterate our recommendation that sustainable funding of specialist women's services should be a priority.

Lord Hylton requested clarity regarding the funding of women's centres in a written parliamentary question (House of Lords 5633, 29 January 2016). Answered by Baroness Evans for the government on 11 February 2016, the message was clear:

> The Government believes that future funding for women's centres should lie at the local level, as local experts know what works in their community and how best to deliver services. We are encouraging and supporting areas to bring together local agencies in the criminal justice, statutory and third sectors to develop a joined up, multi-agency approach to address the often complex needs of female offenders.

In January 2017, the closure of the Asha Centre in Worcester (a forerunner to TW) due to difficulty in finding funding demonstrated the uncertainty and dismay concerning provision for women offenders in the community.

Protected commercial interests obstruct access to a full picture of how different CRCs are addressing necessary women's services. It is clear that community service providers have struggled to engage with some CRCs and that some CRCs have created their own programmes for women rather than investing in existing community provision. London CRC, for example, has created a Structured Supervision Programme for women. This is perhaps contrary to expectations, given governmental support for community-based services for women to 'get going' following the TW demonstration project and the inspiration and impetus from the Corston Report.

The All Party Parliamentary Group on Women in the Penal System (2016), comprising MPs and members of the House of Lords from all parties, having received evidence from academics and practitioners, expressed serious concerns about the future of provision for women offenders in the community, especially the 'one-stop shops' championed by the Corston Report. Drawing on evidence from CRCs directly, there has been concern that the needs of, and quality services for, women have not been adequately safeguarded. The Public Accounts Committee reached the same conclusion (PAC 2016). Some CRCs are reported to have interpreted their duties towards women narrowly, offering the option of a female supervisor but nothing further. Evidence from women's centres is recorded as overwhelmingly negative. This includes no funding or time-limited funding from CRCs; contracts for lower quality services than hitherto offered; and pressure to form consortia of women's centres, with considerable investment of time in the task, only to be informed that centres would be contracted individually (APPG 2016).

In addition to this gloomy picture of backward steps, in 2016, HM Inspectorate of Probation conducted a thematic inspection of provision and quality of services in the community for women who offend. The inspectors acknowledged the significant boost to women's services following the Corston Report. A previous thematic inspection (HMIP 2011) noted both achievements and inconsistencies in provision, highlighting the fact that specific performance measures were unclear. In this most recent thematic inspection, the team found a lack of strategic focus on women, no clear government policy, and 'basic' rather than 'strategic' Community Rehabilitation Company contractual provisions specific to women. The report also noted that outcome measures specific to women were still unclear. In the Foreword, Dame Glenys Stacey observes,

> Since the implementation of the Transforming Rehabilitation programme, dedicated funding for women's community services has virtually disappeared, and provision is mixed and uncertain...Women's Centres are particularly vulnerable and some have already lost funding, yet they have an important role to play. We found cases where they had been pivotal in

turning women away from crime and helping them to rebuild their lives…
In our view, women's centres need both funding and strategic support, so
that they fulfil their potential with this group of women.

(HMIP 2016: 4)

A second major theme is that new figures demonstrate that the number of
women recalled to custody following release had increased by over two-thirds
(68 per cent) since late 2014 (MOJ 2017b). Women recalled to custody now account for 8 per cent of the total women's prison population. The dramatic rise
follows changes introduced by the Offender Rehabilitation Act 2014 with its
new mandated post-custody supervision for all serving sentences of more than
one day. Women are recalled not only because they commit a further offence
but also if they breach the conditions of their licence whilst under supervision.
This includes missing an appointment with probation staff. Just over a quarter of
women, 27 per cent, were recalled for a further criminal charge (MOJ 2017b).

There is also concern about the recent increase in the use of suspended sentences alongside a decrease in community sentences. The Prison Reform Trust
(2017) observes that suspended prison sentences given to women had doubled in
the last decade, whilst community orders had nearly halved. Because suspended
sentences require compliance with court-ordered stipulations, with the threat of
custody for any breach of sentence conditions, their increased use risks driving
up the women's prison population due to breaches and recalls. Add to this the
strong evidence from the front-line organisation Women in Prison (2017) that
prison does not work for women and accumulates problems for the future with
dire need for more investment in community services, it is clear that the Corston
Report remains highly relevant to contemporary policy-making.

Conclusion: three steps forwards, four steps backwards?

Historically, as the introduction to this book notes, women have been seen as
'correctional afterthoughts' in developments of penal policy and practice. More
recently, however, there has been evidence of some positive impact on the effectiveness of criminal justice interventions with women offenders. There have
been significant efforts to focus more directly on what is known about women's
needs and to develop practice-based initiatives that address these needs. Building on earlier progress, Corston's 2007 Report had an inspiring influence on
subsequent developments. Yet the recent Rehabilitation Revolution, which reshaped probation and community support for offenders, risks reversing these
positive steps. The parliamentary *Inquiry into Preventing Unnecessary Criminalisation of Women* (APPG 2015) boldly suggested that the companies now supplying
community-based support and supervision lack both knowledge and experience in relation to women in conflict with the law and their gender-specific
needs. Following concerns raised by the inspectorates of probation and prisons,
the government committed to reviewing the contracts under which providers

are commissioned to deliver rehabilitation services for offenders released from prison. At the time of writing, a further government strategy for women in the criminal justice system is due to be published. It is important that the positive developments discussed earlier are not lost. For instance, budgets for women's services could be ring-fenced and transferred to the National Probation Service to commission programmes both locally and regionally, drawing on the services that have had such positive impact on women's lives, utilising the knowledge and good practice that has been developed over the years and reflecting the principles and values inherent in the Corston Report.

Notes

1 The Sentencing Guidelines Council became the Sentencing Council in 2003.
2 This was originally developed under the leadership of Jenny Roberts, Chief Proba-tion Officer Hereford, and Worcestershire Probation (and known as the West Mercia Community-Based Programme for Women Offenders). See Roberts (2002).
3 Women's Breakout: http://womensbreakout.org.uk.
4 The Women Specific Conditional Caution (WSCC) was introduced as a pilot in three sites in 2008: two in the West Yorkshire Police Service and one in Merseyside Police Service. The WSCC is a pre-court disposal for low-level, low-risk women offenders; it is widely seen as a positive response to the Corston (2007) recommenda-tions (see Easton et al. (2010) for details of the evaluation).
5 The successful bidder in the Durham Tees Valley area was a joint venture without a private sector company.
6 Add action withdrew from the Purple Futures Partnership in April 2015 *'due to a failure to agree the detail of subcontracting arrangements'*.
7 See https://data.gov.uk/sib_knowledge_box/payment-results-definition.
8 Clinks is an umbrella organisation that supports voluntary organisations that work alongside people in the criminal justice system: www.clinks.org/review2016.

References

ACOP (1993) *Partnership: Purpose, Principles, Contractual Arrangements*, London: ACOP.

Alcock, P. (2010) *Partnership and Mainstreaming: Voluntary Action under New Labour* Working Paper 32, Birmingham, UK: Third Sector Research Centre.

All Party Parliamentary Group on Women in the Penal System (2015) *Report on the In-quiry into Preventing Unnecessary Criminalisation of Women*, London: Howard League for Penal Reform.

All Party Parliamentary Group on Women in the Penal System (2016) *Is This the End of Women's Centres?*, London: Howard League for Penal Reform.

Burke, L. and Collett, S. (2015) *Delivering Rehabilitation: The Politics, Governance and Con-trol of Crime*, Abingdon, UK: Routledge.

Carlen, P. (1983) *Women's Imprisonment: A Study in Social Control*, London: Routledge and Kegan Paul.

Carlen, P. (1990) *Alternatives to Women's Imprisonment*, Buckingham: Open University Press.

Carlen, P. and Worrall, A. (1987) *Gender, Crime, and Justice*, Buckingham: Open University Press.

Carlen, P. and Worrall, A. (2004) *Analysing Women's Imprisonment*, Cullompton, UK: Willan.

Carter, P. (2003) *Managing Offenders, Reducing Crime: A New Approach (Correctional Services Review)*, London: Home Office.

Clinks (2013) *Run Ragged,* London: Clinks.

Clinks (2014) *Who Cares? Where Next for Women Offender Services?*, London: Clinks.

Corston, J. (2007) *The Corston Report: A Review of Women with Particular Vulnerabilities in the Criminal Justice System*, London: Home Office.

Deakin, J. and Spencer, J. (2003) 'Women behind bars: explanations and implications', *Howard Journal of Crime and Justice*, 42(2): 123–136.

Department of Justice (2010) *Women's Offending Behaviour in Northern Ireland: A Strategy to Manage Women Offenders and Those Vulnerable to Offending Behaviour 2010–2014*, Belfast: DOJ.

Dobash, R. P., Dobash, R. E. and Gutteridge, S. (1986) *The Imprisonment of Women*, Oxford: Blackwell.

Dominey, J. (2012) 'A mixed market for probation services: can lessons from the recent past help shape the near future?', *Probation Journal*, 59(4): 339–354.

Dominey, J. and Gelsthorpe, L. (2017) 'Competing to control in the community: what chance for a culture of care?' In A. Hucklesby and S. Lister (Eds.), *Private Sector Involvement in Criminal Justice*, London: Palgrave.

Douglas, N., Plugge, E. and Fitzpatrick, R. (2009) 'The impact of imprisonment on health – what do women prisoners say?', *Journal of Epidemiology and Community Health*, 63(9): 749–754.

Easton, H. and Matthews, R. (2011) *Evaluation of the Inspire Women's Project*, London: London South Bank University.

Easton, H., Silvestri, M., Evans, K., Matthews, R. and Walklate, S. (2010) *Conditional Cautions: Evaluation of the Women's Specific Condition Pilot*, London: MOJ Research Series 14/10.

Fox, C. and Albertson, K. (2012) 'Is payment by results the most efficient way to address the challenges faced by the criminal justice sector?', *Probation Journal*, 59(4): 355–373.

Gelsthorpe, L., and Hedderman, C. (2012) 'Providing for women offenders. The risks of adopting a payment by results approach', *Probation Journal*, 59, 374–390.

Gelsthorpe, L. and Morris, A. (2002) 'Women's imprisonment in England and Wales. A penal paradox', *Criminology & Criminal Justice*, 2(3): 277–301.

Gelsthorpe L., Sharpe, G. and Roberts, J. (2007) *Provision for Women Offenders in the Community*. London: Fawcett Commission.

Grace, S., Page, G., Lloyd, C., Templeton, L., Kougali, Z., McKeganey, N., Liebling, A., Roberts, P. and Russell, C. (2016) 'Establishing a 'Corstonian' continuous care package for drug using female prisoners: linking Drug Recovery Wings and Women's Community Services', *Criminology and Criminal Justice*, 16(5): 602–621.

Hedderman, C. (2004) 'Why are more women being sentenced to custody?' In G. McIvor (Ed.), *Women Who Offend*. London: Jessica Kingsley.

Hedderman, C. (2010) 'Government policy on women offenders: labour's legacy and the Coalition's challenge', *Punishment & Society*, 12(4): 485–500.

Hedderman, C. and Gunby, C. (2013) 'Diverting women from custody: the importance of understanding sentencers' perspectives', *Probation Journal*, 60(4): 425–438.

Hedderman, C. Gunby, C. and Shelton, N. (2011) 'What women want: the importance of qualitative approaches in evaluating work with women offenders', *Criminology and Criminal Justice*, 11(1): 3–19.

Hedderman, C., Palmer, E., Hollin, C. with assistance of Gunby, C., Shelton, N. and Askari, M. (2008) *Implementing Services for Women Offenders and Those 'At Risk' of Offending: Action Research with Together Women*, London: MOJ Research Series 12/08.

Heidensohn, F. (1985) *Women and Crime*, London: Macmillan.

HM Inspectorate of Probation (2011) *Thematic Inspection Report: Equal but Different? An Inspection of Alternatives to Custody for Women Offenders*, Manchester: HMIP.

HM Inspectorate of Probation (2016) *A Thematic Inspection of the Provision and Quality of Services in the Community for Women Who Offend*, Manchester: HMIP.

Home Office (1990a) *Supervision and Punishment in the Community,* Cm966, London: Home Office.

Home Office (1990b) *Partnership in Dealing with Offenders in the Community*, London: Home Office.

Home Office (1992) *Partnership in Dealing with Offenders in the Community: A Decision Document*, London: Home Office.

Home Office (2004) *Women's Offending Reduction Programme (WORP) Action Plan*, London: Home Office.

House of Commons Committee of Public Accounts (2016) *Transforming Rehabilitation: Seventeenth Report of Session 2016–17*, London: House of Commons.

House of Commons Justice Committee Justice (2015) *Thirteenth Report. Women offenders. Follow-Up: Government's Response to the Committee's Thirteenth Report of Session 2014–15*, London: House of Commons.

House of Lords (Written Question from Lord Hylton) 5633, 29 January, 2016.

Inspire (2017) Brighton Women's Centre. www.womenscentre.org.uk/services/inspire/.

Jolliffe, D., Hedderman, C., Palmer, E. and Hollin, C. (2011) *Re-offending Analysis of Women Offenders Referred to Together Women (TW) and the Scope to Divert from Custody*, Ministry of Justice Research Series 11/11, London: MOJ.

Loucks, N., Malloch, M., McIvor, G. and Gelsthorpe, L. (2006) *Evaluation of the 218 Centre*, Edinburgh: Scottish Executive.

McCoy, E., Jones, L. and McVeigh, J. (2013) *Evaluation of the Liverpool Women's Turnaround Project*, Liverpool: Liverpool John Moores University.

Ministry of Justice (2007) *The Government's Response to the Report by Baroness Corston of a Review of Women with Particular Vulnerabilities in the Criminal Justice System*, Cmnd 7261, London: TSO.

Ministry of Justice (2010) *Breaking the Cycle: Effective Punishment, Rehabilitation and Sentencing of Offenders*, Cm 7972, London: MOJ.

Ministry of Justice (2011) *Competition Strategy for Offender Services*, London: MOJ.

Ministry of Justice (2012a) *Compendium of Re-offending Statistics and Analysis*, London: MOJ.

Ministry of Justice (2012b) *Punishment and Reform: Effective Probation Services*, Consultation Paper CP7/2012, London: MOJ.

Ministry of Justice (2013) *Transforming Rehabilitation: A Strategy for Reform*, Cm 8619, London: MOJ.

Ministry of Justice (2014) 'Voluntary sector at forefront of fight against reoffending' *Press Release:* https://www.gov.uk/government/news/voluntary-sector-at-forefront-of-new-fight-against-reoffending [Accessed 23 August, 2017].

Ministry of Justice (2016) *Statistics on Women and the Criminal Justice System 2015. A Ministry of Justice Publication under Section 95 of the Criminal Justice Act 1991*, London: MOJ.

Ministry of Justice (2017a) *Justice Data Lab Analysis: Re-offending Behaviour after Participation in the Brighton Women's Centre Inspire Programme* (April 2017), London: MOJ.

Ministry of Justice (2017b) *Offender Management Statistics Quarterly July–September 2016*, London: MoJ.

National Offender Management Service (2012) *A Distinct Approach: A Guide for Working with Women Offenders*, London: NOMS.

National Offender Management Service (NOMS) (2015) *Better Outcomes for Women Offenders*, London: NOMS.

New Economics Foundation (2008) *Unlocking Value*, London: NEF.

New Labour (1997) *Manifesto*, labourmanifesto.com. Accessed: 29 June 2017.

Nicholles, N. and Whitehead, S. (2012) *Women's Community Services: A Wise Commission*, London: NEF.

Open University (2008–9) 'Endless new criminal laws, a massive increase in people jailed, and a rise in the fear of crime', *Society Matters*, 11(4).

Page, G. (2013) *Risks, Needs and Emotional Rewards: Complexity and Crisis in the Drug Interventions Programme*, Unpublished PhD, University of Cambridge.

Panayotopoulos-Cassiotou, M. (2008) European Union session document: Report on the situation of women in prison and the impact of the imprisonment of parents on social and family life (2007/2116(INI).

Prison Reform Trust (2015) *Prison Reform Trust Response to HM Inspectorate of Probation's Call for Evidence on Work with Women Offenders*, London: PRT.

Prison Reform Trust (2016) *Prison Factfile. Bromley Briefings*, London: PRT.

Prison Reform Trust (2017) *Why Focus on Reducing Women's Imprisonment?* Briefing, London: PRT.

Quaker Council for European Affairs (2007) *Women in Prison: A Review of the Conditions in Member States of the Council of Europe*, Brussels: QCEA.

Roberts, J. (2002) 'Women-centred: the West Mercia community-based programme for women offenders.' in P. Carlen (Ed.), *Women and Punishment: The Struggle for Justice*, Cullompton: Willan.

Robinson, G., Burke, L. and Millings, M. (2016) 'Criminal justice identities in transition: the case of devolved probation services in England and Wales', *British Journal of Criminology*, 56(1): 161–178.

Rumgay, J. (2004) *The Asha Centre: Report of an Evaluation*, Worcester, UK: Asha Centre.

Smart, C. (1976) *Women, Crime and Criminology*, London: Routledge and Kegan Paul.

Social Exclusion Unit (2002) *Reducing Re-Offending by Ex-Prisoners*, London: Office of the Deputy Prime Minister.

Stewart, L. and Gobeil, R. (2015) *Effective Interventions for Women Offenders: A Rapid Evidence Assessment*, NOMS Analytical Summary, July 2015.

Women in Prison (2017) *Corston+10. The Corston Report 10 Years On*, London: WIP.

Women's Policy Team (2006) *Women's Offending Reduction Programme: 2006 Review of Progress*, London: Home Office.

Worrall, A. (1990) *Offending Women*, London: Routledge.

Worrall, A. (1997) *Punishment in the Community*, Harlow, UK: Addison-Wesley Longman.

Worrall, A. and Gelsthorpe, L. (2009) ''What works' with women offenders: The past 30 years', *Probation Journal*, 56: 329–345.

3

FROM 'TROUBLED' WOMEN TO FAILING INSTITUTIONS

The necessary narrative shift for the decarceration of women post-Corston

Becky Clarke and Kathryn Chadwick

Introduction

We sit and write this chapter in autumn 2016 in the knowledge that a young woman, Celeste Craig, became the nineteenth woman to die in prison in England and Wales (E&W) in the previous 12 months (Abbit 2016). More women are dying in prisons in E&W than at any time since Baroness Jean Corston's review was published in 2007 (Inquest 2016). This leaves us feeling sad, angry and deeply motivated to question what has happened in the intervening 10 years.

As discussed throughout this book, women constitute a small proportion of the overall prison population. Most women prisoners have histories of experiencing violence and abuse. The majority are serving short sentences for non-violent offences, such as theft, fraud and handling. Many will return to prison within a year (HMIP 2016). 60 per cent of women leave prison without a home (PRT and WIP 2016). Women in Prison[1] note that many women prisoners are primary carers, imprisonment having devastating consequences for their children. Different groups of women experience the criminal justice system disproportionately at all levels. A recent Ministry of Justice (MOJ) report highlights that Black women are 25 per cent more likely than white women to be imprisoned for some offences, exposing the excessive criminalisation of women in particular communities (Uhrig 2016).

There is a context to the imprisonment of criminalised women. Most are socially, politically and economically disadvantaged, which is reflective of their gendered roles in the home or family and position within patriarchal and neo-colonial capitalist structures. Trauma and exploitation are reproduced by institutions that fail to adequately respond to women who experience exclusion and marginalisation (Scraton 2016). Poverty, homelessness, poor mental health, fractured families, ongoing abuse and violence: these become points of intervention by the state, but all too often, the response is to criminalise. As Marie Segrave and Bree Carlton (2010: 289) argue, 'the justice system separates and decontextualizes women's actions from the broader social and structural context of their lives'.

There have been ongoing efforts to expose the particular relationship between criminalised women and the state's power to punish through the use of the prison, from the early empirical work by Pat Carlen at Cornton Vale Prison in Scotland (1983) through to more contemporary studies, such as Segrave and Carlton's research in Victoria, Australia (2010) and Linda Moore and Phil Scraton's in Maghaberry and Hydebank Wood prisons in Northern Ireland (2014). The aforementioned, revealed the gendered experience of criminalisation and punishment. What is evident is that the pains and harms of imprisonment for women have remained consistent over time (Malloch and McIvor 2013).

In 1987, Kathryn Chadwick and Cath Little, focusing on the criminalisation of women, outlined the significance and impact of patriarchal ideologies and their institutionalisation within the criminal justice system. As Carlen (1990) argues, the positioning of criminalised women in relation to the state must reveal the intersections of gender, class and 'race'. Further, the shift within neoliberalism to a responsibilising agenda dissipates the state's role in addressing discrimination, inequalities and marginalisation by making individuals accountable for their own choices, lives and personal and even societal failures. The reliance on punitive responses to structural inequalities is evident, not only in penal policy but in other state processes and practices, such as welfare.

As recognised by Corston, women's experiences are central, their voices and biographies essential in contextualising how lives are 'affected by legacies of abuse, neglect, poverty and institutionalisation' (Segrave and Carlton 2010: 290). To move towards decarceration, explanations of offending that focus only on individual characteristics must be rejected. Instead there is a need to prioritise a deeper scrutiny of state power. Such an approach moves beyond the experiential to recognise the structural relations that are so significant to understanding women's agency (see also Wright 2013). It establishes the continued significance of economic marginalisation as well as the impact of postcolonialism for minority ethnic women and patriarchal relations for all women. Thus, the focus is on the processes that create and reinforce criminalised status alongside an examination of lived experiences of social and state control. By using the term 'criminalised women', the state's decision through its institutions to regulate, control and punish is recognised.

This chapter explores whether the Corston review decontextualised women's imprisonment from broader social structures, albeit unintentionally, thus reinforcing the belief that the site for intervention, if women's imprisonment is to be reduced, is the individual woman, her life and her choices. The liberal reform position central to Corston and the wider official discourse concerning women's imprisonment are considered and ultimately rejected. A critical, radical analysis is adopted, prioritising the significance of state power (see Coleman et al. 2010) and processes of criminalisation in understanding both women's imprisonment and the failure to implement Corston's proposals. It is suggested that not only are criminalised women let down by the state but also that official discourse focusing on women's lives and choices rather than structural contexts and institutional failings leads to continued reliance on punitive responses to manage inequalities.

Corston's narrative: the risks of 'othering' criminalised women

Corston's good intentions are clear from the outset:

> that if ever I could do anything to help address the needs of women in contact with the criminal justice system, and their incarceration in our state institutions, whether in a police cell, psychiatric hospital or prison, then I would do so.
>
> *(2007: i)*

Her review provides a straightforward reporting of the lives of women in prison, enabling the 'problem' to be identified, understood and translated into policy or practice responses by the government. The focus is the relationship between the realities of women's lives, historical and present, and their 'offending' behaviour. This approach, however, simplifies the complex, contextualised and often hidden experiences of criminalised women.[2] Women's accounts reveal the messy and complicated relationships between personal trauma and 'support' or unwanted interventions by state institutions and processes of criminalisation. As Segrave and Carlton (2010: 291) state,

> Institutional intervention featured in women's lives from a young age, along with the constant presence and intervention of welfare and criminal justice agencies... Yet while state intervention was a constant in the women's lives from an early age, this was never experienced nor intended as a positive or supportive attempt to assist young women to address traumatic experiences.

What follows explores the narrative of Corston's review, considering the extent to which these issues were taken into account. It identifies the features of the policy narrative that have endured and the extent to which these may be a barrier to women's decarceration.

Corston's starting point was clear: 'My method has been to listen to as many people as possible with expertise and experience working with women throughout the criminal justice system' (2007: Foreword pi). Closer analysis reveals that within the report, the voices of criminalised women are absent. Occasionally, the direct voice of a woman in prison is noted. Regarding education for example, Corston (2007: 45) comments, 'A young woman I met in prison during my review, who had suffered an appalling childhood of abuse, drugs and abandonment, understood what she had missed and said to me, "I shouldn't be here. I should be in college"'. Taken out of context, however, such glimpses offer little understanding of the relationship between imprisonment and the women's lives. In another example, Corston (2007: 21) notes that

One prison officer I met told me that he knew of one woman in prison who had been born in the mother and baby unit at the same prison. Another told me that he had once had in his care three generations of women from the same family, a mother, her mother and her daughter.

In reproducing such interpretations uncritically, women become the 'object', their lives in the prison de-historicised and decontextualised (Krumer-Nevo and Sidi 2012).

Early on in the review process, Corston acknowledges that it may be 'unhelpful' to label women as 'vulnerable' or in ways that render them 'undeserving' (Letter to Baroness Scotland, cited in Corston 2007: 15). Yet throughout the report, the language of vulnerabilities remains, the lens staying focussed on the 'vulnerable' women. This approach privileges more powerful voices from within the institution of the prison: 'Who are these women? Staff at Brockhill described to me some of the common features of the women received at the establishment' (Corston 2007: 26).[3] The accounts of those who work within the prison are often underpinned by care and concern, yet the interpretation of the problem by professionals focuses on women's relationships and behaviours, obscuring the historic trajectories and role of failed institutions. Instead, it is women's histories of abuse and their addiction and abjection that are foregrounded.

Corston's discussion of criminalised women's direct contributions to the review is condensed into a series of bullet points. They are stark and revealing, speaking volumes about a failed system and damaging institutions, such as mental health issues being managed through criminal courts, children being removed and women being 'treated like children' as well as poverty and destitution, strip-searching in prisons and emotional lives characterised by loneliness, loss, fear and guilt. This information is particularly significant, but it is passed over quickly, obscured in policy recommendations and rhetoric. Focussing narrowly on women themselves, their complex needs, vulnerabilities and choices, Corston's narrative neglects the contexts and structures that shape them. By decontextualising and compartmentalising women's lives, complexity is reduced, and something vital is lost.

Without clear reason or explanation, key academic publications at the time of the review are omitted. These include those studies that engage in critical analysis of penal institutions (Carlen and Worrall 2004; Scraton and Moore 2004) and those that provide clear warnings regarding the limitations of gendered criminal justice reform strategies (Carlen and Tombs 2006). Discussion of the 'Creating Choices' initiative in Canada by their Task Force on Federally Sentenced Women, for example, is absent. As Kelly Hannah-Moffat (2002: 203) noted (five years prior to Corston's review), 'This well intentioned reform initiative inadvertently reinforces traditional conceptualisations of punishment and further entrenches our reliance on the prison (or in this case more 'women centred prisons') as a solution.'

Fixing criminalised women – 'turning ("troubled") lives around'

> Most of the women in prisons are troubled rather than troublesome, and
> the way to break the cycle of offending is to better support these women to
> get their lives back on track.
>
> *(Corston September 2016)*

This statement from Corston, quoted in a recent interview, illustrates two central features to the policy discourse applied to criminalised women in the intervening decade since her report. The first layer is the use of the idiom of 'troubled', reflective of the increased use of such terms as 'troubled lives' and 'troubled families' in policy and media narratives (Casey 2012a,b; IPPR 2015). Such representations serve to fix marginalised groups as the object and transform the debate into stigmatising behavioural labels (Krumer-Nevo and Benjamin 2010). The use of the label often goes together with the second feature: the popular policy rhetoric of 'getting lives back on track', often termed 'turning lives around' (Cameron 2011). It is these features of the narrative concerning criminalised women that underpin Corston's strategy, echoed by other privileged voices both within and outside of state institutions, that are critiqued in this chapter.

Implicit in this rhetoric is the onus on women prisoners to engage with 'new' gender-responsive interventions, to take up the choices on offer and to change their lives. It is a continuation of an enduring official discourse surrounding criminalised women, reflected in a Home Office document from the turn of the millennium:

> The characteristics of women prisoners suggest that experiences such as
> poverty, abuse and drug addiction lead some women to believe that their
> options are limited. Many offending behaviour programmes are designed
> to help offenders see there are always positive choices open to them that do
> not involve crime. At the same time, across government, we are tackling
> the aspects of social exclusion that make some women believe their options
> are limited.
>
> *(Home Office 2000: 7 cited in Carlen and Tombs 2006: 239)*

The approach is framed in terms of 'empowerment', of 'giving' agency to women – if only criminalised women would see the choices open to them and be confident to take them. For Corston, the success of her strategy lies in the purposeful resolve to engage women and support them to 'turn their lives around'. As she states, some women will be 'hard to reach and will require persistence and determination and, above all, tolerance, if we are to assist them to turn around their lives' (Corston 2007: 54). This exposes a very thin line between agency and responsibility (Krumer-Nevo and Benjamin 2010). What is clear is that such strategies are not about the empowerment that might develop from a collective voice or about challenging systems of economic or political oppression. It is a narrative that fails to accept agency in women's lives, telling them that they have the capacity to change and insisting that they *should* use that capacity. This ignores the structural determinants in women's lives that restrict agency. It also fails to accept that women's exercise of agency may lead to other choices and outcomes.

The use and assumed *doxa* of the policy discourse of 'turning lives around' has become routine. In just three days in November of 2016, three key protagonists in the debate around women's imprisonment used this phrase: a politician, a campaign organisation and a prison governor. On 3 November, in her Prison Reform speech as Secretary of State for Justice, Liz Truss MP reflected that she had 'chatted to some women offenders at HMP Bronzefield[4] who were learning percentages for the first time in their lives'. She concluded that 'We must now get better at helping offenders abandon crime once and for all…only then can we say that prisoners are getting the best chance of turning their lives around' (Truss 2016). The following day, the campaign group Women in Prison responded to the Justice Secretary's speech. They reasserted the need to engage with the more 'radical' of Corston's recommendations yet reiterated the narrative of the White Paper,[5] expressing enthusiasm for collaborating with the government to make the criminal justice system 'work for all of us by giving women who offend the best chance of turning their lives around' (WIP 2016).

The tension at the heart of this rhetoric is exposed in a media article published on 2 November, the day before the Justice Secretary's Prison Reform speech. The Governor of HMP Eastwood Park, a local women's prison situated in the English Cotswolds, argued that longer sentences were required in order for staff to rehabilitate women in her prison: 'It's absolutely impossible in a few short weeks to turn somebody's life around and undo decades of abuse' (BBC 2016). HMP Eastwood Park had earlier been the focus of a prison letter to *Inside Time* (*Inside Time* Mailbag 6 January 2015):

> I am writing about the shortage of staff here at Eastwood Park. For the last few weeks we have been banged up for over 22 hours per day, only getting unlocked first thing in the morning from 8am to 9.30am for breakfast, meds, shower and exercise – then back behind the door. We now only have association on Tuesday and Friday from 5pm to 6.45pm, this is for 109 women to get food, shower, use the telephone, and get medication and hot water! It is difficult to keep in touch with our families as there are only 3 phones working on the wing, so the queues of women trying to use the phone in such a short space of time are long and stressful. The governor has told us that nothing can be done about the bang-up situation as there are not enough staff.

This letter followed an Independent Monitoring Board annual report (IMB 2014), published a year earlier, highlighting the recent deaths of three women in HMP Eastwood Park and an increase in the opening of Assessment, Care in

Custody and Teamwork (ACCT) self-harm documents, acknowledging that this might have been due to the restricted regime and its impact on women. This is the institution in which women, it was claimed, required more time to enable them to 'turn their lives around'.

A fundamental barrier to the decarceration of women is precisely this narrative of 'turning (troubled) lives around'. The language and policy rhetoric, once established, is enduring: 'people are fixed in such a position by means of power relations and power structures' (Krumer-Nevo and Benjamin 2010: 696). It is only through a conscious effort to understand the significance of representations of criminalised women and their lives, the currency of the 'troubled' woman and her 'complex' needs, that the risks of othering can be identified and resisted. Narratives that foreground the process of criminalisation, as part of ongoing experiences of trauma and institutional failures in the lives of women, are necessary to support a radical change in women's imprisonment.

From 'criminal women' to the criminalisation of women: the political and economic context of women's lives

This section explores what happens when the processes involved in the criminalisation of women, placing an emphasis on the historical, social, economic and political contexts, are foregrounded. Can such an approach challenge the dominant conceptualisation that focuses on women's individual experiences, their 'complex' needs, vulnerabilities and pathways into lawbreaking? It is argued that the modes of analysis used by Chadwick and Little (1987) to examine the criminalisation of women in the 1980s, with the emphasis on patriarchy, economic marginalisation and racism, remain relevant. As Carlen (2008: 185) reminds us, 'female prisoners are disproportionately poor, Black and with backgrounds involving childhood institutionalisation.'

In particular historical moments, the impact of structural relations – of patriarchal forces, economic marginalisation, racist ideologies – are intensified. The period of the 1980s in the UK under the Thatcher government was such a period (Hall et al. 1978; Scraton 1987; Hall 1988). The political and economic context to the global financial crisis of 2008 provides a similar conjuncture. A range of recent evidence exposes the gendered nature of the current UK government's 'austerity' project. The Fawcett Society (2012), for example, refers to austerity and the 'triple jeopardy' experienced by women who face disproportionate benefit cuts, job losses and reduced services. It provides evidence to show that women's unemployment is the highest it has been for 25 years and that over 75 per cent of spending cuts have come from women's incomes (for example, by reducing paid benefits, council tax discounts or the topping up of earnings through tax credits). Further empirical evidence demonstrates that the situation for women is getting worse as a consequence of employment and welfare policies within the work programme (Centre for Economic and Social Inclusion 2014), the outcome of the roll out of universal credit (CPAG 2011; WBG 2016) and the ratcheting up of the 'troubled families' policy (DCLG 2014). Together, this impacts women whose everyday realities are marked by poverty and marginalisation.

Early feminist criminology, including Susan Edward's 1981 analysis of women in poverty and later developed by Carlen and Dee Cook (1989), demonstrated how the cumulative impact of benefit policies, access to employment and women's roles in the home and as carers was relevant to their criminalisation. Whilst important in recognising the gendered relations of economic policies, such analysis implies that the 'crisis in the gender regime' is a universally experienced phenomenon (Walby 2015), and does not effectively engage in the intersections of gender and other structural relations.

The work of Amina Mama (1984) and more recent empirical research by Awugo Emejulu and Leah Bassel (2016) demonstrates the significance of the relationship between the British state and Black and Minority Ethnic (BME) women at times of economic crisis. As one of the participants in their recent study notes, 'the problems that minority ethnic women face are more structured in nature and therefore beyond the power of the community themselves to actually change' (migrant activist cited in Emejulu and Bassel 2016: 91). Minority women report how current 'austerity' policies affect their lives through pressures of care work and paid employment, and the casual nature of this work, and how this relates to a commitment to study or engage in political activity (Emejulu and Bassel 2016). The lives of minority ethnic women are affected disproportionately by housing and health cuts and the impact of funding cuts on the availability of specialist legal advice or services for survivors of violence (Sandhu et al. 2013). This 'cumulative impact of poverty, ethnicity and gender' has worsened in the context of the 'austerity' policies of the UK Conservative Government (Women's Budget Group 2016).

This work clearly demonstrates the significance of both the current moment of political or economic crisis and its position in a longer trajectory of historical relations between economically marginalised and racialised groups of women and the British state. Given the significance of such marginalisation upon processes of criminalisation, it is clear that particular communities of women are increasingly at risk of criminalisation and imprisonment.

Criminalisation of women – the significance of home and family

In 1987, Chadwick and Little argued that expectations around women's role and functions within the family relating to sexuality, motherhood and childbirth 'not only form a strong economic and ideological construction but permeate throughout state institutions and create the foundations upon which the political management and regulation of women is institutionalised' (1987: 259). Using case studies of women claiming state benefits, women involved in prostitution and women protesters, they noted how both social and state control facilitated the process by which women are criminalised. Each case study demonstrated the processes by which certain behaviours became criminalised, particularly those in which women were deemed to have stepped outside the traditional roles assigned to them in the family and home.

The following analysis updates this work, providing contemporary examples of the gendered process of criminalisation. These have been selected in part because they demonstrate the continuities of such relations, the synergies between penal and welfare policies and the impact on women at risk of criminalisation. It is important to note the intended unification of these policies at a local level, in particular the drive by local professionals and civil servants to integrate Troubled Families policies with criminal justice reforms for women. This is clearly seen within the Women Offender Model Board based in Manchester, which oversees the implementation of a local 'women offender' strategy.[6] This group is able to access and resource analysis of local criminal justice data, uncovering gendered processes of criminalisation. This local data has repeatedly raised the significance of, among other issues, television (TV) licensing and truancy convictions for women.

In the years after Chadwick and Little's (1987) analysis was published, there has been evidence of state institutions regulating citizens through gendered penal and welfare policies that result in the criminalisation of particular women and girls (see Hudson 1988; Worrall 1990; Chigwada-Bailey 1997; Phoenix 2012; Malloch and McIvor 2013). Rona Epstein's (2014) recent work on the imprisonment of mothers with dependent children exposes the continued criminalisation and imprisonment of women for crimes of 'council tax default', 'benefit fraud' and 'non-payment of fines'. This highlights the continued policing and punishment of economically marginalised women. This is further illustrated by MOJ official data that demonstrates the ongoing and disproportionate criminalisation of women for the non-payment of TV licences. The MOJ reported that in 2015, of 189,349 defendants prosecuted, 70 per cent were women. The number and proportion of women criminalised for this offence continues to increase. In an attempt to explain this discrepancy, the MOJ (2016a: 141) suggested that women are 'more likely to be at home when enforcement officers call.'

The ongoing focus on the family home as an appropriate site for behavioural change, and the merging of penal and welfare strategies, is starkly illustrated by the UK government's recent Troubled Families Programme. Launched in April 2012, costing £448 million, families who met one or more of the following criteria were targeted: those in which members were perceived as being involved in youth crime or antisocial behaviour, in which children were recorded as regularly truanting or not in school, or in which there was an adult on out of work benefits or who was perceived as causing high costs to the taxpayer. The practical implication of this policy for those targeted is being the focus of a multi-agency team, consisting of social services, housing workers, health practitioners and, importantly, criminal justice agencies, such as the police and or probation services. The day-to-day experience is of 'intensive support and intervention from dedicated, assertive and persistent workers' (Casey 2012a: 3), with members of the integrated team in the family home every day, sometimes multiple times each day, monitoring behaviour, advising and, when ignored, sanctioning the behaviours of the family. The concern is the consequences and impact of such penal-welfare policies and practice on women. Even when the wider policy is found to fail on its own terms of 'turning lives around' (Crossley 2015), as was the consequence of benefit snoopers in the 1980s, the impact of having partnerships of penal and welfare practitioners intrusively in the family home facilitates a gendered process of criminalisation.

The Troubled Families Programme reflects a wider shift to an authoritarian stance against perceived incivilities, youth crime and antisocial behaviour (Jamieson and Yates 2009). This shift has included an increase in criminal offences, not just for young people but also for those deemed responsible for them. One example of this is the charge and conviction of parents for their child's truancy from school. A Freedom of Information request by the BBC in 2015 reported that 10 women had been jailed for having been found guilty of child truancy offences in 2014 and that women comprised 58 per cent of those fined in 2014 for such offences. Of the 16,850 prosecutions for the offence of truancy in 2015, 70 per cent were of women. In the same year, eight parents convicted of truancy were sentenced to immediate custody; all eight were women (MOJ 2016a). The MOJ suggests the differential can be explained by women more usually being a lone parent. This assumption is challenged by the MOJ's own data as the disproportionate criminalisation of women remains evident in families where both parents are living with a child (MOJ 2016a).

Whether it is the criminal justice policy that translates women's experiences of victimisation into 'criminogenic needs' or the Troubled Families programme, which translates the 'pathways to poverty' into reimagined 'risks', the strategy remains consistent. It is one of pathology, requiring women – and it is mainly women who are held responsible within those families targeted – to receive this support or face sanctions, including imprisonment and/or eviction. The social and political contexts are ignored. It is their choices, their behaviours and their attentiveness to the 'needs of the family' that remain the focus: 'historically, women have been expected to subject themselves, first and perennially to the family – in obedience to the rhetoric that good mothers make good families make good societies' (Carlen 1995: 216). These examples, spanning 30 years, demonstrate how women's criminalisation and imprisonment remains directly related to their role and responsibility within the institutions of the home and family.

Criminalisation of women – intersections of 'race' and gender

Discussions of racial disproportionality in the policies and practice in the criminal justice system are at the heart of a debate that seeks to position the processes of criminalisation at the centre of analysis (Williams and Clarke 2016). Much of the empirical evidence concentrates on men, and the limited empirical work examining the experiences of minority ethnic women requires updating. This evidence, however, cannot be ignored as it clearly exposes the intersections of race and gender in processes of criminalisation. Whether it is Black women's experience of policing (Chigwada-Bailey 1997), representations of minority women by probation staff in their court reports (Hudson 1988) or racialised stereotypes that underpin prison staff practices (Genders and Player 1989), these studies reveal how the criminalisation of poor Black women is not simply a result of 'additive forces' but is contextual of those social, political and economic forces that bear down on their lives (Anderson and Collins 1995).

An examination of official statistics demonstrates that in 2002, BME women constituted less than 8 per cent of the female population in the UK but close to 31 per cent of female prisoners. A high proportion were identified as being Foreign National women, with Black British women making up less than 12 per cent of the prison population although representing just 2 per cent of wider population in the UK at that time (Chigwada-Bailey 2003). In more recently published official data, the position of minority ethnic women is less clear: For a start, the information is held across a number of disparate publications on 'women', 'race' and 'equalities' in the criminal justice system, all with differing reporting time-frames (MOJ 2013, 2014, 2016a,b). What is evident, however, is that between the ages of 21–49 years, BME women make up approximately 18 per cent of the prison population; this drops to less than 10 per cent for under 21 and over 50 age groups (MOJ 2013: 8).

It is not clear whether this data includes Foreign National prisoners. The publication of statistics on women indicates that in 2007, the proportion of Foreign Nationals in the female population had increased to a high of 22 per cent, dropping to less than 15 per cent in 2014 and then to 11 per cent in 2016. Yet whether this reveals a reduction of Foreign National women's incarceration is obscured by the significant increase in immigration detention during this period.[7] Are these Foreign National women now in detention centres such as Yarl's Wood? If so, this would challenge any suggestion of decarceration. Similarly, it is not possible to examine how these changes in the prison population relate to the experiences of British-born minority ethnic women.

What is revealed in this discussion of data relating to the criminalisation of minority ethnic women is, as advised by Mama (1984: 36), 'not simply a matter of going into detail about Black women as a sub group'. Instead, the available evidence reveals the very specific role that the criminalisation of BME and migrant women plays in the rationalisation of the continuing nature of these penal processes and apparatus. There exists research that seeks to explore the experiences of racialised communities of women and of Foreign National women in prison (PRT 2012) as well as the criminalisation of migrant women (Hales and Gelsthorpe 2012) and their experiences of immigration detention (Bosworth and Kellezi 2015). Yet, if such work is to translate into radical agendas for fundamental change, it must serve a critical research agenda that examines the institutional contexts and responses to these communities of women and reveals the gendered and racialised nature of power and punishment.

At the time of writing, in response to the current review on racial bias in the criminal justice system, chaired by Labour Party Member of Parliament (MP) David Lammy, the government published a one-off set of data that reveals new evidence regarding disproportionate criminal justice contact and outcomes for minority ethnic women (Uhrig 2016). The analysis reveals that 'Black women were about 2.3 times more likely to receive a custodial sentence for drug offences compared to white women' (Uhrig 2016: 22), with this disparity being racialised specifically to Black women and greater than that experienced by any minority group of men. The report concludes,

> Taken together, this analysis implies that disproportionality in prison for BAME [Black, Asian and Minority Ethnic] men and Black women convicted of drugs offences can be traced back to a combination of disproportionate arrest and disproportionate custodial sentencing at the Crown Court.
>
> *(p. 22)*

This recent evidence exposes the need to develop a detailed understanding regarding the current impact of processes of criminalisation for racialised groups of women. Without this, it is not possible to understand the distinct impact of criminalisation and authoritatively challenge the imprisonment of women. This should be at the heart of any debate on decarceration and the impact of Corston, yet to date, it has garnered little if any consideration.

The success of Corston is often cited as being the development of a network of women's centres across E&W as a result of her review (APPG 2015). Arguably, these centres offer a space for women to receive community-based punishment and access to the wider services. In the best scenario, women might be diverted from the process of criminalisation. Yet there is emerging evidence that minority ethnic women are absent from such centres. As indicated previously, in Manchester, a Whole System Approach has been developed to divert women into women's centres at all points in the process via police triage, problem-solving courts in some areas and probation case management as well as Through the Gate from prison (Kinsella et al. 2015). The interim evaluation indicated that of the 640 women referred to the women's centres in the first 10 months of the project, just 51 women (8 per cent) were from minority ethnic communities. Given both the ethnic make-up of the local communities and the disproportionate numbers of minority women in prison, this data is cause for concern and raises questions 'as to whether younger women (18–24-year-old) and BME women have the same opportunities to access the support on offer at the women's centres' (Kinsella et al. 2015: 3). Similar patterns are evident in the youth justice context. Following a recent period of youth decarceration, analysis of which young people remain in custody demonstrates that it is increasingly, disproportionately those from BME backgrounds: almost 50 per cent of all juvenile prisoners in some locations and those with histories of being 'looked after' by the state

(Taylor 2016). These cumulative findings expose discriminatory practices that drive processes of criminalisation differently according to the structural relations of gender, 'race', age and class.

Conclusion

By examining the narrative of Corston's review and positioning it within a longer historical and political trajectory of the criminalisation of women, this chapter has sought to establish that Corston's review and resulting strategy was neither radical nor fundamental. Rather, it retained an established liberal and piece-meal approach that has consistently had little impact on the entrenched processes of criminalisation and punishment for women in E&W. As Sandra Acker's (1983: 66) analysis of gender and education demonstrates, implementary approaches 'do not address questions about the underlying reasons for domination and subordination patterns.' What has been argued here is that the liberal penal reform agenda has failed to acknowledge and respond to the class-based, racialised and gendered structural relations that shape the lives of criminalised women. The post-Corston minimal reform agenda has been reconstituted, thereby frustrating attempts at decarceration while having no discernible impact on women's incarceration. In fact, by June 2017, as we finalise the chapter, the statistics reveal that the female prison population in E&W has risen to levels not seen for five years: to almost 4,000 women (PRT 2017).

The continuities in this reform debate are striking. Rather than being radical, Corston's strategy reflects the concerns already raised within previous reviews (see HMIP 1997, 2001; Wedderburn 2000), which are consistent across a range of state and reform agendas (Fawcett Commission 2009; HMIP 2010; PRT 2011, 2014, 2015; APPG 2015). A longer historical lens demonstrates the endurance of the reformist narrative. As early as 1922, the first woman inspector of women's prisons, Dr Mary Gordon, questioned the purpose of prison for women:

> If the system had a good effect on any prisoner, I failed to mark it. I have no shadow of a doubt of its power to demoralize, or of its cruelty. It appears to me not to belong to this time or civilisation at all.
> *(Gordon 1922a: xi in Cheney 2010: 115)*

Consistent with these reports and commissions, including Corston's, Gordon focused on the characteristics of criminalised women:

> poor health, poverty, low self-esteem ("an unconscious feeling of inferiority"), substance abuse involving alcohol and drugs, being victims of men from "vampire trades", suffering from mania and hysterical psychoses, a tendency to self-harm and attempt suicide, and being socially disadvantaged.
> *(Gordon 1922 in Cheney 2010: 131)*

From 1922 to 2017, the narrative from both official state discourse and a range of alternative accounts remains consistent. The research discussed here reveals that the failure to reduce women's imprisonment and implement decarceration arises in part from a reform agenda that places the agency of individual women at the heart of strategies that assume their capacity to make informed choices to 'turn their lives around'. As Gordon observed, 'Why do we talk so loudly about reform and put up with so little action? Why are we as sure as we are that, when our criminal fails to be reformed, the fault is his and not ours?' (Gordon 1922a: cited in Cheney 2010: 134). While reformist debates are derived from within the state, it is likely that, rather than challenging or dismantling problematic dynamics and narratives, 'gender-responsive' approaches reflect gendered, class-based and racialised discourses of responsibility, risk management and punishment (Hannah-Moffat 2002). What is required is a narrative informed by critiques of the institutions that fail women, exposing the specific racist practices that result in the disproportionate criminalisation of Black women and how economically marginalised women's experiences of welfare intervention, often in both their childhood and adult lives, is tied to their punishment. This debate has been consistent but ignored and marginalised from the reform agenda.

The failure to implement Corston's strategy has been much criticised (WIP 2012; Coles 2013; APPG 2015). The community of individuals and organisations committed to reducing women's imprisonment should shift the lens from individual women and focus on state practices and responses, whether penal or welfare, thus revealing the underlying dynamics of criminalisation. Critical and urgently required is a brake on the process of 'othering', derived in the narrative of 'troubled' women, replaced by collective work exposing and challenging the failing institutions that intervene harmfully in women's lives. It should reveal the hidden role of institutions, legislation, policies and practices, of social services, local authorities, health services, the police, the courts and the prison. These shape women's lives and reproduce ongoing economic marginalisation, racism and experiences of loss, abuse, trauma, under-protection and domination (Segrave and Carlton 2010). Agency and empowerment of women is not simply a statement of 'women making better choices' or having a responsibility to 'turn their lives around' but a collective abolitionist strategy demanding the changes necessary in communities and (where possible without compromising visionary abolitionist goals) within state institutions to address the marginalisation and the disproportionate criminalisation of women.

Essentially, this includes ensuring that women's voices are heard and accepted, not in ways where the terms are already set by objectifying official discourse (Krumer-Nevo and Benjamin 2010) but by uncovering and exposing the realities of institutions, power and injustice. While this work is for all women (Pate 2013) – in fact, all those (women and men) who are committed to principles of social justice and human rights – such debates must be led by those with experience of criminalisation and incarceration, including minority perspectives that must be afforded more than a tokenistic voice in critical analysis and discourse

(Phillips and Bowling 2003; Krumer-Nevo and Sidi 2012). It is only by fore-grounding the experiences of those failed by institutions and by responding to the tensions that are presented when individuals speak truth to power (Scraton 2007) that strategies for change and action can be secured.

The ongoing tension remains: Can 'we', or should 'we', continue with the reforms made possible by the type of pragmatic recommendations advocated for by Corston? They might offer some respite to some incarcerated women, help-ing them to survive prison and the harms of punishment. Yet, by focussing on minimal change, is the potential for a more fundamental critique and response delayed?

As the writing of this chapter began, a woman took her life in HMP Styal. During the process of writing, a further two women took their lives in English prisons. In November 2016, Sarah Burke was found dead, three weeks into her prison sentence at HMP Drake Hall in Staffordshire (Eccleston 2016), and in December 2016, Jenny Swift a transgender woman, was found dead whilst on re-mand in HMP Doncaster, an all-male establishment (Halliday 2017). The reform debate in E&W has failed criminalised women. From Gordon to Corston and beyond, the shared narrative demonstrates the seemingly immovable connection between the reform agenda and institutionalised state power and practices. Our call is one for change: change to the long-standing narrative, propelling forward new voices and a collective endeavour to redirect and re-energise the debate. Thus, new strategies, able to drive truly radical agendas and place activism at the forefront of an abolitionist vision, can be initiated and progressed.

Notes

1 'Women in Prison' was established in 1983, aiming to support women to avoid, sur-vive and exit the criminal justice system and campaign for the radical changes needed to deliver justice for women. Open letter to the *Times* newspaper (3/11/2016).

2 See this book's Introduction and Chapter 1 for detailed discussion of Corston's method on pp. 1–31.

3 HMP Brockhill was a small, state-run women's prison in the Midlands. In February of 2004, it featured in a national newspaper in a comment piece (Bright 2004) that exposed the prison as having some of the 'worst conditions in the prison system'. Staff and prisoners highlighted a lack of sanitary facilities (only two of the 170 cells had a toilet), and there was no drug detoxification unit and significant inadequacies in ad-dressing the levels of self-harm in the institution. Less than two months later, in April 2004, Sheena Kotecha (aged 22) took her own life. She was one of the 20 women to take their own lives in prisons in E&W that year. HMP Brockhill was re-rolled to a male establishment in 2006, just after Corston's visit and while her review was still underway. The prison closed in 2011.

4 HMP Bronzefield in Middlesex is a privately run local prison managed by Sodexo Justice Services. The last two Independent Monitoring Board reports (IMB, 2014, 2015) describe it as a 'modern establishment which is not overcrowded'. Both reports note concerns regarding the number of women prisoners with unmet mental health needs, some of whom are identified as requiring secure hospital places rather than imprisonment.

5 www.gov.uk/government/publications/prison-safety-and-reform.

6 http://archive.agma.gov.uk/cms_media/files/121031_tj4_women_offenders. pdf?static=1.
7 Yarl's Wood Immigration Removal Centre is a privately run detention centre in Bedfordshire, England. Over 400 adult women and family groups are detained here indefinitely whilst they appeal their immigration status in the UK. Campaign organisations, journalists and academics have worked with female detainees to reveal the degrading and dehumanising treatment at the facility (Canning 2014). A collective of over 2,000 campaigners protested outside Yarl's Wood in September 2016, demanding it be shut down following multiple accusations of sexual harassment and abuse of women detainees.

References

Abbit, B. (2016) 'Celeste Craig begged for help but ended up dead in a prison cell', *Manchester Evening News* 27 September 2016. www.manchestereveningnews.co.uk/ news/greater-manchester-news/celeste-craig-styal-prison-death-12089950.

Acker, S. (1983) 'Women and teaching: a semi-detached sociology of a semi-profession', in S. Walker and L. Barton (eds.) *Gender, Class and Education*, London: Falmer.

All Party Parliamentary Group (2015) *Report on the Inquiry into Preventing Unnecessary Criminalisation of Women*, London: Howard League for Penal Reform.

Anderson, M. L. and Collins, P. H. (1995) *Race, Class and Gender*, 2nd Edition. Belmont, CA: Wadsworth.

BBC (2015) 'School truancies lead to rise in prosecution of parents', www.bbc.co.uk/ news/education-33861985.

BBC (2016) 'Prison governor wants longer sentences to help female inmates', www.bbc. co.uk/news/uk-england-bristol-37832877.

Bosworth, M. and Kellezi, B. (2015) *Quality of Life in Detention Results from MQLD Questionnaire Data Collected in IRC Campsfield House, IRC Yarl's Wood, IRC Colnbrook, and IRC Dover, September 2013–August 2014*, Oxford: Oxford University. http://artsonline. monash.edu.au/thebordercrossingobservatory/files/2015/02/2015MQLD_Bosworth- and-Kellezi_.pdf.

Bright, M. (2004) 'Women burn, strangle and stab themselves in jail hell', *The Guardian*, 8 February 2004, www.theguardian.com/uk/2004/feb/08/ukcrime.prisonsand probation1.

Cameron, D. (2011) *PM's Speech on the Fightback after the Riots*, www.gov.uk/government/ speeches/pms-speech-on-the-fightback-after-the-riots.

Canning, V. (2014) 'Women, asylum and the harms of detention', *Criminal Justice Matters*, 98: 10–11.

Carlen, P. (1983) *Women's Imprisonment: A Study in Social Control*, London: Routledge.

Carlen, P. (1990) *Alternatives to Women's Imprisonment*, Milton Keynes: Open University Press.

Carlen, P. (1995) 'Women, crime, feminism and realism' in N. Naffine (ed.) *Gender, Crime and Feminism*, Aldershot: Dartmouth Press.

Carlen, P. (2008) 'Gender, class, racism and criminal justice: against global and gender-centric theories, for post structuralist perspectives', in K. Evans and J. Jamiesen (eds.) *Gender and Crime, a Reader*, Maidenhead: Open University Press.

Carlen, P. and Cook, D. (1989) *Paying for Crime*, Milton Keynes: Open University Press.

Carlen, P., Hicks, J., O'Dwyer, J., Christina, D. and Tchaikovsky, C. (1985) *Criminal Women*, Cambridge: Polity Press.

Carlen, P. and Tombs, J. (2006) 'Reconfigurations of penality: the ongoing case of women's imprisonment', *Theoretical Criminology*, 10(3): 337–360.

Carlen, P. and Worrall, A. (2004) *Analysing Women's Imprisonment*, Cullompton: Willan.

Casey, L. (2012a) *Listening to Troubled Families, London: Department for Communities and Local Government,* www.gov.uk/government/uploads/system/uploads/attachment_data/file/6151/2183663.pdf.

Casey, L. (2012b) *Working with Troubled Families,* www.gov.uk/government/uploads/system/uploads/attachment_data/file/66113/121214_Working_with_troubled_families_FINAL_v2.pdf.

Centre for Economic and Social Inclusion (2014) *Work Programme Statistics: Inclusion Analysis.* www.learningandwork.org.uk/sites/niace_en/files/resources/WP%20statistics%20briefing%20September%202014.pdf.

Chadwick, K., Clarke, B., O'Hara, T. and Wood, A. (2015) *An Evaluation of the 'Triangle Project': A National Service for Women in Prison in England and Wales,* London: Women in Prison.

Chadwick, K. and Little, C. (1987) 'The criminalisation of women', in P. Scraton (ed.) *Law, Order and the Authoritarian State,* Milton Keynes: Open University Press.

Cheney, D. (2010) 'Dr Mary Louisa Gordon (1861–1941): a feminist approach in prison', *Feminist Legal Studies,* 18: 115–136.

Chigwada-Bailey, R. (1997) *Black Women's Experiences of Criminal Justice: Discourse on Disadvantage,* Hampshire: Waterside Press.

Child Poverty Action Group (2011) *Universal Credit: The Gender Impact.* www.cpag.org.uk/content/universal-credit-gender-impact-0.

Coleman, R., Sim, J., Tombs, S. and Whyte, D. (2010) *State, Power, Crime,* London: Sage.

Coles, D. (2013) 'Deaths of women in prison: the human rights issues arising', in M. Malloch and G. McIvor (eds.) *Women Punishment and Social Justice,* London: Routledge.

Corston, J. (2007) *The Corston Report: A Review of Women with Particular Vulnerabilities in the Criminal Justice System,* London: Home Office.

Corston, J. (2016) Women in Jail More Troubled Than Troublesome. *The Sydney Morning Herald,* 14th September 2016. www.smh.com.au/comment/harriet-wran-an-example-of-the-sort-of-woman-who-goes-to-prison-20160912-grek5o.html.

Crossley, S. (2015) *The Troubled Families Programme: The Perfect Social Policy?* www.crimeandjustice.org.uk/sites/crimeandjustice.org.uk/files/The%20Troubled%20Families%20Programme, %20Nov%202015.pdf.

Department for Communities and Local Government (2014) *Troubled Families Programme Expanded to Help Younger Children,* DCLG Press Release. www.gov.uk/government/news/troubled-families-programme-expanded-to-help-younger-children.

Eccleston, B. (2016) 'Crack addict found dead in prison three weeks into sentence for attacking OAPs' *The Coventry Telegraph,* 12 December 2016. www.coventrytelegraph.net/news/crack-addict-found-dead-prison-12308823.

Emejulu, A. and Bassel, L. (2016) 'Minority women, austerity and activism', *Race and Class,* 57(2): 86–95.

Epstein, R. (2014) *Mothers in Prison: The Sentencing of Mothers and the Rights of the Child. Howard League Working Paper.* http://howardleague.org/wp-content/uploads/2016/04/HLWP_3_2014.pdf.

Fawcett Commission (2009) *Engendering Justice – From Policy to Practice: Final Report of the Commission on Women and the Criminal Justice System,* London: The Fawcett Society.

Fawcett Commission (2012) *The Impact of Austerity on Women.* Fawcett Society Policy Briefing. www.fawcettsociety.org.uk/wp-content/uploads/2013/02/The-Impact-of-Austerity-on-Women-19th-March-2012.pdf.

Genders, E. and Player, E. (1989) *Race Relations in Prison,* Oxford: Clarendon Press.

Hales, L. and Gelsthorpe, L. (2012) *The Criminalisation of Migrant Women.* Institute of Criminology, University of Cambridge. www.crim.cam.ac.uk/people/academic_ research/loraine_gelsthorpe/criminalreport29july12.pdf.

Hall, S. (1988) *The Hard Road to Renewal: Thatcherism and the Crisis of the Left,* London: Verso.

Hall, S., Critcher, C., Jefferson, T., Clarke, J. and Roberts, B. (1978) *Policing the Crisis,* London and Basingstoke: Macmillan.

Halliday, J. (2017) 'Transgender woman found dead in cell at Doncaster prison', *The Guardian* 5th January 2017. https://www.theguardian.com/society/2017/jan/05/ transgender-woman-jenny-swift-found-dead-at-doncaster-prison.

Hannah-Moffat, K. (2002) 'Creating choices: reflecting on choices' in P. Carlen (ed.) *Women and Punishment: The Struggle for Justice,* Cullompton: Willan.

HM Inspectorate of Prisons (1997) *Women in Prison: A Thematic Review,* London: Home Office.

HM Inspectorate of Prisons (2001) *Follow-Up on Women in Prison: A Thematic Review,* London: Home Office.

HM Inspectorate of Prisons (2010) *Women in Prison: A Short Thematic Review,* London: Home Office.

HM Inspectorate of Probation and HM Inspectorate of Prisons (2016) *A Joint Thematic Inspection of Through the Gate Resettlement Services for Short-Term Prisoners,* London: Home Office.

Hudson, B. (1988) *Content Analysis of Social Enquiry Reports Written in the Borough of Haringey.* Middlesex Area Probation Service. Unpublished report.

Independent Monitoring Board (2014) IMB Annual Report: HMP Eastwood Park 2013– 14, www.imb.org.uk/reports/2014-annual-reports/page/2/.

Inquest (2016) Deaths of Women in Prison: England and Wales (1990 to date). www. inquest.org.uk/statistics/deaths-of-women-in-prison. Accessed 10 December 2016.

Inside Time (2015) www.insidetime.org/shortage-of-staff-at-hmp-eastwood-park/.

Kinsella, R., O'Keefe, C., Lowthian, J., Clarke, B. and Ellison, M. (2015) *Evaluation of the Whole System Approach for Women Offenders: Interim Report. Manchester City Council.* www.shu.ac.uk/research/specialisms/hallam-centre-for-community-justice/ reports/evaluation-of-the-whole-system-approach-for-women-offenders-interim- report.

Krumer-Nevo, M. and Benjamin, O. (2010) 'Critical poverty knowledge: contesting othering and social distancing', *Current Sociology,* 58(5): 693–714.

Krumer-Nevo, M. and Sidi, M. (2012) 'Writing against othering', *Qualitative Inquiry,* 18(4): 299–309.

Levi, R. and Waldman, A. (eds.) (2016) *Inside This Place, Not of It: Narratives from Women's Prisons,* London: VERSO, Voice of Witness Series.

McNeil, C. and Hunter, J. (2015) *Breaking Boundaries: Towards a 'Troubled Lives' Programme for People Facing Multiple and Complex Needs,* London: Institute for Public Policy.

Malloch, M. and McIvor, G. (eds.) (2013) *Women Punishment and Social Justice,* London: Routledge.

Mama, A. (1984) 'Black women, the economic crisis and the British state', *Feminist Review,* Special Issue 17: 22–34.

Ministry of Justice (2013) *Equalities Report,* www.gov.uk/government/uploads/ system/uploads/attachment_data/file/380129/noms-offender-equalities-annual- report-2013-14.pdf.

Ministry of Justice (2014) *Statistics on Race and the Criminal Justice System 2014,* www.gov. uk/government/uploads/system/uploads/attachment_data/file/480250/bulletin.pdf.

Ministry of Justice (2016a) *Statistics on Women and the Criminal Justice System 2015,* www.gov.uk/government/uploads/system/uploads/attachment_data/file/572043/women-and-the-criminal-justice-system-statistics-2015.pdf.

Ministry of Justice (2016b) *Offender Management Statistics Quarterly: January to March 2016,* www.gov.uk/government/uploads/system/uploads/attachment_data/file/541499/offender-management-statistics-quarterly-bulletin-jan2-mar-2016.pdf.

Moore, L. and Scraton, P. (2014) *The Incarceration of Women: Punishing Bodies, Breaking Spirits,* Basingstoke: Palgrave.

Pate, K. (2013) 'Women, punishment and social justice: why should you care?' in M. Malloch and G. McIvor (eds.) *Women Punishment and Social Justice,* London: Routledge.

Phillips, C. and Bowling, B. (2003) Racism, ethnicity and criminology. *Developing Minority Perspectives British Journal of Criminology,* 43(2): 269–290.

Phoenix, J. (2012). *Out of place: the policing and criminalisation of sexually exploited girls and young women.* The Howard League for Penal Reform.

Prison Reform Trust (2011) *Reforming Women's Justice: The Final Report of the Women's Justice Taskforce,* London: PRT.

Prison Reform Trust (2012) *No Way Out for Foreign National Women Behind Bars,* Prison Reform Trust Website. www.prisonreformtrust.org.uk/ProjectsResearch/Women/Comment/NoWayOutforeignnationalwomen.

Prison Reform Trust (2014) *Brighter Futures,* London: PRT.

Prison Reform Trust (2015) *Transforming Lives: Reducing Women's Imprisonment,* London: PRT.

Prison Reform Trust (2017) *Women's Prison Population Close to 4,000 after Rapid Twelve-Month Rise,* Prison Reform Trust Website. www.prisonreformtrust.org.uk/PressPolicy/News/vw/1/ItemID/444.

Prison Reform Trust & Women in Prison (2016) *Home Truths: Housing for Women in the Criminal Justice System,* London: PRT.

Sandhu, K. Stephenson, M. and Harrison, J. (2013) *Layers of Inequality,* www2.warwick.ac.uk/fac/soc/law/research/centres/chrp/publications/layers_of_inequality_report.pdf.

Scraton, P. (ed.) (1987) *Introduction to Law, Order and the Authoritarian State,* Milton Keynes: Open University Press.

Scraton, P. (2016). 'Bearing witness to the 'pain of others': researching power, violence and resistance in a women's prison', *International Journal for Crime, Justice and Social Democracy,* 5(1): 5–20.

Segrave, M. and Carlton, B. (2010) *Women, Trauma, Criminalisation and Imprisonment, Current Issues in Criminal Justice* 22(2): 287–305.

Taylor, C. (2016) Review of the Youth Justice System in England and Wales. Ministry of Justice. www.gov.uk/government/uploads/system/uploads/attachment_data/file/577103/youth-justice-review-final-report.pdf.

Truss, L. (2016) Prison reform speech. www.gov.uk/government/speeches/prison-reform-justice-secretary-speech.

Uhrig, N. (2016) *Black, Asian and Minority Ethnic disproportionality in the Criminal Justice System in England and Wales,* London: Ministry of Justice.

Walby, S. (2015) *Crisis,* Cambridge: Polity Press.

Wedderburn Report (2000) *Justice for Women: The Need for Reform,* London: Prison Reform Trust.

Williams, P. and Clarke, B. (2016) *Dangerous Associations: Joint Enterprise, Gangs and Racism,* London: Centre for Crime and Justice Studies.

Women in Prison (2012) *Traffic Light Review of Corston Report 5 Years On,* London: WIP.

Women in Prison (2016) Response to reform speech, www.womeninprison.org.uk/news-and-campaigns.php?s=2016–11–04–justice-secretary-statement.

Women's Budget Group (2016) http://wbg.org.uk/wp-content/uploads/2016/03/WBG_2016Budget_Response_PDF.pdf.

Worrall, A. (1990) *Offending Women: Female Lawbreakers and the Criminal Justice System*, London: Routledge.

Wright, S. (2013) *Being Set Up to Fail? The Role of the Criminal Justice System in Perpetuating Cycles of Repeat Criminalisation for Substance-Addicted Women*, London: Howard League for Penal Reform ECAN Bulletin, Issue 18, January.

4

THE IMPRISONMENT OF WOMEN IN SCOTLAND

Restructure, reform or abolish?

Margaret Malloch

Introduction

Abolitionism is a challenging term to define, with some confusion surrounding the boundaries between reform agendas and abolitionist calls for change. Many advocates of reform publicly state that they are not abolitionists while appearing to be. Attempting to address the harms of existing systems is not the same as setting out new visions. However, those claiming to be abolitionists frequently find themselves supporting pragmatic reforms. For Ruggiero (2010: 7), 'abolitionism is not only a strategy, or a set of demands, aimed at the reduction (or suppression) of custody, it is also a perspective, a philosophy, an approach which challenges conventional definitions of crime.'

The imprisonment of women is an issue that has had significant potential for reform, although it has had limited effect to date. It is also an issue held up by those who claim to be abolitionists as a feasible starting point in the abolitionist agenda. The key reasons are the relatively low numbers of women in prison, about 5 per cent of the total prison population, and the fact that generally, with notable exceptions, women tend not to fit the stereotype of the 'dangerous other' (Garland 2002). The use of imprisonment and noncustodial disposals for women in Scotland has been an ongoing focus of attention for policy-makers and penal reformers and has remained so in the decade since the publication of the Corston Report. The report, like similar enquiries into the circumstances of women in prison in Scotland, focussed on the 'vulnerabilities' that were a feature of the lives of many women in conflict with the law and drawn into the criminal justice system.

Baroness Jean Corston (p. 15, para 1.4) recognised the controversy surrounding the use of the term 'vulnerable,' setting out the following from the outset:

> I have declined to define "vulnerable" as required by my terms of reference and my review encompasses all those women *whom I consider to be*

inappropriately located in prison. I prefer to consider these women in terms of their "vulnerabilities", which fall into three categories. First, domestic circumstances and problems such as domestic violence, child-care issues, being a single-parent; second, personal circumstances such as mental illness, low self-esteem, eating disorders, substance misuse; and third, socioeconomic factors such as poverty, isolation and unemployment. When women are experiencing a combination of factors from each of these three types of vulnerabilities, it is likely to lead to a crisis point that ultimately results in prison.

(emphasis added)

Notably, she continues, 'It is these underlying issues that must be addressed by helping women develop resilience, life skills and emotional literacy.'

This dichotomy between acknowledgement of the domestic, personal and socioeconomic factors of women's lives and the 'solutions' proposed forms the basis of this chapter. It explores the claim that some women are 'inappropriately placed in prison' while retaining the seemingly default notion of individual deficit and the potential for addressing this through the justice system. This contradictory stance obscures claims of system failure and of the punitive basis of imprisonment, resulting in newly introduced concepts in Scotland of 'community custody.' The chapter reflects on abolitionist claims that if prison is inappropriate, instead of designing new forms of custody or more developed forms of 'punishment in the community,' those who are 'inappropriately' incarcerated should be released.

Background

Until recently, the national prison for women in Scotland was Her Majesty's Prison (HMP) Cornton Vale, holding adult and young women prisoners from throughout the country. Current developments have led to the relocation of women to dedicated sections of prisons in Edinburgh, Grampian, Greenock and Polmont Young Offenders Institution (YOI) and, as the chapter outlines, concerted efforts to reduce the overall female prison population. Accounting for approximately 4 per cent of the overall prison population, the number of women in custody in Scotland has reduced, with a notable reduction for young women prisoners.

There is significant evidence to illustrate that many women in the criminal justice system, and specifically those who are committed to prison, have significant experiences of poverty, problematic drug and alcohol use, mental health problems, abuse, violence and bereavement. This is reflected in the attention given to women's 'needs' within the context of the criminal justice system, either through programmes and interventions in prison or in specifically devised services for 'women offenders' in the community. Despite widespread acknowledgement of the significance of social problems (poverty and inequality) in relation to women's criminalisation, inquiries have consistently focussed on the penal context, even though most people involved recognise the limitations of addressing social justice issues via the criminal justice system (Carlen 2008). On-going attempts have been made to respond to the persistently increasing female prison population and the severe social circumstances that many women prisoners appear to have experienced prior to encountering the criminal justice system (Loucks 1997; Bloom et al. 2003).

While reformers argue in favour of rehabilitative interventions aimed at meeting the needs of the poor and marginalised, to integrate them into 'normal' society, abolitionists query why it is the poor and dispossessed that disproportionately end up in prison, why 'rehabilitation' efforts are focussed on the poor and why the poor are already punished by social inequalities and structures when clearly the enforcement of the law is itself discriminatory. There is also a conceptual issue of 'time' underpinning both reform and abolition. Most of the reports that have been conducted into the female prison estate (discussed further below) occurred in response to critical situations (the deaths of young women in HMP and YOI Cornton Vale and HMP Styal) in which urgent action was required. Calls for reform are introduced within this context in which longer-term strategic change may be aspired to, but short-term intervention is required. Notably, Stan Cohen (1985: 252) acknowledged the importance of being 'pragmatic about short-term possibilities' and 'genuinely utopian about constructing long-term alternatives.'

The case for penal reform

> I do not believe, like some campaigners, that no women should be held in custody. There are some crimes for which custody is the only resort in the interests of justice and public protection, but I was dismayed to see so many women frequently sentenced for short periods of time for very minor offences, causing chaos and disruption to their lives and families, without any realistic chance of addressing the causes of their criminality. I acknowledge that some low-level offending women are persistent offenders who breach their bail conditions and this cannot be ignored. But breach is ratcheting up the use of custody to little avail and there are alternative community solutions which I explore in my report.
>
> *(Corston 2007: foreword)*

Corston acknowledged the deleterious impact of imprisonment on women, a situation recognised across the United Kingdom (UK), as well as internationally, and one that has led to a widely shared desire to reduce the female prison population. This issue has exercised policy-makers, practitioners and academics since the 1980s in Scotland (e.g. Carlen 1983; Dobash et al. 1986). Much attention on women and the criminal justice system in Scotland has focussed on the problems of custody and, related to that, recommendations to improve practice in prison. Successive reports by HM Inspectorate of Prisons for Scotland (2007, 2009, 2011) have identified specific problems, many of which have been addressed and/or resolved over time.[1]

While Corston is cited as having a significant impact on debates and discussions about the imprisonment of women, Scotland has had its own journey in responding to the seemingly inevitable circumstances of women in the criminal justice system. Much activity in Scotland preceded the Corston Report, bringing significant discussion and debate. Calls for change in the application of women's punishment were reinforced with the series of reports produced following the deaths of seven young women within a 30-month period at HMP and YOI Cornton Vale between June 1995 and December 1997.[2] Many similarities exist regarding the circumstances of the women who died in Scotland, which led to the publication of *Women Offenders: A Safer Way* (Social Work Services and Prison Inspectorates 1998), and the Corston Report, following the deaths of six women in HMP Styal between August 2002 and August 2003.[3] *Women Offenders: A Safer Way* highlighted particular concerns for drug users in Cornton Vale and recognised the high number of problem drug users who were repeatedly incarcerated. The review went beyond the confines of the prison, with most of the Inspectorates' recommendations aimed directly at increasing services to support the use of bail, reducing fine default, inter-agency cooperation to address key issues, tailoring social work services to meet the needs of women, separate collation of statistics/data on women, and an end to the use of prison custody for under-18s. The Inspectorates suggested that a reduction in available prison places, coupled with an increased provision of community sentencing options, could shrink the prison population at Cornton Vale to '100 or less on a daily basis by the end of the year 2000' (Social Work and Prison Inspectorates 1998: 53).

In 2002, a Ministerial Group on Women's Offending, established to take forward these recommendations, produced an updated report, *A Better Way*, which considered ways of keeping women out of prison, reflecting on recommendations made by a dedicated Inter-Agency Forum, such as prevention and early intervention (including responses to prostitution and the particular circumstances of young women and the use of arrest referral, diversion and bail); community disposals (supervised attendance orders, structured deferred sentences, drug treatment and testing orders, drug courts, restricted liberty orders, a 'time-out' centre (later to become the 218 Centre);[4] and specialised services for women. Aftercare provisions and the importance of facilitating access to community-based services in relation to substance misuse, accommodation, employment and training, education, benefits and finance and health-related needs were highlighted.[5]

Highlighting innovative initiatives

Corston's review of the imprisonment of women drew on evaluations of innovative initiatives in Scotland, referring to the use of Drug Courts in Scotland and the 218 ('time-out') Centre (Loucks et al. 2006). The 218 Centre in Glasgow was considered by Corston in the context of her discussion of women's community centres (which also included Calderdale in Halifax and Asha in Hereford and Worcester), influencing her vision for a 'distinct, radically different, visibly-led, strategic, proportionate, holistic, woman-centred, integrated approach.' Corston described the management of Cornton Vale prison as a 'holistic' and 'human rights' approach that, for her, was 'common sense' (2007: 18, para 2.6).

The publication of the Corston Report was received with considerable interest across the UK. While the identification of good pockets of practice in Scotland (i.e. the 218 Centre) meant that Scottish policy-makers were able to acknowledge the positive developments that had taken place in Scotland, they were exercised by the ongoing issues facing women in prison and the failure of community disposals to have any significant impact on the rising numbers of women in prison. In 2011, Gill McIvor and Michele Burman reported that women did not appear to be committing more serious offences but received more severe sentences than they had previously. It was acknowledged that the circumstances of disadvantage that feature in the lives of many women drawn into the criminal justice system (individualised as 'criminogenic factors') might contribute to their criminalisation.

Attempts to address these problems continued in Scotland after the publication of the Corston Report in England and Wales and in the aftermath of other notable enquiries in Scotland. The 2008 Report of the Scottish Prison Commission, although not focussed specifically on women, had concluded that current uses of imprisonment were not working and recommended that the Scottish government pursue a policy of reducing the prison population while also supporting relevant statutory bodies and investing resources in local communities. In 2009, the Scottish Parliament Equal Opportunities Committee produced a report, *Female Offenders in the Criminal Justice System* (Equal Opportunities Committee 2009), focussing on the quality of mental healthcare for women in prison, which argued that more provisions for short-term and remand prisoners were required (especially in relation to literacy and numeracy skills) and also called for a speech and language therapy programme to be piloted.[6] As with previous reports, the Equal Opportunities Committee called for consideration to be given to statutory support for women on short-term sentences on release, increased support for children of prisoners, improvement of visitor facilities and more action to stop the circulation of drugs in prison. It also considered sentencing, alternatives to imprisonment, prevention of reoffending, gender equality duty and leadership in relation to the provision of services for women.

In 2012, the Commission on Women Offenders collated extensive evidence on women in the criminal justice system, which was distilled into its published report. While cognisant of Corston, it built on previous reports of enquiries carried out in Scotland. Recommendations were wide-ranging and covered 'service redesign' in the community.[7] The Commission also made recommendations in relation to alternatives to prosecution, including new powers for police to divert women to community justice centres with conditional cautions and alternatives to remand ('bail supervision plus', further examination of electronic monitoring as a condition of bail, communication and awareness of alternatives to remand in custody).

Other areas on which the Commission made recommendations were sentencing[8] and leadership/structures/delivery, including the establishment of a national Community Justice service: a National Community Justice and Prison Delivery Board to promote integration between the Scottish Prison Service (SPS) and the community justice system. It was recommended that each key agency appoint a senior director with responsibility for women and that annual reports on implementation be produced by the Cabinet Secretary for Justice. A number of recommendations of specific relevance to the prison were also set out, including the reiteration of previous concerns about links between mental health programmes and interventions in prison and the community, the use of remand, and staff training as well as, significantly, a call to replace Cornton Vale with a smaller, specialist prison. The reformist emphasis of the report also attempted to look beyond the prison and recognised the limitations of the criminal justice system.

While areas beyond the criminal justice system were recognised by the Corston Report, previous reports in Scotland and the later report by the Commission on Women Offenders as contributing to the escalating female prison population and the circumstances of women drawn into it, government responses to the central recommendations of both Corston and the Commission were located firmly within a reformist framework.

Both the Corston Report and the Commission on Women Offenders drew attention to the provision of services within the community, referring to their 'fragmentation,' a recurrent theme in other jurisdictions. For example, the Social Exclusion Unit (2002) acknowledged that women in prison were most likely to be among the most socially disadvantaged and least likely to have their needs addressed in prison. Corston noted (para 4.16),

> There is a wealth of knowledge, research, experience, good practice and expertise throughout all of the agencies working with women in the criminal justice system but much good work is being carried out in isolation, with duplication of effort, little coordination and, in some cases, in ignorance of identical work being carried out elsewhere. [...] It is essential that a central body gets to grips with this basic administrative task.

In Scotland, the Justice Committee (2012) questioned 'what works' in terms of alternatives to custody. During the presentation of evidence, Elish Angiolini, who had chaired the Commission on Women Offenders, commented on the fragmented nature of interventions. She noted that there were many good services in existence, but they were often fragmented and amorphous, with monitoring and evaluation directed towards the needs of funders rather than sufficiently aimed at evaluation of what was making a difference. The duplication and disparate nature of interventions meant that sentencers were not always aware of alternatives at the point of sentencing nor could the government provide an overview of alternatives. 'That disparate, fragmented picture leads to a lack of cohesion and understanding, as well as a limited value in the research that is carried out' (Justice Committee 2012: 1578).

Related to the fragmentation of services was the need identified by both Corston and the Commission for strategic oversight and clear forms of leadership in directing the female penal estate. This had been noted by the Prison Reform Trust in 2011. Angiolini, in evidence to the Justice Committee, claimed (2012: 1585), 'A chief executive is needed to drive the whole dynamic forward so that community justice alternatives become a central part of the justice system rather than the marginalised Cinderella that they are at present.'

This issue had also been identified by Corston (2007: para 4.38) who noted,

> None of the pathway leads were able to demonstrate to me that they have a specific high-level strategy for women. Virtually nothing was said about the particular difficulties or restraints faced in dealing with women, who are a tiny minority at every stage within the criminal justice system.

Of the Women's Offending Reduction Programme (WORP) (England and Wales), set out to deliver a 'joined-up' response to women in the justice system, Corston (2007: 47) noted,

> (I)t is disappointing that the WORP has not been able to achieve more, despite the best efforts of the small dedicated team of four whose enthusiasm and commitment is exemplary. Without authority, power or backing at the highest levels the team is unable to effect change in the policies and priorities of others even within its own organisation, leaving aside the myriad of other government departments and agencies involved.

Government responses to both enquiries also engaged with governance issues. The Government Response to the Corston Report (MOJ 2007) identified key issues as the need for high-level governance and better mechanisms for cross-departmental working, an Inter-Ministerial Group to provide governance, the establishment of a 'Women's Commission' and the appointment of a 'champion' for women to drive forward the changes. In England and Wales, the government established an Inter-Ministerial Group to provide governance, establishment of a cross-departmental unit within the Ministry of Justice to coordinate and monitor work and a Ministerial Champion with responsibility for women and criminal justice matters. Rather than challenging the use of custody, both Corston and the Commission argued for new forms of custody, intended to be facilitated by a reduction in the number of women sent to prison as the result of other reforms. Corston (2007: 3.34) stated,

> Like many other commentators I have concluded that the present structure of relatively large, self-contained institutions that are sparsely distributed

across the country will become even less appropriate as the female prison population reduces as my recommendations are implemented. The existing system of women's prisons should be dismantled and replaced by smaller secure units for the minority of women from whom the public requires protection.

Corston, like others before her (e.g. Social Work Services and Prisons Inspectorates for Scotland 1998), considered that her proposed penal reforms would result in a significant reduction in the number of women imprisoned, and, accordingly, the female prison estate would require radical restructuring, resulting from the number of women likely to be imprisoned. *Women Offenders: A Safer Way* (Social Work Services and Prisons Inspectorates for Scotland 1998) proposed a 'twin-track' approach that consisted of *both* the development and enhancement of community disposals *and* a reduction of the number of available prison places to support the use of community disposals. The Prison Reform Trust (2011: 3) had also called for 'the planned closure of women's prisons to be accelerated and the money reinvested to support women's centres and other effective services for women offenders and vulnerable women in the community.' Failure to pursue both elements – as noted by the Social Work Services and Prisons Inspectorates and suggested by evidence from progressive work in Canada, the US and elsewhere – simply results in the expansion of the number of women in prison. The failure of reforms has often served to legitimise punishment as the only way to respond to social problems, thereby expanding the penal system. This has been particularly troublesome in the case of the criminal justice response to women (Carlen and Tombs 2006).

The Commission on Women Offenders called for the closure of Cornton Vale and for its replacement with a smaller institution, more suited to the needs of women, reflecting similar calls by Corston. The proposed closure of Cornton Vale and its replacement with smaller units across Scotland has noticeable parallels to Canada, following the closure of Kingston Prison for Women (which, like Cornton Vale, was deemed 'unfit for purpose') and its replacement with smaller institutions (Correctional Service Canada 1990). Importantly, while feminist scholars and activists were involved in the development of the policy and ethos of *Creating Choices* (Correctional Service Canada, 1990), the 'penal interpretations' that characterised its implementation have been criticised for returning to the narrow paradigm of individualising problems rather than challenging the injustices and inequalities that contribute to processes of criminalisation, with particular consequences for women (Hannah-Moffat and Shaw 2000; Hannah-Moffat 2001, 2008).

There have been several attempts to develop alternative forms of custody throughout the UK (e.g. Women in Prison 2012; Lidell Thomson 2015; Wilson 2015). As prison reformers have consistently argued, it is inadvisable to make prison an attractive option for sentencers, especially given the current disparity in evidencing 'effective practice.' While community provisions are under pressure to show they 'work,' prisons have no similar requirement, and indeed, in Scotland, there is no recorded data on the number of women who lose their jobs, tenancy, home (through repossession) or have their children taken into care as a consequence of their imprisonment. Consideration of the use of remand is ongoing, and the Commission highlighted this area as being particularly problematic, suggesting that custodial remand could actually mitigate the potentially deterrent impact of imprisonment.

Corston's most significant recommendation regarding women in prison was that existing women's prisons should be replaced with geographically dispersed, small, multi-functional custodial centres[9]. The government's response was an agreement to *consider* the future of the women's custodial estate and *explore* the potential scope, aims and objectives of the proposed new units. While accepting 'in principle' the underlying intent that custodial provision in the women's estate must be configured appropriately to meet women's needs, their response was to give this issue further consideration.

By contrast, following the publication of the Commission's report, the SPS was proactive from the outset, commissioning Reid Howie Associates (2012) to chair a series of meetings across the country, intended to consider the Commission Recommendations. They developed plans for a 300–350-bed prison for women (HMP Inverclyde), aiming to provide a 'state of the art' prison for women, meeting all their needs in one location. This brought about a mixed response, with some applauding the comprehensive design of the new proposed prison and others, notably prison reformers, challenging the ethos of the prison and arguing that this would work to increase rather than reduce the female prison population.

In 2014, Cabinet Secretary for Justice Michael Matheson announced a halt to the development at Inverclyde. Following his announcement, much activity followed as the SPS again took the lead, along with the Scottish government, re-viewing plans for women, with meetings convened across the country to discuss what should happen next. There has been determination across all agencies to maintain momentum for change. An international symposium was convened to consider how best to move forward following the decision to halt plans for HMP Inverclyde, producing a report, *From Vision to Reality: Transforming Scotland's Care of Women in Custody* (SPS 2015). In response to the Commission on Women Offenders' (2012) recommendations on community provisions, mentoring schemes and community justice services were established. A recent evaluation by the Institute for Research in Social Services (IRISS) (Dryden and Souness 2015) reiterated the challenges of short-term funding and highlighted good practice.

The speed with which SPS led the debate on alternatives to the proposed HMP Inverclyde was notable. By comparison, in terms of community provisions, the fragmentation of community resources and the different policy areas that come under the remit of different systems have implications for the potential of 'joined-up' approaches to tackle the key problems more broadly facing women. At the time of writing, developments are in hand for a national prison (80–100 places), small regional facilities for the west, east and north of the country (50 places each) and community-based residential units (each providing 15–30 places, totalling 150 places), with young women accommodated separately from adult prisoners (Wilson 2015). It is unclear when HMP Cornton Vale will close, and therefore women will continue to be held in designated areas of local male prisons.

While prison is generally viewed as a static feature at the centre of criminal justice policy, the implementation of resources in the community is fragmented and often short term. Similarly, in Canada, following the closure of the Kingston Prison for Women, the Expert Committee (2007: 16) concluded that more focus was required to build community capacity and increase creativity at grass-roots level: 'The Committee is left with the impression that there is a lack of co-ordinated effort on the community side relative to what we have observed at the institutions'.

Tensions between reform and abolition

Loraine Gelsthorpe (2004) highlights that when women are asked why they have 'offended,' the most common reasons cited are use of drugs/alcohol, the need for money for drugs/alcohol and general lack of financial support. This, coupled with lack of accommodation/housing for those released from prison, serves to maintain cycles of criminalisation. A feature of both Corston and the Commission on Women Offender reports was the shared acknowledgement of the role that poverty and social deprivation played in the criminalisation of women. Poverty was one of the three categories used to define 'vulnerabilities' by Corston (2007) (alongside 'domestic circumstances,' such as domestic violence, single-parent or childcare issues and personal circumstances, such as mental illness, low self-esteem or substance misuse). Yet the limitations of their scope in making recommendations are evident. Acknowledging the wider circumstances of women's lives, Angiolini (Justice Committee 2012: 1589) notes that 'Those are much wider issues that the Commission could not deal with.' References to 'structural change' in the context of recommendations referred to better delivery of services and stronger leadership rather than sociopolitical transformations.

The increasing burden of economic pressure on the poorest families and growing inequality between rich and poor is evidenced by the dramatic growth in the use of food banks across Scotland, with a significant increase in the number of people turning to food banks for emergency aid in recent years (All Party Parliamentary Group 2014). Current welfare cuts in Scotland have had particular impact on women (and children) as a consequence of recent changes in benefit entitlement, which have wider implications in terms of the inter-relationship of poverty and mental ill health as well as inadequate housing and physical and mental illness.

A key recommendation from the Social Work Services and Prisons Inspectorates (2008) was that expansion of community provisions should be accompanied by a cap on prison places. This was intended to ensure that community resources were used in place of custody, thus avoiding potential problems of 'net-widening,' in which increased numbers of women were drawn into the criminal justice system to access resources that were absent from local communities. This cap has never been introduced (see Tombs 2004). Updates on the implementation of the Transforming Rehabilitation agenda in England and Wales also noted concerns that more women may be drawn into the criminal justice system and remain there for longer (All Party Parliamentary Group 2015).

Although there has been significant investment in community provisions in Scotland, funding provided in two-year cycles causes considerable uncertainty for workers and service-users alike, allowing little time for services to continue beyond a setup and pilot phase. Short-term interventions are unable to evidence longer-term impact (Loucks et al. 2006; Hedderman et al. 2008, 2011; Easton and Mathews 2010, 2011; Burgess et al. 2011; Dryden and Souness 2015). 'Alternatives,' suggested as significant innovations within the system, are often absorbed into it in a way that softens them yet, at the same time, deflects the initial critiques within which they originated. This process also impedes the transformation from short to long-term goals.

In Scotland, the Reducing Reoffending Change Fund (RRCF) was set up as part of the government's preventative approach to tackling some of Scotland's most challenging problems. This £10 million fund has been used to provide mentoring services across Scotland 'to help them ["offenders"] to turn their lives around and to become responsible contributing citizens' (Cabinet Secretary for Justice 2013: 1). £2.7 million of this funding has been used to support 'Shine,' a national mentoring service for women.

The emphasis on mentoring denotes a return to addressing individual's 'vulnerabilities' through interventions with community services, a key recommendation from the Commission on Women Offenders:

> The Commission noted the potential for a mentor to work with each individual to address their criminogenic and non-criminogenic needs, engage effectively with community justice services and assist their access to public services that will support their ongoing rehabilitation and reintegration. The aim is to encourage women participating in the programme to consider their own offending behaviour and, as a result, reduce their offending in the future.
>
> *(Cabinet Secretary for Justice 2013: 2)*

Approximately £3 million was allocated to support local criminal justice partners across Scotland to develop, extend or restructure services for women within the criminal justice system, aimed at responding to the Commission's ambition of coordinated, multi-agency working in a holistic response to women's needs. However, the language of 'criminal justice' retains a positivist basis of 'offending' and 'offenders' and determines responses within a limited framework of reform, individualising problems and their solutions.

Transformation of limited visions

Attempts to reduce the female prison population have been reflected in a plethora of reviews, reports and inquiries into the imprisonment of women and potential reforms. Key reports have been based on extensive consultation and evidence-gathering and in discussion with women in the criminal justice system, practitioners, service providers and commissioners, representatives/leaders of key agencies and academics. Evidence has included national and international contributions that located the Scottish situation within an international context. Alongside this, academic research and analysis, evaluation and service monitoring have contributed to these key reports. Although as Corston (2007: 16) noted, 'There can be few topics that have been so exhaustively researched, to such little practical effect, as the plight of women in the criminal justice system.'

While prison populations have increased, attempts to enhance community disposals have continued without evident success in reducing the female prison population significantly, although recent restructuring in Scotland did initially show some reduction in the number of women in custody. Consistent features of all reports and inquiries into women in prison in Scotland have identified the need for appropriate mental health facilities, provisions for problem drug users in prisons linked into the community, appropriate education and training, reduction of use of remand and short-term prison sentences, improved access to/for families and provisions for visitors that cater for children. Each has highlighted the need to develop resources in the community and to ensure effective transitions between prisons and the community. All have indicated that the female prison population could be reduced significantly without detriment to the safety of local communities.

For any effective change to take place and be sustained, there is a requirement for actual engagement beyond the criminal justice system, based on a recognition of the limitations of criminal justice agencies to secure change in isolation. Political momentum towards more radical and far-reaching reform is required through addressing the inequalities and disadvantages that are features of many local populations where 'communities' have been fragmented. To maintain this momentum it is vital that when radical interventions are proposed, they are able to retain that radical potential. These are challenges evident in Scotland, as indicated above, but also elsewhere, following Corston (2007), including Correctional Service Canada (2009) where strategies for change, and the innovations within them, have been diluted. The focuses of Corston, the Commission and international experiences highlight the fragmentation of services and resources, taking little account of the wider fragmentation of communities. It is beyond the scope of such reform agendas to try to resolve this deep and pervasive problem.

It is important to return to Ruggiero's (2010: 7) definition of abolitionism as being 'not only a strategy, or a set of demands, aimed at the reduction (or suppression) of custody, it is also a perspective, a philosophy, an approach which challenges conventional definitions of crime.'

This fits with the need for an approach that goes beyond, but may include, practical initiatives. As Thomas Mathiesen (1974) has advocated previously alternative visions must be sketched out, rather than elaborate blueprints constructed (see this book's concluding chapter (Scraton and Carlton) for further discussion). Fundamentally, the context that surrounds and defines current criminal justice approaches needs to be transformed for a shift from reformism to abolitionism to take place. There needs to be a wider acknowledgement that the prison in particular, and the criminal justice system in general, does not meet its own objectives in terms of crime reduction or control.

It is the fundamental base of 'criminal justice' that requires interrogation to move beyond the existing mindset that maintains a dysfunctional prison system with limited room to manoeuvre in the direction of innovative change. Until this is challenged, the 'ontological reality of crime' goes unchallenged (Hulsman 1986). The depth to which the punitive discourse reaches is evident when consideration is given to the suggestion made by Mathieson and Kristian Hjemdal (2016: 146) to 'adjust the efforts of society as help to the victim *rather than* punishment of the offender' (emphasis in original). The instinctive discomfort that this concept can generate speaks volumes, illuminating a broad tradition within criminal justice of acknowledging the significance of the victims of 'crime' but, in practice, dedicating few resources to actually addressing their needs in the longer term (i.e. beyond court processes). Given the recognised circumstances of many women in prison, experiences of victimisation could certainly have been recognised earlier (i.e. prior to events resulting in custodial sentences), which would have had the potential to make a significant social impact. However, there appears little likelihood that within the current penal context, attention to the 'offender,' be it to punish or 'rehabilitate,' will be shifted towards ensuring the needs of the 'victim' are either identified and/or addressed.

Finally, it is the broader structural issues – social, political and economic – that determine the throughput of the criminal justice system. Any attempt at reform that does not address this necessarily will be limited. It is important to challenge the 'uplifting liberalism' for those at the top of the social structure and 'punitive paternalism' for those at the bottom (Wacquant 2012). However, current developments across the UK have highlighted the tendency to integrate prison and community penalties, and consequently, the wider social context remains obscure and unchallenged. The 'vulnerabilities' identified by Corston and the Commission on Women Offenders have been 'decoupled' from structural relationships and 'recoupled' with individual risks and/or deficits in their implementation, if not in the quest for a different approach to women in the criminal justice system. There is a growing frustration, however, with attempts to set out radical ideals that are translated into piecemeal practical reforms, in which individualising theories are used to justify the dilution of far-reaching change. Indeed, this has formed the basis for a more critical shift towards abolitionism and utopia (Malloch and Munro 2013; Malloch 2016). Until there is a shift in consciousness, this dystopian setup is likely to remain as the status quo.

This requires a reframing of 'reform' to recognise the limitations of attempting to make radical change within a wider penal system that appears to be highly resistant to reductions in scale or scope. While both Corston and the Commission for Women Offenders sought to highlight reforms to the criminal justice system as it applied to women, much like developments in Canada and elsewhere (see Malloch and McIvor 2013), their strategies relied on practical interventions within community initiatives and the governance of community justice more broadly. Their aspiration was that these developments would result in a reduction in the number of women sentenced to custody due to the availability and indeed efficacy of community disposals. This would allow a radical transformation of the penal estate as it applied to women, due directly to a reduction in the numbers sentenced to custody. Ultimately, fewer women in custody would enable a rethinking of the use of custody, with a different form of custodial experience emerging. With the majority of women experiencing community-based interventions, their 'vulnerabilities' would be better addressed but would continue to be dealt with under the auspices of the criminal justice system. Those who required separation from society would therefore be recipients of a more humane and needs-based response. However, while this may promise some potential for change, the broader and deeper structural constraints ensure that such change is limited and limiting. Rather than focussing, as so much criminological work does, on how best to ameliorate the individualised 'vulnerabilities' that characterise the lives of women in conflict with the law, attention would be better directed towards focussing on and actively contesting the vulnerabilities that are a direct result of inequitable and destructive social, political and economic systems. Vulnerabilities that emerge as a consequence of community fragmentation, punitive welfare reforms that most heavily impact the poorest and an attention to the misdemeanours of one section of society purposefully distracts from the war-manufacturing, capital-accumulating frenzy at the top of the economic ladder.

Abolitionism, going beyond reforms or reductions in penal populations, requires a shift in consciousness that questions what comes to be defined as a 'crime,' turning attention towards the harms that do not result in such a definition. This is accompanied by the requirement to explore the broader structures of society and the economic and social injustices that characterise widespread inequalities and divisions. The liberal project of reform does not consider the wider context of what actually constitutes 'justice' in a society defined by class and gender inequalities that restrict access to social and economic resources. Processes of criminalisation must be interrogated from this position. This requires rethinking the central concepts of 'crime' and 'punishment' and critiquing notions of 'rehabilitation.' Just as a conscious paradigm shift is required to imagine what it would be like to have a justice system that prioritised attention and social resources to helping the victim rather than punishing the offender, an abolitionist approach requires envisaging a society without prisons rather than the development of a more palatable prison system.

Notes

1 For example, during the 1990s, the absence of an open estate for women, lack of appropriate educational opportunities for women in prison, the need to address the specific 'needs and aptitudes' of women and calls for consideration of small local units (referring specifically to Aberdeen, Inverness and Dumfries) were highlighted (for example, HM Inspectorate of Prisons for Scotland 1995). Issues, such as training opportunities for women, visiting arrangements and ongoing concern about medical care (especially in relation to psychiatric and psychological problems), have featured consistently in Inspectorate Reports throughout the 1990s and 2000s.
2 At that time, Scotland's national prison for women.
3 See also Prisons and Probation Ombudsman for England and Wales (2003).
4 Plans for rollout across the country did not come to fruition (see Malloch et al. 2008).
5 The average daily female prison population at this time (2002) was 201.
6 It often seems that inquiries and their recommendations are influenced by the expertise of those conducting the inquiry.
7 To include Community Justice Centres, multidisciplinary teams and key workers, intensive mentoring, supported accommodation, national service-level agreement for the provision of psychiatric reports, development of mental health services to address the needs of women with personality disorders and mental health training for criminal justice professionals.
8 Recommendations on sentencing included the piloting of a problem-solving summary criminal court, rapid criminal justice social work reports, subsequent progress review hearings, introduction of composite custody and community sentence, suspended sentences and training for Judicial Studies Committee.
9 See also Scottish Prisons Commission (2008).

References

All Party Parliamentary Group on Hunger and Food Poverty (2014) *Feeding Britain: A Strategy for Zero Hunger in England, Wales, Scotland and Northern Ireland*, London: The Children's Society.

All Party Parliamentary Group on Women in the Penal System (2015) *Report on the Inquiry into Preventing Unnecessary Criminalisation of Women*, London: Howard League.

Bloom, B., Owen, B. and Covington, C. (2003) *Gender Responsive Strategies: Research, Practice and Guiding Principles for Women Offenders*, Washington DC: National Institute of Corrections.

Burgess, C., Malloch, M. and McIvor, G. (2011) *Women in Focus: An Evaluation*, Irvine, CA: South West Scotland Community Justice Authority.

Cabinet Secretary for Justice (2013) *Second Annual Progress Report*, Edinburgh: Scottish Parliament Justice Committee.

Carlen, P. (1983) *Women's Imprisonment: A Study in Social Control*, London: Routledge and Kegan Paul.

Carlen, P. (2008) *Imaginary Penalities*, Cullompton: Willan Publishing.

Carlen, P. and Tombs, J. (2006) 'Reconfigurations of Penality,' *Theoretical Criminology*, 10(3): 337–360.

Cohen, S. (1985) *Visions of Social Control*, Cambridge: Polity Press.

Commission on Women Offenders (2012) *Commission on Women Offenders: Final Report*, Edinburgh: Scottish Government.

Correctional Service Canada (1990) *Creating Choices*, Ottawa, ON: CSC.

Corston, J. (2007) *The Corston Report: A Review of Women with Particular Vulnerabilities in the Criminal Justice System*, London: Home Office.

Dobash, R., Dobash, R. and Gutteridge, S. (1986) *The Imprisonment of Women*, London: Wiley-Blackwell.

Dryden, R. and Souness, C. (2015) *Evaluation of Sixteen Women's Community Justice Services in Scotland*, Edinburgh: Scottish Government.

Easton, H. and Matthews, R. (2010) *Evaluation of the 218 Service*, Edinburgh: Scottish Government Social Research.

Easton, H. and Matthews, R. (2011) *Evaluation of the Inspire Women's Project*, London: South Bank University.

Equal Opportunities Committee (2009) *Female Offenders in the Criminal Justice System*, Edinburgh: Scottish Parliament.

Expert Committee Review (2007) *The Expert Committee Review of the Correctional Service of Canada's Ten-Year Status Report on Women's Corrections 1996–2006*, Ottawa, ON: Correctional Services Canada.

Garland, D. (2002) *The Culture of Control*, Oxford: Oxford University Press.

Gelsthorpe, L. (2004) 'Female Offending: A Theoretical Overview,' in G. McIvor (ed.) *Women Who Offend*, London: Jessica Kingsley Publishers.

Hannah-Moffat, K. (2001) *Punishment in Disguise: Penal Governance and Federal Imprisonment of Women in Canada*, Toronto: University of Toronto Press.

Hannah-Moffat, K. (2008) 'Re-imagining Gendered Penalities,' in P. Carlen (ed.) *Imaginary Penalities*, Cullompton: Willan Publishing.

Hannah-Moffat, K. and Shaw, M. (2000) *An Ideal Prison? Critical Essays on Women's Imprisonment in Canada*, Halifax, NS: Fernwood Publishing Company.

Hedderman, C., Gunby, C. and Shelton, N. (2011) 'What Women Want: The Importance of Qualitative Approaches in Evaluating Work with Women Offenders', *Criminology and Criminal Justice* 11(1): 3–19.

Hedderman, C., Palmer, E. and Hollin, C. (2008) Implementing Services for Women Offenders and Those 'At Risk' of Offending: Action Research with Together Women, Ministry of Justice Research Series 12/08, London: Ministry of Justice.

HM Inspectorate of Prisons for Scotland (1995) *Thematic Study: Custody and Training of Female Prisoners and Young Offenders in Scotland*, Edinburgh: Scottish Office.

HM Inspectorate of Prisons for Scotland (2007) *HMP and YOI Cornton Vale Inspection: 19–20 March 2007*, Edinburgh: Scottish Executive.

HM Inspectorate of Prisons for Scotland (2009) *HMP and YOI Cornton Vale Inspection: 21–29 September 2009*, Edinburgh: Scottish Executive.

HM Inspectorate of Prisons for Scotland (2011) *HMP and YOI Cornton Vale Follow-up Inspection: 1–4 February 2011*, Edinburgh: Scottish Executive.

Hulsman, L. (1986) 'Critical Criminology and the Concept of Crime,' *Contemporary Crises*, 10(1): 63–80.

Justice Committee (2012) *Official Report: Discussion of the Commission on Women Offenders* (Final Report 2012), Edinburgh: Scottish Parliament 26 June 2012.

Lidell Thomson Consultancy (2015) *Consultation Report: The Future of the Female Custodial Estate*, Edinburgh: Scottish Government.

Loucks, N. (1997) *Research into Drugs and Alcohol, Violence and Bullying, Suicides and Self-Injury and Backgrounds of Abuse*, Edinburgh: Scottish Prison Service Occasional Papers Report No. 1/98.

Loucks, N., Malloch, M., McIvor, G. and Gelsthorpe, L. (2006) *Evaluation of the 218 Centre*, Edinburgh: Scottish Executive Social Research.

Malloch, M. (2016) 'Justice for Women: a Penal Utopia?' *Justice, Power and Resistance* Foundation Volume (September 2016) pp. 151–169.

Malloch, M. and McIvor, G. (eds) (2013) *Women, Punishment and Social Justice,* Abingdon: Routledge.

Malloch, M., McIvor, G., Loucks, N. (2008) 'Time Out for Women: Innovation in Scotland in a Context of Change,' *The Howard Journal,* 47(4): 383–399.

Malloch, M. and Munroe, B. (2013) *Crime, Critique and Utopia,* Basingstoke: Palgrave Macmillan.

Mathiesen, T. (1974) *The Politics of Abolition,* Oxford: Martin Robertson.

Mathieson, T. and Hjemdal, O. (2016) 'A New Look at Victim and Offender,' *Justice, Power and Resistance,* Foundation Vol. 1: 137–150.

McIvor, G. and Burman, M. (2011) *The Drivers of Women's Imprisonment,* Stirling: Scottish Centre for Crime and Justice Research.

Ministerial Group on Women's Offending (2002) *A Better Way,* Edinburgh: Scottish Executive.

Ministry of Justice (2007) *The Government's Response to the Report by Baroness Corston,* London: Ministry of Justice.

Prison Reform Trust (2011) *Reforming Women's Justice: Final Report of the Women's Justice Taskforce,* London: Prison Reform Trust.

Prisons and Probation Ombudsman for England and Wales (2003) *The Death in Custody of a Woman and the Series of Deaths in HMP/YOI Styal August 2002–2003,* London: Home Office.

Reid Howie Associates (2012) *Women Offenders in Custody: Analysis of Consultation Findings,* Edinburgh: Scottish Prison Service.

Ruggiero, V. (2010) *Penal Abolitionism,* Oxford: Oxford University Press.

Scottish Prisons Commission (2008) *Scotland's Choice,* Edinburgh: Scottish Prisons Commission.

Scottish Prison Service (2015), *From Vision to Reality,* Edinburgh: SPS.

Social Exclusion Unit (2002) *Reducing Re-Offending by Ex-Prisoners,* London: Office of the Deputy Prime Minister.

Social Work Services and Prisons Inspectorates for Scotland (1998) *Women Offenders – A Safer Way,* Edinburgh: Scottish Office.

Tombs, J. (2004) 'From "A Safer to a Better Way": Transformations in Penal Policy for Women,' in G. McIvor (ed.) *Women Who Offend: Research Highlights in Social Work,* 44. London: Jessica Kingsley.

Wacquant, L. (2012) 'Three Steps towards an Anthropology of Actually Existing Neoliberalism,' *Social Anthropology,* 19(4): 66–79.

Wilson, T. (2015) *International Review of Custodial Models for Women: Key Messages for Scotland,* Edinburgh: Scottish Government Social Research.

Women in Prison (2012) *Report on the Roundtable on Small Custodial Units,* London: Women in Prison 15 May.

5

POST-CORSTON REFLECTIONS ON REMANDED WOMEN'S EXPERIENCES IN NORTHERN IRELAND

Gillian McNaull

Introduction

Custodial remand, the pretrial phase when a prisoner has yet to be convicted of a crime and retains the presumption of innocence, presents a challenge to the principles of social justice. Not only are those remanded to custody 'deprived of their liberty'; often, they find themselves 'subjected to the worst conditions' despite previous calls for 'improved and separate facilities' for remand prisoners (Ashworth 2015: 329). As Baroness Jean Corston (2007: i) states in her review of vulnerable women in the criminal justice system,

> There are many women in prison, either on remand or serving sentences for minor, non-violent offences, for whom prison is both disproportionate and inappropriate. Many of them suffer poor physical and mental health or substance abuse, or both. Large numbers have endured violent or sexual abuse or had chaotic childhoods. Many have been in care. I have concluded that we are rightly exercised about paedophiles, but seem to have little sympathy, understanding or interest in those who have been their victims, many of whom end up in prison.

Awareness has been raised about the vulnerability of imprisoned women in terms of the issues they import into the prison and regarding the impact of imprisonment in compounding and creating vulnerability (Corston 2007; Scraton and Moore 2007; Carlton and Seagrave 2013). Custodial remand is recognised widely as a significant driving force in the upward trajectory of women committed to prison (Edgar 2004; Kerr 2014). It has contributed to the disproportionate increase of women's imprisonment in recent decades throughout England and Wales (E&W) (Howard League of Penal Reform 2011) and Northern Ireland

(Kerr 2014; Moore and Wahidin 2015). Corston (2007: 3) notes that 'proportionately more women than men are remanded in custody'. For her (Corston 2007: 8), the 'overuse' of remand reflects a necessity for more alternative disposals alongside 'bail placements' suitable to women's needs, with 'more supported accommodation' to reduce risk of reoffending.

This chapter examines current practices for remanded women in Northern Ireland. It is derived in empirical research conducted by the author in Ash House, Northern Ireland's only women's prison unit. Ash House is situated within Hydebank Wood Secure College (formerly Young Offender Centre), a custodial institution for young men. Locating a women's unit within a predominantly male institution has been criticised repeatedly by inspections and independent organisations (Prison Review Team 2011; Moore and Scraton 2014). The research included interviews with 25 remanded women between October 2015 and March 2016. The proportion of women remanded to custody has decreased significantly since the extent of remand was raised in 2011 as a defining feature of imprisonment in Northern Ireland (Owers et al. 2011). However, while remanded women comprise 25–30 per cent of the women's daily prison population, in annual terms, they constitute 57 per cent of women who enter the prison (DOJNI 2015), and Northern Ireland's remand rates remain the highest in the United Kingdom (UK) (Campbell 2016).

With reference to Corston, the chapter explores the failure in Northern Ireland to implement previous recommendations to ensure women's diversion into community sanctions and gender-responsive imprisonment. The section 'Dismantling Women's Offending Pathways' interrogates conceptualisations of 'pathways' to custody through analysis of women's lived experiences prior to imprisonment. It is argued that, despite official acknowledgement of these 'pathways' (DOJNI 2010), the continued focus on individualised explanations of crime fails to recognise Northern Ireland's distinct political, economic and historical conditions. From the late 1960s, ethno-national conflict[1] embedded the region in sectarian violence and military occupation. 'The Conflict'[2] produced a 'unique prison system', 'shaped by sectarianism', staffed by 'overwhelmingly' male, Protestant prison officers who were considered viable targets by Republican paramilitaries (Moore and Scraton 2014: 73). Punitive conditions were imposed on women prisoners: first, in Armagh gaol, followed by Mourne House Unit in Maghaberry (high-security male prison) and from 2004, in Ash House (Moore and Scraton 2014). The section 'The Space In Between' explores women's experiences within this distinct penal context, challenging conceptions of the gender-specific reform that Corston had envisaged and noting the continued marginalisation of women within a male-focused system. In conclusion, it is argued that despite recognition of experiences of poverty, violence and harm in the production of women's 'offending', Corston's (2007) approach maintains existing narratives and practices that enmesh women within a criminal justice framework, reifying their 'offender' status and reproducing the logic of punishing marginalised women.

Dismantling women's offending pathways

Within the UK, the anticipation is that 25 per cent of prisoners held on remand will be acquitted or will receive a community sentence (Prison Reform Trust (PRT) 2016: 19). Yet, whilst 74 per cent of prisoners remanded from Crown Court go on to receive a prison sentence, only 15 per cent of remanded prisoners tried at magistrates' courts will be sentenced to custody (PRT 2013: 3). For women prisoners, 84 per cent are imprisoned for non-violent offences (PRT 2016: 30), with Elaine Player considering that the fact that 6 out of 10 remanded women are subsequently acquitted or given a non-custodial sentence highlights the dissonance between bail and sentencing decisions, with women committed to custody for reasons other than the severity of their crime (Player 2007: 403). Reasons for remand include 'no fixed abode', lack of bail address or detox placement, perceived 'risk' to oneself and assessment for mental capacity (Player 2007). Corston (2007) questions high remand rates that result in low levels of custodial sentencing. For her, women's remand reflects lack of parity in due process, presenting ethical and moral challenges with court decisions to remand women in custody often 'inequitable and lacking common sense' (p. 9). However, rather than resisting the capture of vulnerable women within the 'offending behaviour' paradigm, Corston continued to problematise the individual and her environment, justifying criminal justice responses to the 'risks' such women posed.

Drawing inspiration from Corston, a similar conceptualisation of individualised 'offending pathways' was adopted by the Northern Ireland Department of Justice (DOJNI) in its 2010 'Strategy to Manage Women Offenders and those Vulnerable to Offending Behaviour'. The Strategy identified nine 'pathways' to offending: accommodation; education, training and employment; health and mental health; alcohol and substance misuse; finance, benefits and debts; children and family; attitudes, thinking and behaviours; supporting women who have been abused, raped or have experienced domestic violence; and supporting women who have been involved in prostitution. The DOJNI (2010: 8) commented that 'addressing these issues is vital to ensuring that women are properly supported to lead law-abiding lives, and to reducing levels of re-offending'. The Strategy proposed diversion from custody via 'a range of women-centred interventions available within the community', thus producing 'a better experience and outcome for those women who receive a custodial sentence' (p. 17). These interventions would be delivered through a 'strategic framework for reducing offending aimed at targeting pathways that contribute to offending and reoffending' (p. 23). It also proposed the development of a 'gender-specific approach to the management of women in custody', with 'gender-specific standards and guidance for those working with women offenders' (p. 55). However, while acknowledging that remanded women constituted 61 per cent of all female receptions, new initiatives failed to include the experiences of women remanded to custody, a gap raised by the 'stakeholder engagement' that formed an element of the 'Reducing Women Offenders 2013–2016' refreshed strategy (DOJNI 2013: 17).

The Strategy also failed to address the distinct intersection of oppressions experienced by women prisoners in Northern Ireland, manifested not only within structural conditions of poverty, systemic gendered inequality and disabling responses to mental health and capacity but also through distinctive frameworks of sectarianism and the conservative Christian patriarchy. This context punishes marginalised women not just for their 'crime' but also for the 'double deviance' (Carlen 1983) of nonconformity to heteronormative gender roles.

For many women interviewed for the study, their socioeconomic marginalisation was a defining feature of their lives before prison, characteristics mirrored by preceding research on imprisoned women in Northern Ireland (Scraton and Moore 2007; Kerr 2014; Moore and Scraton 2014; Campbell 2016; O'Neill 2016). Of the 25 women interviewed, 19 were not working or in education, with 12 self-reporting receipt of Disability Living Allowance. Fifteen women had experienced homelessness, nine of whom were living in a hostel or were homeless at the time of arrest. Four had advanced to insecure accommodation, lost in the process of remand. Six women with secure housing prior to their committal had become homeless due to either bail conditions precluding them from returning home or, in two cases, fear of paramilitary reprisal. Only four women would return to their 'home' post-release.

For remanded women, experiences extend beyond material oppression, incorporating demonisation and stigma as the women endure the 'traditional distinction between deserving and undeserving poor' (Jones 1984: 285). For imprisoned women, the presumed 'deviance' projected through the moralisation of poverty is compounded by their gender and the consequent power differentials. Many of the women interviewed had experienced sexual abuse, domestic violence and the loss of their children to state 'care' or family members, resulting in mental ill health, self-harm and addiction. Their lives were steeped in gendered experiences of violence, trauma and loss. However, for 'criminal women', deviation from cultural expectations extends beyond the crime of which they are accused, emphasising a form of 'double deviance' as they depart from normative narratives of femininity and womanhood (Carlen 1983; Heidensohn 1985; Lloyd 1995; Chesney-Lind 1999).

In Northern Ireland, negative gendered experiences are compounded by a profound hegemonic sociocultural framework related to the conflict and the magnification of socioeconomic deprivation with the legacy of war and subsequent under-investment (Tomlinson 2013). Ethno-nationalist discourses rooted in twin patriarchal religions, Protestantism and Catholicism, produce 'normative models of sexuality and gender' geared towards 'ideals of motherhood, domesticity and chastity' (Ashe 2009: 5). These heterosexist discourses stigmatise and regulate women's behaviour, producing 'a highly regulated sexual landscape characterised by limited sexual rights' (Kitchin and Lysaght, in Ashe 2009: 5). This is evident in the threat to women's autonomy posed by existing abortion legislation and vociferous obstruction of reform (Ward 2013) through failure to adopt legislative acceptance of lesbian, gay, bisexual and transgender (LGBT) marriage and efforts to compound LGBT discrimination (Hayes and Nagle 2015). It also includes legislation undermining sex workers' rights (Ellison 2015). While women in Northern Ireland experience the same intersections of class, gender, 'race' and disability discrimination that prevail elsewhere, they also bear additional oppressions emanating from religion and sectarianism.

During a period of transition from conflict, women continue to experience these systemic features (Rooney 2011), with transitional justice debates neglecting the persistent impact on women and children (Ni Aolain cited in Moore and Wahidin 2015). Women who grew up in rural and urban working-class communities during 'the Troubles' incurred the everyday experience of colonial occupation with its associated militarisation (Harris and Healy 2001). The threat of paramilitary violence and control remains 'post-conflict' (Ward 2013). Segregated interface communities experienced a 'levelling downwards' of poverty (Rooney 2011) through lack of investment and impeded structural growth. This was gendered and often related to single parenthood alongside disability and ill health (Hillyard et al. 2003). In a context of pervasive violence, these features intertwined with experience of death and injury of close personal contacts, with over half the adult population having witnessed violent events (Tomlinson 2013). Enduring such experiences has significantly raised deprivation levels, heightened unemployment rates and increased risk of physical and mental ill health (Tomlinson 2013: 2). 'Hidden' legacies of mental ill health and addiction are routine as individuals find mechanisms to cope with day-to-day survival (Ward 2013). Men's alcohol and drug use feeds into domestic and sexual violence (Ward 2013). In transitional working-class communities, young women endure not only continued paramilitarism but also the risks of sexual exploitation and illegal drug use (Ward 2013).

For the women participants in this research, the Conflict was an additional layer to their marginalisation, ominously overshadowing other factors. All but four participants were from Northern Ireland, the Conflict forming the backdrop to their lives. For some women, their experience went beyond the implicit infusion of everyday life to include explicit experiences of violence that persisted in transitional society. Due to their religious background, Loana's family had been forced out of Northern Ireland by paramilitaries. When she moved back from England, paramilitary control continued:

> I've been put out of all my homes by paramilitaries. I was in my town and because I brought a Catholic home they forced me out... Twenty-four hours to get out or I was going to get shot. I'm looking over my shoulder all the time.[3]

Loana experienced paramilitary control of her behaviour, sexuality and relationships, challenging her agency to make decisions. Common to other women, this entailed physical violence, social exclusion and symbolic condemnation of gendered 'deviance'.

Women faced a vein of harm and trauma running through their lives, affecting their mental health and leading to addiction, self-harm and suicidal ideation. Incarcerated women's experiences extend beyond 'discrete' incidents of trauma. Their pre-custody lives often reflect 'cumulative trauma' amassed from cycles of childhood abuse, experience of sexual and domestic violence, separation from children and state intervention and institutionalisation (Carlton and Segrave 2011: 553). As Corston's (2007) recommendations and DOJNI (2010) policy exemplify, there is a broad consensus that responses to imprisoned women should overcome 'victim/perpetrator dichotomies', acknowledging the trauma prevalent in women's lives. However, what often unfolds is a policy discourse 'preoccupied with gender specific "risks"' that produce women's criminogenity (Corcoran and Fox 2013: 139). For vulnerable women, this manifests as a conflation of 'need' and 'risk', with the dangers to the women recast as dangers they pose (Cooper 2014: 15). What emerges from this risk/need paradigm is a discourse on 'social lack' and 'individual deficits' in the multivariant forms of trauma, addiction, relationship choices and mental illness, transforming 'social need' into 'lifestyle risks' that are 'inherently criminogenic' (Corcoran 2010: 242). This detracts from the 'societal failings' underpinning these 'needs,' 'paradoxically making the structural nature of crime-related deprivation less visible' (Corcoran 2010: 242).

This institutionalised response to marginalised women is one element of a shift that has transformed the welfare state into a security state, with social issues redefined as risks to be managed via coercion (Hallsworth and Lea in Bell 2014). Within neoliberal society, 'risk' and 'public protection' dominate criminal justice discourse and practice (McAlinden and Dwyer 2015: 322). Actuarial methods are used in the development of 'subjective disciplinary techniques of governing' (Hannah-Moffat 1999: 73), with 'correctional interpretations of women's needs as potential or modified risk factors' becoming 'central to the efficient management of incarcerated women' (p. 88). Women classified as 'a risk' receive a variety of 'risk reduction' corrective mechanisms from risk-needs programmes (Hannah-Moffat in O'Malley 2009: 12) through to incapacitation as a way of 'neutralising' risk (Feeley and Simon in O'Malley 2009). Thus, women move through a range of institutions of governance, occupying what Michel Foucault conceives as a 'carceral archipelago', with punishment exerted via an individual's contact with the 'social body' (Foucault 1977: 298). Women's journeys through the state's institutions initiate their exclusion from schools and families, institutional care, mental health facilities and homeless hostels, finally extending to the prison. Each strand of governance enacts mechanisms on a particular aspect of the women's conduct, setting in motion monitoring, judgement and control before processing them to the next point of exclusion, moving 'gradually from the correction of irregularities to the punishment of crime' (Foucault 1977: 298). Risk has become a component of governance that 'imagines' problems in a particular way (O'Malley 2009: 5). What is governed for remanded women is not necessarily the physical manifestation of behaviour but the *potential* for deviant conduct. This recasts experiences of marginalisation and harm as deficiencies to be managed pastorally and punitively. The risk paradigm legitimises a 'waste-management' response to the surplus populations of neoliberalism, through material containment (Drake and Muncie 2010: 117), while producing a symbolic 'blaming system' responsive to 'intolerable levels of risk' (Sparks in Drake and Muncie 2010: 129).

Thus, many women interviewed considered that their vulnerability was related to responsive punishment and control by state agencies because harms were redefined throughout their lives and reconceptualised as 'risk' posed. Seventeen of the 25 women had experienced bereavement and loss, spanning their childhoods and continuing into adulthood, exacerbating harms incurred in early years. Seventeen had suffered regularly from gendered violence – including domestic abuse, sexual abuse and/or rape. Twelve had experienced domestic violence within intimate relationships, often interrelated with the violence of the Conflict. They developed 'negative' coping mechanisms and enduring mental health issues. Eighteen women had drug and/or alcohol addictions, with 15 receiving a dual diagnosis of co-existing mental health and substance use issues. Children were central to the loss experienced by many women. Nineteen were mothers, and 17 did not have custody prior to imprisonment. Some women had lost custody to violent partners or had several children removed by the state, while others had previously passed caring responsibilities to family members. With their identities as mothers compromised, they became stigmatised and marginalised in their communities, their violation of 'female gender roles' and societal normative values recasting their identities as 'mad', 'sad' and 'bad' (Lloyd 1995; Gelsthorpe 2004; Scott and Codd 2010).

When pastoral care was exerted, it focused on 'attitudes, thinking and behaviours' (DOJNI 2010), adjusting women's cognitive responses and moral behaviour through Cognitive Behavioural Therapy (CBT) and 'empowerment' courses. Thus, survivors participated in rehabilitation from 'victimhood', which held them responsible and decoupled from 'the context of communal violence, sectarianism or conflict' (Moore and Wahidin 2015: 290). This perpetuated 'the psy-ing of women's social marginalization' while diverting 'attention from systemic oppression' (Pollack 2007: 170). These 'soft' state responses involved pastoral management, resulting in increased social control and leading to further policing until women were eventually enmeshed in the 'carceral net' (Cohen 1985). Twenty of the women interviewed were prescribed psychopharmaceutical medication, unsurprising in a region with one of the highest antidepressant prescription rates in the world (McClure 2014). Eighteen participants were diagnosed with depression and/or anxiety, two were diagnosed as bipolar, and one woman suffered from disassociative identity disorder. However, in the health and social care sector, 'a preoccupation with "what comes first" results in potential service users being excluded from help', with access often refused to 'service users' who 'misuse substances' (Crome et al. 2009: 3). Five women experienced behaviour control through the 'diagnostic technology' of 'personality disorder' (McBride 2015: 1), a 'contested and controversial' psychiatric label 'used to categorise people assessed to experience impairments of the "self"' and dysfunctions in 'interpersonal functioning' (McBride 2015: 9). The label is pernicious, and in Northern Ireland it brings stigmatisation, reducing pathways for mental health support. Unlike legislation in other UK jurisdictions, the NI Mental Health Order (1986) excludes personality disorder, which is considered 'chronic' and 'untreatable' (McBride 2015: 9), thus segregating those diagnosed from other mental health service users. The management of personality disorder via criminal justice relegates them to a forensic setting for 'rehabilitation'. The criminalisation of the 'medical' and the medicalisation of the 'criminal' subjects women to a 'layering of institutional control' through 'multi-institutional management' (Medina and McCranie 2011: 139).

Angela, for example, had been in conflict with the law throughout her life, hospitalised in an acute mental healthcare unit on multiple occasions. Yet her mental health history was judged as a 'pathway' to criminal behaviour, with her last sentence imposing mental health treatment as a condition for her release. On release, Angela discovered that her marginalisation in the community had not decreased. She remained dependent on hostel provision. There was no panacea for the 'personal journey' she had been impelled to undergo to achieve 'rehabilitation'. Her life outside remained unchanged: a mundane trudge to the probation officer, mental health services and addiction services. She stated, 'It just annoys me that I did all that work last time and I was still on my back, it was like out of one prison and into another'. Angela's experience was typical: the structural impediments to integration into mainstream society remained, as did systemic inequalities.

While women are remanded in custody for reasons beyond the severity of crime – from no fixed abode, 'chaotic' lifestyle, risk to self and psychiatric assessment – this can be connected to behaviour leading them to meet the threshold of imprisonment. What transpired for some women interviewed was the escalation of their behaviour because of interactions with criminal justice services responding to their 'deviant' acts. Edwin Lemert (1951) characterises this process as primary and secondary deviation, a framework differentiating between 'original causes' and 'effective causes' of deviant acts. For many women, their primary deviation – public disorder, being drunk, being in mental health crisis, drug use and/or lack of accommodation – led to prison once they were absorbed into the criminal justice system. What followed was 'secondary deviation': 'deviant behaviour or a role based upon it as a means of defence, attack or adjustment to the overt and covert problems created by the consequent societal reaction' (Lemert in Newburn 2009: 212). Typical of other women's experiences, Sarah described how in a vulnerable situation at the time of her arrest,

> I was feeling suicidal...I had a drink and went to the bridge. Two men pulled me down and phoned the police. The police came and checked my pockets because I am not allowed a lighter as a bail condition,

> because of the fire last time. When I was coming over the bridge onto the pavement, my leg accidentally touched one of the officers and she said 'Assault!' I said 'I was just trying to climb over here. I didn't do anything deliberately!'

For women like Sarah with a dual diagnosis, their mental health issues are demoted, replaced by a crime control response, emphasising the deviancy attached to alcohol use. Sarah's involvement with the criminal justice system stemmed from her attempted suicide. She had attempted to burn herself alive and was charged with damage to Housing Executive property.[4] Initially bailed, she continued to attempt suicide, breaching her bail conditions and leading to an escalation of criminal charges. Not only does the severity of the arrest process layer more harm on women who have experienced trauma, it also cements the state's conception of deviant behaviours which deserve punishment. Beyond these harmful effects, criminalisation tightens the snare in which marginalised women become trapped.

As the previous discussion demonstrates, women continue to be remanded to custody for the reasons Corston had raised as problematic. Despite highlighting the need to 'demand convincing evidence that the defendant is fit for custody ... for petty offences that will in all likelihood not attract a custodial sentence' (Corston 2007: 9), women like Loana, Angela and Sarah continue to be remanded for reasons not related to severity of crime. This reveals the practice of sending a woman to prison as a "place of safety" or "for her own good" that Corston considered 'appalling', advocating that it 'must stop'. Yet, in the course of the research, three participants, including Sarah, were remanded for offences directly related to suicide attempts. Three women were imprisoned while the court awaited psychiatric and/or social work reports. Women considered to have insufficient mental capacity for imprisonment waited for weeks to be transferred from prison to mental health facilities. Rosemary, aged 58 with learning disabilities, had been arrested for knocking on her neighbour's windows when she was lonely and found herself incarcerated because 'decisions are sometimes taken in court based on insufficient information' (Corston 2007: 56). Women were imprisoned for safety or because courts considered that there was no alternative accommodation. Numerous women were remanded to prison awaiting courts to process their bail applications.

Corston found that bail information schemes in women's prisons were poor, and this was the case in Hydebank Wood. Kate was granted bail but was awaiting a housing referral months later as no one took responsibility for her paperwork. It became apparent that this was the responsibility of the sentence manager:

> I went down to see her... for the first time in three months. She said it was a form she would have to fill in, and she said nobody told her she needed to do that, or it would have been done a couple of months ago. It will be the end of February before I get out now.

Natalia also experienced the effects of no bail information or help in place prior to her release:

> They let me out at 6.30/7pm into reception, they said, 'You have to go now'. I said, 'Where do you want me to go? I have nowhere to go? I have no place to go?' I couldn't go to my town to stay with my family because of bail conditions…

As Corston (2007: 66) considered, for marginalised women, 'bailing them out of their home area could be as disruptive as remanding them in custody'. However, this remained an overwhelming issue for women in Northern Ireland, many of whom faced bail restrictions or paramilitary threat preventing their bail. Despite Corston's consideration that bail support service provision was 'unacceptably arbitrary' (p. 56), in 2016, remanded women in Northern Ireland continued to experience a gap in service provision, undermining aims of 'resettlement' and 'reducing offending'. In effect, they were cast out with no support and no appropriate housing.

Significant for Corston (2007: 56) was the community deficit that led some women to 'prefer to be in prison' rather than experience the paucity of secure provision outside the prison walls. As Natalia stated, 'I have that little out there that it is actually better for me in this hole.' Corston (2007: 56) considered that

> Prison should be more tolerable for those women who need to be there but I believe that it is not the place for respite, for access to services which should be available in the community and nor should it become a home for those very unfortunate women who simply have nowhere else to go.

An examination of remanded women's experiences highlights the paradoxical nature of projecting agency onto those who have limited choices. The continued focus on individuals' behaviour in response to 'offending' overlooks the contextual conditions producing such 'pathways' (Moore and Wahidin 2015), justifying the containment of the 'detritus of contemporary capitalism' (Davis 2003), condemning further those who experience harm caused by structural failings.

The space in-between – women's experiences of prison

As discussed above, Corston's (2007: 9) core recommendation was that custody for women 'must be reserved for serious and violent offenders who pose a threat to the public', challenging the presumption that women should be 'sent to prison for their own good, to teach them a lesson, for their own safety or to access services'. For women for whom prison was deemed 'necessary', Corston recommended a government strategy to 'replace existing women's prisons with suitable, geographically dispersed, small, multi-functional custodial centres' (p. 35). She made several proposals to generate a gender-appropriate environment:

'investment in more rigorous training and ongoing support and supervision for all those charged with meeting the complex needs of women' (p. 13). For those imprisoned, 'the conditions should be clean and hygienic with improvements to sanitation arrangements addressed as a matter of urgency', with strip-searching of women 'reduced to the absolute minimum compatible with security' (p. 35).

Corston (2007: 56) recognised the distinct issues faced by women on remand, annually averaging 65 per cent of receptions. This population experiences heightened gendered vulnerability. Approximately 50 per cent of remanded women receive no family visits, compared to a quarter of remanded men. 44 per cent will have attempted suicide previously, compared to 27 per cent of remanded men (p. 56). The disproportionate vulnerability of remanded women causes heightened 'sleep problems, depressive ideas, depression, lack of concentration and forgetfulness ... obsessive symptoms, panic and phobias'. Remanded women who had been in prison for less than a month showed an 82 per cent incidence of neurotic symptoms. Remanded women were also at increased risk of medicalisation, twice as likely to be medicated with 'hypnotics and anxiolytics', with 14 per cent receiving antipsychotic medication (p. 73). Corston also referenced high rates of self-harm and suicidal ideation among the remand population, noting that 50 per cent of prison suicides occurred during remand (p. 18). Regarding the official response to these issues, Corston (p. 75) considered 'a therapeutic environment and treating substance addiction holistically' appropriate treatment for those with drug use issues. Women vulnerable to self-harm require 'a therapeutic environment with properly trained multidisciplinary staff at an appropriate staffing level', with the diversion from custody of self-harming women whose offending is at a lower-level and the care of self-harming women with more serious offending led by the National Health Service (NHS), either in an NHS resource or shared multi-disciplinary care in prison (p. 76).

The DOJNI (2010: 55) aimed at 'Developing a gender-specific approach to the management of women in custody', responding to Corston as follows:

> Baroness Corston acknowledged, however, that 'prisons are being asked to do the impossible'... many are simply too ill for prison to be an appropriate location for them ... While such women continue to be given custodial sentences, NIPS recognises that it is critical to find ways to improve their experience of custody and to respond to the considerable vulnerabilities that they often present.

The initiatives proposed by the DOJNI in response to women's gendered needs included a commitment to building 'a new, purpose-built women's prison facility' while, in the interim, 'implementing a process of incremental change within the current facilities available to women at Hydebank Wood'; producing gender-specific standards to underpin the prison's 'gender-specific approach to all areas of custody', including 'gender-specific guidance for staff working with women prisoners'; and developing 'staff-training in gender-specific issues' introduced in 2009 'across a wide range of disciplines and service providers' (DOJNI 2010: 55–59).

These policies were part of a broader transformation of the Northern Ireland Prison Service (NIPS), which embarked on a three-year 'change programme' in 2012. In March 2016, the recommendations of the 'Prison Review Team Final Report' (Prison Review Team 2011) were signed off by the Prison Reform Oversight Committee. Justice Minister David Ford (2016: 34) declared, 'with 90% of the recommendations signed off, we have seen significant progress, and the prison system today, in Northern Ireland, is very different from the one that I inherited on devolution in April 2010'. However, in Hydebank Wood, which was transitioning from a young offenders' centre to a 'secure college', with 'prisoners' rebranded as 'students', well-established attitudes persisted beneath the veneer. The changes introduced for young male offenders were not designed or implemented equitably nor were they applied in a gender-responsive context. Rather, reforms were left to 'trickle-down' to women.

A revised response to the arrival and committal procedures was initiated. Arrival at prison is experienced as a time of uncertainty, with prisoners concerned for their safety, facing deprivation of freedom and autonomy and feeling separation and loss (Harvey 2012: 27). Women prisoners suffer disorientation and fear, experiencing vulnerability, 'shock from their arrest or sentence' and insecurity regarding family arrangements (Scraton and Moore 2007: 51). Corston (2007: 29) considered that these issues were compounded by 'crowding, noise and the threatening atmosphere', which were exacerbated by 'sharing cells with women with mental health problems and who self-harmed' and by the experience of sharing close quarters with women 'who were suffering severe drug withdrawal or seizures' as well as those with 'delusional or psychotic' features. This was the reality in Ash House, with its mixed population of vulnerable prisoners and new committals confined together on the committal landing. Despite an overhaul of committal practise, the experience for some women was inadequate, as Cindy commented:

> This is my first time in prison. I felt scared of everything. The alarms, the people talking on tannoys, the look of the place, seeing that there is no way to get out … I came in on a Saturday and I was told I would be locked early at 5/5.30 [pm] … Basically I was fine until I tried to go to sleep and then the voices in my head started going, it just hit me that I was locked again and I didn't know that you were allowed out during the week and had stuff to do or anything. It was the not knowing.

This 'not knowing' was also experienced by Agnes. Entering prison without information on the induction process, environment or regime, she experienced significant uncertainty. While all new committals should be placed on the same landing, when the committal landing's 'safer cell' is occupied those entering prison with vulnerabilities are often placed in an observation cell on another landing. Agnes stated,

I came straight from Knockbracken[5] to here. I was immediately put on a SPAR (Supporting Prisoners at Risk[6]), but there were too many people on SPARs on A2, so I was put into A3 on arrival. I didn't leave my room for 2 days; I didn't wash or anything … in A2, they know you are new and explain things. I only found out things as I asked, it took a really long time.

The committal landing is designed to meet specific entry needs of prisoners. Moreover, the Northern Ireland Prison Rules (1995) state that where possible, 'untried prisoners shall be kept out of contact with other prisoners as far as this can reasonably be done' (Rule 99). For those women who suffered suicidal ideation, the provision of one observation cell on the committal landing prevented them from settling. As Agnes indicated, this meant they were allocated to a landing with sentenced and settled prisoners.

Meanwhile, the anticipated therapeutic environment for women prisoners did not materialise. Rather, the transformation into 'Hydebank Wood Secure College' evolved, with resources funnelled into a framework essentially designed, implemented and focused around the needs of the young men with whom women prisoners shared the site. It was unclear whether this outcome was intended from inception. At the opening of the 'secure college', both the Justice Minister and Director General of the Prison Service focussed on the transition from 'Young Offender Institute'. Neglecting any reference to women prisoners, they referred to the college solely in terms of 'young offenders' who would be given 'hope for the future' (Ford in *Belfast Telegraph* 2015). What emerged was an institutional transformation into a 'secure college'. Women of all ages received the same educational framework developed for young male offenders by the external providers, Belfast Metropolitan College (BMC). Thus, women were allocated work/training in joinery, painting and decorating, horticulture, plumbing, bricklaying and hair and beauty alongside classes including literacy, art and crafts, ceramics, ICT[7] and cookery. They also worked within the prison, including its kitchens, recycling and cleaning. While committals were not always allocated work, the 'governor's orders' were that all prisoners should be occupied in work or in classes during the daily regime.

Although opportunities for purposeful activity are welcome for most women in prison, for those with mental health or drug detoxification issues such activities may be experienced as punitive. Women commented on inadequate content and inconsistent implementation. Provision was neither gender-specific nor tailored to the needs of older women or young women defined within the NEET profile (not in education, employment or training). Despite prison rules regarding their status, remanded women received financial punishment and extended periods of lock-up if they failed to comply with the secure college regime. Alice stated,

[…] now people with mental health problems like me still have to go to work, even if we don't feel like it. Before that you got 11 pounds no matter what, and if you worked you got more. But now you have to work all day, every day for 11 pounds.

Two punitive elements emerged from the process. First, despite mental health issues, women were compelled to leave the landing and go to work/study or face being locked in their cells. This was significant for remand prisoners disproportionately affected by vulnerabilities (PRT 2012: 22). 80 per cent of the women interviewed received medication for at least one mental health issue. Second, the payment they received for working in the prison was often their sole income beyond the basic provision of the prison service. Further, social exclusion is a significant issue for remand populations, who are more likely to have been living in unstable accommodation arrangements prior to imprisonment (PRT 2012: 23). Remanded prisoners are five times more likely to have been living in hostels prior to incarceration (NACRO in PRT 2012: 23). Socioeconomic marginalisation was evident with over 20 interviewees in long-term unemployment, a significant number of whom were in receipt of disability allowance, with others close to 'retirement'. A 'secure college', seemingly positive in providing generic purposeful activity, was far from an ideal environment for these women.

While 'full attendance' was presented in a recent Criminal Justice Inspection Northern Ireland (CJINI) report (2016) as evidence of the college's success, it failed to recognise the lack of agency experienced by women being compelled to participate. Further, staff illness and the turnover of the remand population created an environment that was not conducive to successful outcomes for women prisoners. What emerged was an 'imaginary penality' (Carlen 2008). The 'secure college' was not the most appropriate response to women's imprisonment and was unresponsive to the distinct needs of vulnerable women highlighted by the Corston Report and, subsequently, by the DOJNI (2010) 'Gender Specific Strategy'. This did not mean the outcome was benign, characterised only by the absence of promised 'transformation'. As Alice experienced, the framework introduced a punitive element for those women assessed in the community as unfit for work but compelled into education by the threat of 'lock-up' and denied income. Yet a rehabilitative therapeutic framework, tailored and responsive to their distinct needs, remained absent.

Many aspects of the women's lives were impacted negatively by sharing the site with young men. Hydebank Wood was a campus designed and enacted through a 'young offender' lens, focusing on male 'pathways' to crime and failing to provide a women-focussed environment. Fundamentally, this was reflected in the generic diet within the institution, as a kitchen staff member explained, 'What women want to eat and what young offenders want to eat are completely different...The boys are hungry and need something substantial.'

Concerning risks posed by gender and movement within the prison campus, it was women rather than young men who were constrained. Sharing the site with young men led to women experiencing inappropriate attention. As Mayte, a survivor of domestic violence, stated, 'There was an incident one time, when I was asked to do a job round the prison and the young offenders were very rude making comments to me … It was a sexual gesture and I was in bits'. The environment was unresponsive to the needs of women, particularly those who had prior experiences of gendered violence.

Not only did Ash House fail to provide the therapeutic environment envisaged by Corston, it responded to women suffering from self-harm and suicidal ideation with control rather than care. Recent Prisoner Ombudsman for Northern Ireland (PONI) reports raised concerns about the standard of care implemented across the NIPS estate (PONI 2016a,b), with recent CJINI reports (2016: 6) declaring that levels of mental health provision for women 'needed to be much better', with some women being transferred to external mental health facilities. Across NIPS, 'the standard of healthcare and mental health services those in prison receive, continues to be poorer than that available within the community', with 'healthcare failings' considered contributory factors in recent deaths in custody and serious self-harm (Butler 2016). Contrary to Corston's recommendations, remanded women continued to be incarcerated as 'a place of safety' despite awareness that 'the risk of self-harm may be exacerbated rather than reduced as a consequence of imprisonment' (Player 2007: 417).

This was reflected in the experiences of many women interviewed, who commented on the high levels of lock-up they experienced, often from 4pm to 8am during the week, remaining in place from Friday afternoon until Sunday morning, the isolation impacting their mental health. For some women, the oppression of time spent alone behind the door encouraged suicidal feelings, as Cindy explained,

> I attempted to hang myself on a curtain rail and it collapsed and then I was sitting on the bed picking my scabs off and it was bleeding. Then the staff came and asked me if I was ok and if I wanted to talk and I started crying and they got the nurse and she said I was really distressed and a two-bunk room wouldn't cut it.

Consistent with prisons across the NIPS estate, Hydebank Wood engages the SPAR process in response to those who attempt suicide or self-harm. At the acute level of risk, the prison response is an observation cell. This subjects women to what is termed a 'risk appropriate' environment, focussed solely on preventing the prisoner's capacity to take her own life, removing ligature points from cells and installing 24/7 observation cameras. Cindy described this experience:

> Not being able to wear your own clothes. Not being in your own bed, not having any proper covers – not even having a sheet or proper pillow. I was freezing and you can't wear trousers… I got out of the OBs (observation) cell four days ago. I wouldn't tell the staff if I felt suicidal again, because I don't like that cell, I hate it. You feel like you are being punished.

Cindy described the deprivation accompanying intense observation and the degradation associated with the bedding and clothing considered punitive by women on observation. These responses to suicidal prisoners exemplify the prison's continued reliance on strategies of control and surveillance when dealing with vulnerable women's needs. SPAR procedures might prevent a prisoner from taking her own life but fail to provide appropriate therapeutic intervention to respond to *why* prisoners feel suicidal. Scraton (in McCracken 2012) describes the tension between treatment and punishment at Hydebank: 'The contradiction of delivering appropriate care and treatment to prisoners with complex healthcare needs, particularly mental ill-health, in regimes that prioritise discipline and cellular confinement remains'.

Corston's focus was on the diversion of vulnerable women from prison, with the few women requiring detention located within replacement 'small, multifunctional custodial centres' (Corston 2007: 35). A vacuum followed. Ten years on, the anticipated centres had not materialised and female imprisonment rates remained high, with women continuing to be incarcerated in 'relatively large, self-contained institutions … sparsely distributed across the country' (p. 34). In a period of economic austerity, efforts to divert women who pose no threat appear to have been postponed, while attempts to 'improve the prison experience for those who do' has resulted, at best, in ill-designed 'help and caring', with no progress towards 'therapeutic environments to assist them rebuild their lives' (p. 34). At worst, persistent attempts to address women's mental health issues within the punitive carceral framework display disregard of women's distinct needs, with anticipated reform incorporated into a 'secure college' designed for young men.

Conclusion: post-Corston reflections, the failure of reform

Corston (2007: 66) recommended a 'different model of provision', supplied by 'an integrated approach to services' that would 'cut the numbers of women on remand and reduce the risk of re-offending by tackling their criminogenic needs'. This included 'residential women's centres' to accommodate women remanded for reasons including lack of suitable accommodation or fixed address, 'drug treatment or mental health needs that would not be met in the community' and 'low to medium risk offences and awaiting sentence'. Corston (2007: 85) envisaged that such centres would support the 'top end' of non-custodial disposals, anticipating their suitability 'for women either on bail or being released from prison with no suitable accommodation'. In Northern Ireland, these residential centres never materialised. Whilst the much-acclaimed 'Inspire' model of women-centred community provision emerged from a partnership between probation services and the community sector, it did not include the remand population. Rather, it served 'women who are subject to statutory supervision orders, those whose cases have been adjourned for pre-sentence reports and a small number of women on day release from prison' (Kerr 2014: 6). The omission of remanded women from the criteria for referral was counterproductive in reducing offending.

While Corston's recommendation for diversion was significant, her vision was restricted by a criminal justice framework underpinning community alternatives. As discussed above, the women interviewed had been remanded to custody, often for reasons beyond the seriousness of their offences. This compounded their social and economic marginalisation while imposing punishment on their lives and families. Despite recognition of the social harms experienced by many vulnerable women, harms that increase their likelihood of facing imprisonment, the focus of reform remained fixed on assumptions regarding women's deviance, their troubled environments interpreted as 'risk factors', thus necessitating the continuation of their punishment and control.

At a time of ever-reducing community provision, women categorised as 'offending' and requiring punishment will continue to be channelled to prison. It is evidence of the failure of 'reform'. A decade on in Northern Ireland, many of the questions Corston's review sought to raise remain unaddressed. Rather than 'transformation', women's experiences of 'gender-specific' imprisonment reflect mismatched reform alongside an inability to provide appropriate therapeutic settings. In effect, Corston proposed the sanitisation of the punishment administered to women and the initiation of proportionality, which continued to locate women on a carceral continuum where they were considered deserving of punishment. This contrasted with the contextualisation recognised throughout her review. Through the report's adoption of a gender-specific lens that is entwined with recommendations of gender 'appropriate' penal environments and measures, Corston effectively binds women to concepts of punishment, confined by the limits of gender-based reform. As this chapter illustrates, these issues are pertinent, particularly for women on remand, each of whom carries the pretrial presumption of innocence and many of whom have not committed an imprisonable offence. Recognition of the structural determination of their marginalisation and criminalisation should promote their removal from the punitive paradigm of criminal justice responses while progressing enhanced public health, social care and welfare provision for the vulnerabilities this population endures.

Notes

1 The partition of Ireland under the Government of Ireland Act 1920 led to the creation of Northern Ireland, the region of Ireland that would remain under UK governance following the Anglo-Irish Treaty (1921), continuing under that jurisdiction following the creation of the Republic of Ireland in 1949. Following partition, allegations of the Unionist Government's discrimination against Catholics and episodes of violent sectarianism contributed to the civil unrest commencing in 1968, leading to the abandonment of devolution in Northern Ireland and return to Direct Rule (1972).

2 The definition of unrest that occurred in the Northern Ireland region varies, with the local 'euphemism' of 'the troubles' interpreted as 'playing down' the conflict that occurred, keeping it located as a 'local difficulty' of the UK. In contrast, 'the Conflict'

reflects the serious political connotations of the violence that occurred, positioning local issues within larger international struggles (Dickson 2010: 5).

3 All quotes are from women remand prisoners interviewed in the author's research. Interviewee names have been changed to protect anonymity.

4 The Housing Executive is Northern Ireland's strategic housing authority, providing services related to socially rented, privately rented and owner-occupied accommodation. They provide and manage 89,000 social dwellings across the region. At: www. nihe.gov.uk/index/about.htm Accessed 24 August 2017.

5 Knockbracken Healthcare Park provides in-patient services for people with mental health problems from across the Northern Ireland region. At: www.belfasttrust. hscni.net/hospitals/Knockbracken.htm. Accessed 24 August 2017.

6 The Northern Irish Prison Service protective and supportive response to suicidal and self-harming prisoners is governed through the 'Supporting Prisoners at Risk' (SPAR) process. www.justice-ni.gov.uk/sites/default/files/publications/doj/april-2014-suicide-and-self-harm-prevention-policy.pdf.

7 Information and Communications Technology, a class on the students' curriculum.

References

All Party Parliamentary Group on Women in the Penal System and Corston, J. (2011) *Women in the Penal System: Second Report on Women with Particular Vulnerabilities in the Criminal Justice System*, London: Howard League.

Ashe, F. (2009) 'The pedagogical challenges of teaching sexual politics in the context of ethnic division', *Enhancing Learning in the Social Sciences, 2*(2): 1–19.

Ashworth, A. (2015) *Sentencing and Criminal Justice*, 6th edition, Cambridge: Cambridge University Press.

Baldry, E. (2010) 'Women in transition: From prison to…', *Current Issues in Criminal Justice,* 22(2) 253–267.

Bell, E. (2014) 'The Confines of Neo-Liberalism', V. Canning (ed.) *Sites of Confinement*, Weston-Super-Mare, England: European Group.

Butler, M. (2016) 'What's happening to health in Northern Ireland Prisons?' *RightsNI.* Available online at: http://rightsni.org/2016/10/what-is-happening-to-healthcare-in-northern-ireland-prisons/ (accessed 21st November 2016).

Campbell, K. (2016) *The Current Landscape of Support for Women Who Offend in Northern Ireland*, Belfast: VSB Foundation.

Carlen, P. (1983) *Women's Imprisonment: A Study in Social Control*, London: Routledge & Kegan Paul, pp. 39–44.

Carlen, P. (2008) 'Imaginary penalities and risk-crazed governance', P. Carlen (ed.) *Imaginary Penalities*, Cullompton: Willan. pp. 1–25.

Carlton, B. and Segrave, M. (2011) 'Women's survival post-imprisonment: Connecting imprisonment with pains past and present', *Punishment & Society, 13*(5): 551–570.

Carlton, B. and Segrave, M. (eds.) (2013) *Women Exiting Prison: Critical Essays on Gender, Post-Release Support and Survival*, Oxon: Routledge.

Chesney-Lind, M. (1999) 'Media misogyny: Demonizing "Violent" girls and women', J. Ferrell and N. Websdale (eds.) *Making Trouble: Cultural Constructions of Crime, Deviance and Control*, pp. 115–140, New York: Walter De Gruyter Inc.

Cohen, S. (1985) *Visions of Social Control: Crime, Punishment and Classification,* Cambridge: Polity Press.

Cooper, V. (2014) 'Gendered Geographies of Punishment', V. Canning (ed.) *Sites of Confinement*, Weston-Super-Mare, England: European Group.

Corcoran, M. (2010) 'Snakes and ladders: Women's imprisonment and official reform discourse under new labour', *Current Issues in Criminal Justice, 22*(2): 233–251.

Corcoran, M. and Fox, C. (2013) 'A bit neo-liberal, a bit Fabian: Interventionist narratives in a diversionary programme for women', B. Carlton and M. Segrave (eds.) *Women Exiting Prison: Critical Essays on Gender, Post-Release Support and Survival*, Oxon: Routledge, pp. 136–155.

Corston, J. (2007) *The Corston Report: A Review of Women with Particular Vulnerabilities in the Criminal Justice System*, London: Home Office.

Criminal Justice Inspection Northern Ireland (with her Majesty's Chief Inspector of Prisons England and Wales and the Regulation and Quality Improvement Authority) (2016) *Report on an Unannounced Inspection of Ash House Women's Prison Hydebank Wood, 9–19 May 2016*, Belfast: CJINI.

Crome, I., Chambers, P., Frisher, M., Bloor, R. and Roberts, D. (2009) *The Relationship between Dual Diagnoses: Substance Misuse and Dealing with Mental Health Issues*, London: Social Care Institute for Excellence.

Davis, A. (2003) *Are Prisons Obsolete?* New York: Seven Stories.

Department of Justice Northern Ireland (2010) *Women's Offending Behaviour in Northern Ireland: A Strategy to Manage Women Offenders and Those Vulnerable to Offending Behaviour 2010–2013*, Belfast: DOJNI.

Department of Justice Northern Ireland (2013) *Reducing Women's Offending 2013–2016*, Belfast: DOJNI.

Dickson, B. (2010) *The European Convention on Human Rights and the Conflict in Northern Ireland*, Oxford: Oxford University Press.

Drake, D. and Muncie, J. (2010) 'Risk prediction, assessment and management', D. Drake, J. Muncie and L. Westmarland (eds.) *Criminal Justice: Local and Global*, Cullompton: Willan, pp. 105–140.

Edgar, K. (2004) *Lacking Conviction: The Rise of the Women's Remand Population*, London: Prison Reform Trust.

Ellison, G. (2015) 'Criminalizing the payment for sex in Northern Ireland: Sketching the contours of a moral panic', *British Journal of Criminology, 57*(1): 194–214.

Ford, D. (2015) 'College offers young offenders hope', *Belfast Telegraph* April 13 2015. At: www.belfasttelegraph.co.uk/news/northern-ireland/college-offers-young-offenders-hope-31137694.html. Accessed 24 August 2017.

Ford, D. (2016) *Official Report Hansard* Monday 14 March 2016 Volume 113, No 4, Belfast: Northern Ireland Assembly.

Foucault, M. (1977) *Discipline and Punish: The Birth of the Prison*, New York: Vintage.

Gelsthorpe, L. (2004) 'Female offending: A theoretical overview', G. McIvor (ed.) *Women Who Offend*, London: Jessica Kingsley.

Hannah-Moffat, K. (1999) 'Moral agent or actuarial subject: Risk and Canadian women's imprisonment', *Theoretical Criminology, 3*(1): 71–94.

Hannah-Moffat, K. (2010) 'Sacrosanct or flawed: Risk, accountability and gender-responsive penal politics', *Current Issues in Criminal Justice, 22*(2):193–215.

Harris, H. and Healy, E. (eds.) (2001) 'Everyday Resistance', *'Strong About It All…' Rural and Urban Women's Experiences of the Security Forces in Northern Ireland*, Derry: North West Women's / Human Rights Project.

Harvey, J. (2012) *Young Men in Prison: Surviving and Adapting to Life Inside*, 2nd edition, Oxon: Routledge.

Hayes, B.C. and Nagle, J. (2015) 'Ethnonationalism and attitudes towards gay and lesbian rights in Northern Ireland', *Nations and Nationalism, 22*(1): 20–41.

Heidensohn, F. (1985) *Women and Crime*, London: Macmillan.

Hillyard, P., Kelly, G., McLaughlin, E., Patsios, D. and Tomlinson, M. (2003) *Bare Necessities: Poverty and Social Exclusion in Northern Ireland*, Belfast: Democratic Dialogue.

Jones, G. S. (1984) *Outcaste London: A Study in the Relationship between Classes in Victorian Society*, London: Peregrine Books.

Kerr, J. (2014) *The [re] Settlement of Women Prisoners in Northern Ireland: From Rhetoric to Reality*, London: Howard League.

Lemert, E. (1951) *Social Pathology: A Systematic Approach to the Theory of Sociopathic Behaviour*, New York: McGraw-Hill.

Lloyd, A. (1995) *Doubly Deviant, Doubly Damned: Society's Treatment of Violent Women*, London: Penguin Books.

McAlinden, A.M. and Dwyer, C. (eds.) (2015) *Criminal Justice in Transition: The Northern Ireland Context*, London: Bloomsbury Publishing.

McBride, R. S. (2015) *Risk and Recovery in an Era of Convergence: A Critical Discourse Analysis of Personality Disorder Policy and Practice in Northern Ireland* (Doctoral dissertation, Queen's University Belfast).

McClure, J. (2014) 'New Data shows Northern Ireland is a world leader in prescription use', 17 November 2014, *The Detail Online*. At: www.thedetail.tv/articles/new-data-shows-northern-ireland-is-a-world-leader-in-prescription-drug-use. Accessed 24 August 2017.

McCracken, N. (2012) 'Surge in self-harming at Hydebank Wood', *The Detail Online*, At: www.thedetail.tv/articles/surge-in-self-harming-at-hydebank-wood. (Accessed on 21st November 2016).

Medina, T.R. and McCranie, A. (2011) 'Layering control: Medicalization, psychopathy, and the increasing multi-institutional management of social problems', B. A. Pescosolido, J. K. Martin, J. D. McLeod and A. Rogers A. (Eds.) *Handbook of the Sociology of Health, Illness, and Healing*, New York: Springer, pp. 139–158.

Moore, L. and Scraton, P. (2014) *The Incarceration of Women: Punishing Bodies, Breaking Spirits*, Basingstoke: Palgrave Macmillan.

Moore, L. and Wahidin, A. (2015) 'Transition, women and the criminal justice system in Northern Ireland', A. M. McAlinden and C. Dwyer (eds.) *Criminal Justice in Transition: The Northern Ireland Context*, London: Bloomsbury Publishing, pp. 227–301.

Muncie, J. (2008) 'The theory and politics of criminalisation: John Muncie argues that a critical understanding of criminalisation remains crucial', *Criminal Justice Matters*, 74(1), 13–14.

Newburn, T. (2009) *Criminology*, Oxon: Routledge.

Northern Ireland Prison Service (1995) *Prison Rules*, Belfast: Department of Justice.

O'Malley, P. (2009) *Governmentality and Risk. Sydney Law School Research Paper No. 09/98*.

O'Neill, J. (2016) *Time after Time: A Study of Women's Transitions from Custody*, London: The Griffins Society.

Players, E. (2007) 'Remanding women in custody: Concerns for human rights', *Modern Law Review, 70*(3): 402–426.

Pollack, S. (2007) '"I'm just not good in relationships": Victimization discourses and the gendered regulation of criminalized women', *Feminist Criminology*, 2(2) 158–174.

Prison Reform Trust (2012) *Bromley Briefings Prison Factfile*, London: PRT.

Prison Reform Trust (2013) *Bromley Briefings Prison Factfile*, London: PRT.

Prison Reform Trust (2016) *Bromley Briefings Prison Factfile*, London: PRT.

Prison Review Team (2011) *Review of the Northern Ireland Prison Service: Conditions, Management and Oversight of All Prisons, Final Report October 2011*, Belfast: PRT.

Prisoner Ombudsman (2016a) *Investigation Report into the Circumstances Surrounding the Death of Mr Geoffrey Ellison Aged 58 in Magilligan Prison on 28th March 2015*, Belfast: The Prisoner Ombudsman for Northern Ireland.

Prisoner Ombudsman (2016b) *Investigation Report into the Circumstances Surrounding the Death of Patrick Kelly Aged 46 on 20th March 2015*, Belfast: The Prisoner Ombudsman for Northern Ireland.

Rooney, E. (2006) 'Women's equality in Northern Ireland's transition: Intersectionality in theory and place', *Feminist Legal Studies, 14*(3): 353–375.

Rooney, E. (2011) 6th ECPR General Conference: University of Iceland, 25–27 August 2011 Panel Theories of/for Transitional Justice Intersectionality: A Feminist Theory for Transitional Justice? Draft. At: https://ecpr.eu/filestore/paperproposal/fc3dd072-39d7-4fc0-bf34-67ec1f528eae.pdf. Accessed 24 August 2017.

Scott, D. and Codd, H. (2010) *Controversial Issues in Prisons*, Maidenhead: Open University Press.

Scraton, P. and Moore, L. (2005). *The Hurt Inside: The Imprisonment of Women and Girls in Northern Ireland*, Belfast: The Human Rights Commission.

Scraton, P. and Moore, L. (2007) *The Prison Within: The Imprisonment of Women at Hydebank Wood 2004–06*, Belfast: Northern Ireland Human Rights Commission.

Tomlinson, M. (2013) *Legacies of Conflict: Evidence from the Poverty and Social Exclusion Survey*, Belfast: Northern Ireland Assembly.

Wacquant, L. (2009) *Punishing the Poor: The Neoliberal Government of Social Insecurity*, Durham, NC and London: Duke University Press.

Ward, M. (2006) 'Gender, citizenship, and the future of the Northern Ireland peace process', *Éire-Ireland, 41*(1): 262–283.

Ward, M. (2013) 'Excluded and silenced: Women in Northern Ireland after the peace process', *Open Democracy Online*. Available online at: www.opendemocracy.net/5050/margaret-ward/excluded-and-silenced-women-in-northern-ireland-after-peace-process. (Accessed 21st November 2014).

6

CORSTON PRINCIPLES IN CANADA

Creating the carceral Other and moving beyond women in prison

Vicki Chartrand and Jennifer M. Kilty

> When I fed the poor,
> they called me a saint.
> When I asked why the poor had no food,
> they called me a communist.
>
> *(Dom Helder Camar)*

Context and introduction

Traditionally, penal research and practice were critiqued for placing too much emphasis on men, for being gender-blind, and for considering women to be "too few to count" (Adelberg and Currie 1987). Penal practices were argued to give little consideration to how punishment impacted women, while rehabilitative programming stereotypically enlisted women in norms of domestication, motherhood, and femininity (see Smart 1977; Freedman 1981; Edwards 1982; Carlen 1983; Rafter 1983; Strange 1985; Naffine 1997; Hudson 2002; inter alia). Emerging in the late 20th century, a growing body of social and feminist literature began to address the neglect of gendered analyses and disparity in the penal system by highlighting the experiences and circumstances of women in prison. Among this literature and as discussed throughout this collection, the Corston Report (2007) concluded that women in prison require a multi-agency, women-centred, and holistic approach that takes into consideration their multiple and overlapping needs while prioritising decarceration. This sentiment was similarly articulated in Canada 17 years prior in *Creating Choices: The Report of the Task Force on Federally Sentenced Women* (1990). Based on consultations with women's groups, feminists, scholars, advocates, correctional policy makers, frontline staff, and prisoners, the report called for extensive reforms to federal corrections for women in Canada. It described federally sentenced women as generally not posing a serious danger to society, the majority having substance use concerns and many being survivors of sexual abuse, violence, and poverty. In line with social and feminist critique, the report similarly advocated for women-centred, holistic, and non-punitive responses for women in prison.[1]

Today, according to the Correctional Service Canada (CSC), prison operations for women are considered to reflect a *Creating Choices* philosophy with a gender-responsive approach that is supposed to empower women to make healthy lifestyle choices, given their specific needs (CSC 2011: 1). Despite the correctional adoption of a women-centred and community focus, in Canada today, and globally, women are the fastest-growing prison population.[2] Women in prison continue to experience gendered and punitive treatment and, in some cases, more severe penal interventions than men (Kilty 2012; Chunn and Gavigan 2014; Chartrand 2015; Office of the Correctional Investigator (OCI) 2015). As several scholars point out, despite the extensive and unique attention to women in prison, the renewed correctional focus based on social and feminist critique led to a new assemblage of gendered and intersectional punishments (see e.g. Fox 1999; Hannah-Moffat 2001, 2005, 2008; Carlen 2002; Kendall 2002; Pollack and Kendall 2005; Maidment 2006; Dell et al. 2009; Russell and Carlton 2013).

Although progressive on the surface, a gender-responsive approach to women's corrections opened up new correctional sites for the regulation of women that now flow from their multiple and overlapping social, cultural, and economic disadvantages. This is what Pat Carlen (2002) refers to as a mixed economy of the 'therapunitive' and Kelly Hannah-Moffat (2005) describes as a hybrid model of risk/needs whereby 'criminal risks' are linked with 'social needs' as a way to regulate women through individualising and responsibilising penal strategies. As Hannah-Moffat points out,

> Newly formed risk/needs categorizations and subsequent management strategies give rise to a new politics of punishment, in which different risk/needs groupings compete for limited resources, discredit collective group claims to resources, redistribute responsibilities for risk/needs management and legitimate both inclusive and exclusionary penal strategies.

Within a penal framework, women's social disadvantage of victimisation, poverty, and addiction emerge as a self-forming or chosen activity that women must manage themselves according to their penal programmes (see also Smiley 2001; McCorkel 2004). Jill McCorkel (2003) argues that even with penal practices equally applied to women and men, or what she refers to as an 'equality with a vengeance' approach, the discursive practices of penality advance understandings of women as both gender deviant and deviant criminals. With an 'equal' and 'gendered' focus, the more invasive penal practices do not so much disappear as shift to produce and enforce a neoliberal model of life.

While the literature highlights how criminality, gender, and other intersectional categories continue to contribute to women's punishment and regulation in prison, this chapter argues that a women-centred approach to corrections, by virtue of setting women apart as a special category of prisoner, remains consistent with a broader carceral logic that continues to establish norms and target difference, gendered or otherwise. In other words, a shift in penal discourses and practices, as seen with *Creating Choices*, does not necessarily promote an absence of punitive interventions for women in prison but shifts the modalities by which they are prescribed and legitimated. In developing a normative theory of 'women in prison' as part of a political strategy for change, women nonetheless continue to be discursively constituted within carceral divisions that normalise penal interventions with little recognition of the structural oppressions that lead to women's criminalisation and engender punitive responses to women's criminality. Regardless of the emerging discourse or critique that informs its practices, carceral logics are designed to set populations and people apart based on what is considered acceptable, reasonable, and necessary for the greater public health and safety of the time. This is evident in the history of carceral practices of colonial assimilation from eugenics, sterilisation, and the segregation of lawbreakers to the present practices of detention and deportation of immigrants. The above are examples of punishing the poor (Wacquant 2009), the containment of poverty, and the elimination of high-risk populations through indefinite confinement. Through carceral logics, the 'Other' is set apart and marked for treatment, segregation, assimilation, immobilisation, modification, violence, elimination, or salvation (Chartrand 2017).

This chapter considers the carceral impact that the *Creating Choices* philosophy continues to have on women in Canadian federal prisons, nearly three decades after its implementation.[3] It reveals how a holistic, women-centred approach is part of an ongoing carceral logic that seizes on normative discourses to manage women in prison through: (1) therapeutic controls, (2) segregation, and (3) gendered violence. While far removed from the original vision, these carceral logics and practices are legitimated as part of a *Creating Choices* philosophy that promotes the prison as a reasonable remedy to women's social disadvantage. The problematic character of the penal system is exemplified through the case analysis of Ashley Smith who, at the age of 15, was sentenced to one month in juvenile custody for breach of probation for throwing crab apples at a postal worker in Moncton, New Brunswick. While in custody, she accumulated numerous institutional infractions, predominantly for self-injurious behaviour and resisting correctional guards' efforts to subdue her (at times, violently or by spitting or throwing urine), resulting in so much additional time to her sentence that she was held for nearly four years in custody (three years in a youth facility and 11.5 months in federal prison) on this minor index offence. At 19 years old, Ashley died from self-asphyxiation while on suicide watch in her segregation cell as prison staff watched and filmed her from the hall. This case is an exemplar of how the strategies of control, exclusion, and violence are central to the carceral efforts of *Creating Choices* in bringing women into the folds of prison compliance and conformity. Ashley's case shows how the mechanisms used to govern incarcerated women reflect the punitive carceral logic that structures federal corrections for women in Canada.

What follows first problematises how social and feminist discourses about women in prison were taken up and operationalised via carceral logics. How such discourses have been instituted through the problematic and repressive practices of therapeutic control, segregation, and gendered violence is then outlined. It is argued that progressive change to the penal system is not a matter of finding the right logic, discourse, practice, or reform but rather of moving away from carceral logics that continue to legitimate the prison as a reasonable response to women's criminalisation. The abolition of penal systems that rely on penal and punitive interventions and control strategies is advocated, suggesting that any project that seeks to dismantle penal systems must shift critique to criminalising processes while redirecting people and populations away from the prison and carceral systems (e.g. Miller 1991).

The carceral Other

Historically, in Canada and other industrialised countries, women's imprisonment initially emerged to promote feminine respectability and morality for those women considered unruly (Faith 2011). This penal response reflected a bourgeois sentiment that localised women within private spheres of family obligation and male dependence with a focus on strengthening marriage, family bonds, and childrearing (Rafter 1983; Chartrand 2014). With the advent of modern knowledge and the use of statistics, categorisations and divisions, the ongoing refinement of penal classifications increased a capacity to manage women along their social potentials for sex, marriage, and childbearing, while scientific discourses classified deviant women as biologically perverse, sexually aberrant, emotionally disturbed, and intellectually deficient (Dobash et al. 1986). Disorder and the contaminating influences of women prisoners were represented as a social threat and thus as a problem for penal management.

Beginning in the latter part of the 20th century, along with human rights and civil liberties discourses, penal research increasingly focused on women in prison providing explanations for the social factors contributing to women's imprisonment. Research drew attention to the unequal treatment in penal systems and the gendered expectations, paternalism, and harsh treatment women experienced in prison. This avenue of research today is extensive, exploring a number of different areas and topics related to the social experiences and characteristics of women in prison. This includes family and relationships (e.g. O'Connor 1996), prison release and re-entry (e.g. O'Brien and Harm 2002), children and single parenting (e.g. Butler 1994; Goulding 2004), housing and homelessness (e.g. Baldry et al. 2003), health and mental health (e.g. Bloom, Owen and Covington 2004), employment and poverty (e.g. Phillips and Harm 1998), education and literacy (e.g. Case et al. 2005; Frietas et al. 2014; Pollack 2014), HIV/AIDS, Hepatitis C, and other diseases (e.g. Zakaria, Thompson and Borgatta 2010), alcohol and/or drug use and addiction (e.g. Farrell 2000; Messina, Burdon and Prendergast 2003), family violence and histories of abuse (e.g. Aungles 1994), sexual assault and abuse (e.g. Chesney-Lind and Pasko 2004), death and rates of mortality (e.g. Davies and Cook 1999), racialised and cultural differences (e.g. Daly 1993; Richie 2004), victimisation (e.g. Chesney-Lind 2006), poverty (e.g. Chunn and Gavigan 2014), the rarity of charges for violence (e.g. Gelsthorpe and Morris 2002; Comack 2014), counselling and support needs and relations with correctional staff (e.g. Dodge and Pogrebin 2001; Pollack and Kendall 2005), unstructured or unsupervised time and associates (e.g. Severance 2004), violence and self-harm (e.g. Schrader 2005; OCI 2013b), coping strategies (e.g. Brown 2004), everyday requirements, such as identification, banking, budgeting, clothing, and transportation (e.g. Galbraith 2004), disorientation and despair (e.g. Pogrebin and Dodge 2001), stress, stigma, and shame (e.g. O'Brien 2001; Petersilia 2003), self-esteem (e.g. Armytage, Martyres and Feiner 2000), and spiritual needs (e.g. Covington 1998; Dell et al. 2014).

With a growing body of social and feminist critique and penal scholarship committed to developing extensive analysis and understanding of women in prison, Canadian corrections shifted to make use of these new social, cultural, and economic categories for the penal management of women. According to the CSC (2017: 1),

> CSC offers a variety of programs for women offenders, including programs for Aboriginal women. They are designed to address problems that are specific to women and use a modern, holistic approach. Women offenders have diverse needs that affect the way they respond to correctional programs. As a result, our programs for women offenders consider: their social, economic, and cultural situation in society, the importance of relationships in their lives, their unique pathways into crime, the fact that they are more likely than men to experience trauma, victimization, mental health problems, low self-esteem, and have parenting responsibilities.

By shifting discourses of femininity, morality, and disease to broader social, economic, and health categories, women in prison were no longer characterised as 'depraved and disorderly' (Damousi 1997) but as suffering from multiple and overlapping social disadvantages requiring penal interventions. By linking social disadvantage to their 'unique pathways to crime', women in prison are enlisted in essentialising penal discourses and programmes consistent with carceral logics that continue to set them apart from the norm and intervene by the promotion of gendered social norms. This includes interventions in relationships and living skills, problem-solving abilities, alcohol and drug issues, health and mental health, housing, employment, education, vocational training, offence-specific programmes, and recreational activities, among others. Predominantly adapted from social and feminist discourse that developed over the last decade, the prison became the host and remedy for women's social disadvantage.

George Yúdice (1989) argues that a liberal notion of equality that attempts to de-marginalise groups by promoting equal rights, equal pay, and practices of recognition also constructs such groups as those that set minority identities apart from processes and aspects of life valued by the norm. The practice of defining differences and governing the carceral Other has been central to carceral logics and penal practices designed to perpetually exclude targeted populations from free and democratic participation in society. Individuals and groups who do not meet the norm or who cannot be 'corrected', the very women who are sent to prison, are enlisted to other localities that govern through coercion, violence, and physical removal and also through the withholding or denial of social, legal, or economic supports and resources. This logic is reflected in the case of Ashley Smith, for whom an appeal was made when she turned 18 for her to be transferred from youth custody to the adult federal correctional system, where it was believed she would receive better access to mental health treatment and programming. Ashley, however, was housed in segregation for the duration of her time in federal custody, while she continued to tie ligatures around her neck. According to Kim Pate, a lawyer and Executive Director of the Canadian Association of Elizabeth Fry Societies, Ashley was denied any meaningful contact or support while in segregation, was regularly refused a writing instrument to document her grievances, and at times, she was denied access to seeing her family, her lawyers, and other advocates (Pate 2014).

The penal management of women's social disadvantage results in regulatory and punitive responses when women's behaviour is not in line with social programming goals set for them by correctional authorities. For example, women are subject to mandatory psychotherapeutic treatments, compulsory isolation, strip-searches, regular surveillance, and mandatory social programming interventions. Women such as Ashley, who are unable to act according to their correctional plan and the supposed 'good order' of the institution have their behaviour reconstituted via discourses of non-compliance and are then placed in localities of control and exclusion. To develop this argument, three carceral mechanisms (i.e. therapeutic controls, segregation, and gendered violence) are presented. These govern incarcerated women and demonstrate how notions of gender-responsivity are folded into the punitive carceral logic that structures federal corrections for women in Canada.

Therapeutic controls

Therapeutic controls in Canadian federal prisons for women consist mainly of cognitive-behavioural psychological discourses, related (mandatory) programming, as well as the (over)use of psychopharmaceutical medications, including involuntary injections (Pollack and Kendall 2005; Kilty 2012). Cognitive-behavioural programming includes alcohol and drug use, relapse prevention, dependency and lifestyle support, violence management, personal development, anger and depression management, drunk driving, traffic and responsible driver education, life management and living skills, (re)integration, family relationships and parenting, communication and assertiveness, social and legal issues, education, and peer mentoring. Focusing on women's social lives, the cornerstone of therapeutic programming is to encourage women to develop 'healthy pro-social' relationships to reduce the likelihood of reoffending by fostering responsible self-government (Fox 1999; Pollack and Kendall 2005). Several authors have discussed the relevance of "empowerment" strategies in women's prisons as part of those individualising approaches that depoliticise feminist concerns, de-responsibilise the state, and place greater emphasis on women's choices and relationships (e.g. Hannah-Moffat 2001; McCorkel 2004).

While CSC acknowledges the victimisation-criminalisation continuum,[4] in practice, therapeutic programmes effectively deny this logic. As Pollack and Kendall (2005: 75) note, 'If program facilitators acknowledge external factors, such as violence or poverty, they are thought to be feeding in to the offenders' denial and rationalisations of their offence'. Instead, programming encourages women to internalise a 'criminal personality storyline' and to reject alternative constructions of identity and experience. This approach to therapeutic programming demonstrates how treatment is a part of a governing carceral logic that is couched within a punitive framework that structures corrections for women in Canada. As Hannah-Moffat (2008: 213) contends,

> Feminist-inspired approaches seek to incorporate safety into the structure, content and location of the programme (community where possible) and the choice of treatment provider. These issues are all salient to treatment "successes": The RNR (risk-need-responsivity) and gender responsive approaches continue to understate the fact that prisons are not necessarily warm, caring, safe places in which women can be empowered to create meaningful connections. In fact, quite the opposite is typically the case.

In effect, therapeutic programming characterises women's experiences of victimisation, substance use, and structural disadvantage as the result of individual poor choices and flawed thinking patterns that subsequently contribute to their 'pathways into crime'.

Because women's criminality is situated as the result of bad choices and poor reasoning, women in prison are considered to suffer from some form of cognitive or mental pathology. Consequently, this logic also supports the use of psychotropic medications. The OCI (2015) reported that during 2014–2015, 30 per cent of incarcerated women were hospitalised for psychiatric reasons, and 60 per cent were prescribed some form of psychotropic medication to manage their mental health. Earlier reports reveal that prescription patterns increase in the Prairies, where there is a disproportionate number of Aboriginal women in prison (Langner et al. 2002). Heavily medicating incarcerated women to subdue resistant comportment is an implicit security strategy to ensure women do not challenge institutional rules or emotionally tax staff (Kilty 2012). While in federal custody,

Ashley was injected involuntarily with psychotropic medications and physically restrained in the WRAP and the Pinel Board[5] (Sapers 2008) as part of her treatment plan. Within the prison, women's problems must be resolved through behavioural or lifestyle changes, achievable by maintaining a positive attitude and being amenable to normalising interventions, programmes, and therapies. A failure to remain 'pro-social' or 'law-abiding' is not interpreted as a reflection of social vulnerabilities or a lack of service or support but rather as the inability or unwillingness on the part of individual women to empower themselves and is therefore considered evidence of poor personal coping strategies, whereby a more intrusive treatment plan is enacted. This was the case for Ashley.

Segregation

The use of segregation, more commonly known as solitary confinement, is a response to behaviours considered threatening to the security of the institution, staff, or the individual prisoner. It is important to note that the CSC identifies two different types of segregation. The first, disciplinary segregation, isolates a prisoner as a form of punishment, typically for committing or threatening acts of violence against staff or other prisoners and for more serious forms of institutional rule-breaking and destruction of property. The second, administrative segregation, isolates the prisoner 'for their own protection' – either because they requested a time-out from the general population or to facilitate direct monitoring of individuals who are considered to be suicidal or who are in emotional or mental distress. These cells are equipped with 24-hour-a-day closed-circuit television (CCTV) camera surveillance, and there is no qualitative difference between the two types of segregation cells. Thus, the conditions of confinement are the same, and the distinction between disciplinary and administrative segregation is a difference only in status. Similar to disciplinary segregation, women locked in administrative segregation are confined to their cells for 23 hours a day, with only one hour per day to shower and walk within a tiny, individually caged yard. They have no access to programming. Contact with staff only occurs when guards slide meals through the cuffport – a thin slot in the cell door – or when a nurse or warden checks on them once a day via a conversation through the cuffport. Despite these conditions, the CSC claims that administrative segregation is non-punitive, although it is well documented that incarcerated women interpret admission to administration segregation as punishment (OCI 2013b).

When treatment programmes or institutional protocols fail in their desired effect to instil compliance, segregation is used for those who refuse, resist, or cannot manage, cope, or adapt to the prison order. Ashley spent the duration of her time in federal custody (11.5 months) in segregation. To keep her in segregation for this length of time, beyond the 60-day limit stipulated within correctional policy, Ashley was transferred 17 times across five provinces and between three federal penitentiaries, two psychiatric treatment facilities, two external hospitals, and one provincial correctional facility (Sapers 2008). Each time the CSC moved her, they would 'restart the segregation clock' because she was technically not in segregation during transfer. Smith was segregated for a number of reasons, notably due to her repeated acts of self-injury, habitual use of ligatures to self-strangulate, and her efforts to resist carceral authorities, including their use of physical and chemical restraints. The standard correctional policy response to self-injurious behaviour (e.g. 'slashing'/cutting, head banging, or placing instruments under the skin or in bodily orifices) is to strip-search the prisoner to ensure she does not have any items on her person with which she may harm herself and to admit her to administrative segregation, where she can be closely observed, albeit at a distance, via CCTV. Segregating women for having suicidal thoughts or for self-harming is a demonstrably punitive practice that not only ignores the psychological harms of isolation, especially in terms of inciting or aggravating existing inclinations toward self-injurious behaviour (Haney 2003, 2008; Rhodes 2004; Kilty 2006; Shalev 2009; Guenther 2013; OCI 2013b), but also reflects the authoritarian tendencies of a penal system that insists upon enacting a norm. As Linda Moore and Phil Scraton (2013: 15) point out, 'cursing, swearing, insubordination, challenging authority, refusal to work, failure to obey guards' instructions and, "malicious" allegations against guards are examples of "offensive" and "offending" behaviour that lead to offence reports, charges, segregation, and additional prison time'.

Women who fail to meet normative behavioural expectations as set out by institutional policy, correctional programming requirements, and their rehabilitative treatment and release plans are considered high risk and high need. Within carceral logics, this translates into a security threat that is targeted with various control mechanisms, including a heavy reliance on segregation. For example, Indigenous women, who are often documented as being resistant to the correctional regime and make up 35.5 per cent of women in federal custody, are more likely to be classified as maximum security and are significantly more likely to be admitted to segregation, where they accounted for almost half of all admissions in 2014–2015 (OCI 2015). Indigenous women are one of the most disadvantaged groups in Canadian society and in the penal system. They disproportionately experience poverty; physical, sexual, and psychological abuse; poor health; and substance use (Dell et al. 2014). Over the last ten years, use of force incidents against Indigenous women more than tripled, and their rates of self-injury are 17 times higher than for non-Indigenous women (OCI 2015). The greater the disadvantage a woman faces, the less likely an individualising correctional treatment plan will meet her needs and the more likely she is to resist and face a punitive response, such as segregation and even violence.

Gendered violence

Women in prison are broadly considered difficult to manage and resistant to correctional instruction (Snider 2003; Dell et al. 2009). They are often conceptualised as pathological liars, manipulative, abused, needy, aggressive, disadvantaged, unfortunate, conniving, complex, intimidated, vulnerable, and cunning (e.g. Power and Brown 2010; see also Pollack and Kendall 2005; Kilty 2012; Chartrand 2015). These characterisations identify women as simultaneously deprived and dangerous, a combination that constitutes women as both in need and as a social threat (Hannah-Moffat 2001, 2008). With carceral logics that shift between discourses emphasising therapeutic controls, coercive management tactics and women's social pathways into crime, punitive and violent interventions become normalised responses and justified as the only way to ensure both the health and safety of the women and the institution. The OCI (2013a) contends that the culture of punishment in Canadian federal prisons exhibits an over-reliance on uses of force and restraint measures in women's prisons. Thus, women are more likely to be subject to segregation, punishment, and institutional charges than are men.

Violence in the prison is routinely justified and trivialised as a requirement for prison operations and the regulation of women. This is reflected in practices such as:

> [h]igh risk designations, higher classifications, involuntary and forced transfers, deportation, strip-searches, isolation cells, special handling units, behavioural units, solitary confinement, dry cells, transfers to men's prisons, excessive force and lack of medical attention – all of which can culminate into self-harm, suicide and death.
>
> *(Chartrand 2014: 313)*

At Grand Valley Institution for Women, correctional staff repeatedly used force against Ashley in over 150 documented incidents. She was often tasered, pepper-sprayed, strip-searched, and forcibly removed from her cell. The Institutional Emergency Response Team was deployed on several occasions to subdue her and to forcefully prevent her from harming herself by placing her in the WRAP or on the Pinel Board. During many of these violent interactions with staff, Ashley was grabbed, dragged across the floor, lifted off the floor, and called a 'cunt'; also, her head was stepped on, she was struck with a flashlight, her arm was twisted for two minutes after she extended it through the food slot, her fingers were bent back in a move termed 'pain compliance', and her hair was pulled to subdue her (Carlisle 2013). It was later revealed that while in air transport, Ashley was duct taped to her airplane seat with a mesh hood over her head.

Ashley died on 19 October 2007 while in segregation at the Grand Valley Institution for Women in Kitchener, Ontario. She asphyxiated from a hand-fashioned ligature she had tied around her neck while correctional staff filmed her from a few feet away in the hall outside her cell. To avoid confrontation, frontline staff were instructed not to enter Ashley's cell when she tied ligatures until she had passed out. On this occasion, less than 24 hours after she expressed that she was suicidal, staff waited for nearly 30 minutes before removing the ligature, only calling paramedics and performing CPR after she died. The Ashley Smith tragedy reveals that when criminalized women find ways to cope, adapt, challenge, resist, counter, and reshape their experiences in prison, they are governed through coercion, isolation, and violence.

Abolition and anti-carceral logics

Despite advances in the discourses and practices of prison as a consequence of social and feminist critique, penal standardisation continues to regulate women through carceral logics of containment, control, discipline, punishment, rehabilitation, and other logics that set women in prison apart for correction. The prison remains a preferred site for changing women's social context via strategies and programmes of so-called choices that privilege mechanisms of control, segregation, and violence. Those who do not adapt to the standards and procedural norms of the prison are more easily dismissed, depoliticised, or shifted to more strictly regulated punitive sites. From an abolitionist perspective, any critique of penal practices must also offer strategies that challenge the use of a broader carceral logic and response.

When problematic penal practices are externally reviewed and investigated, recommendations are typically made in favour of various penal reforms, such as calls for better institutional management and oversight, external accountability, and increased specialised staff training (e.g. Arbour 1996; OCI 2013a). Such recommendations continue to see some form of carceral response as the appropriate solution. Nowhere is this more evident and problematic than in the CSC's refusal to abolish the use of segregation for criminalised women and prisoners with mental health issues following the recommendations made by both the OCI and the Ontario Coroner's Inquiry after Ashley's 2007 carceral death.

Abolitionist analysis and practice stems from historical movements working to challenge despotic control systems such as slavery, child labour, the death penalty, and the penal system. A penal abolitionist approach starts from the tenet that the current criminal justice system is ideological and unreasonable in the assumption that criminalising and punishing social harms is a productive way to resolve social problems. As Nils Christie (1977) notes, there is no reason to believe that the level of pain inflicted by the state on its citizens is the right or natural course of action. Redress, rather than punishment, is to acknowledge a social harm, the need for accountability, and the fact that some forms of restoration, reparation, or compensation are needed. Abolitionists do not seek solely to improve the conditions of confinement; rather, they challenge carceral logics by bringing focus to state practices that criminalise and problematise non-normative: lifestyle, culture, race, gender, sexuality, class, identity, poverty, and form of survival. In discussing the politics of penal abolition, Thomas Mathiesen (2015: 47) argues that 'finishing' an abolitionist project (i.e. finalising its form and its goals) renders it 'destined to fail' and that only an 'unfinished' approach, which means that the goals, message, and means are never finalised, will progress an abolitionist agenda. This conceptualisation of an 'unfinished' approach resists normative standards and objectives in order to develop ongoing, diverse, locally rooted, and creative responses to social harm. Such a project is able to contradict and compete with the established system and thus the status quo precisely because "its unfolding is still in process" (Mathiesen 2015: 57) and it detracts from carceral regimes that enforce normative expectations. In the same vein, Karlene Faith (2000: 161) distinguishes between projects that are 'reformist reform' (i.e. to improve the conditions of confinement) and those that have 'revolutionary reform potential'. According to Faith, the danger of engaging in reformist reform is that while it may ease certain pains of imprisonment, it simultaneously reinforces existing carceral logics by implying that prisons are improving. On the other hand, a revolutionary reform that seeks to substantially alter existing practices 'benefits women in the long run, strengthens communities, and reduces the number of prisoners'.

By returning focus to state practices and avoiding the currency of carceral logics, a penal abolitionist approach moves from normative standards of citizenship and processes of criminalisation towards responsibilising the state to meet financial and social entitlements and benefits and find more creative and relevant solutions for accountability. For example, Victoria Law (2011) and Emily Thuma (2015) explore several international and US abolitionist grassroots initiatives and strategies in the anti-violence and anti-carceral feminist movement, describing how these address the specific character and diverse needs of local communities without resorting to or relying on the existing criminal justice system or other punitive models. One such initiative is the *Creative Interventions Group*, which developed a site to collect and publicly offer tools and resources that address violence in everyday life, whereby the community offers support and protection to the women who are impacted while holding the perpetrator of violence to account through meetings. This initiative challenges the idea that women are in need of police, criminal, and punitive justice protections that often result in problematising women through erroneous charges or failing to protect them, while another individual is placed in a prison where no accountability in relation to the harm done is addressed. By moving away from a carceral response to local and social problems, more inclusive understandings and practices of justice that aim to foster creative opportunities in living and growing may be nurtured (Faith 2000; Centre for Justice Exchange 2016; Mathiesen 2015).

In Canada, there are ongoing efforts to counter penal formations at both the individual and collective levels and that aim to address the plethora of problems associated with carceral logics. Abolitionist groups across the country have found creative responses to social harm and offer diverse forms of support, accountability, and alternative justice. Bar None Winnipeg is an abolitionist group offering a prison rideshare programme that connects people with rides to visit their friends and loved ones who are in prison. Criminalization and Punishment Education Project is a group that brings students, researchers from Carleton University and the University of Ottawa, and community members together with those affected by criminalisation and punishment to identify key issues as the focus of criminological inquiry, develop collaborative research projects, and plan and carry out related public education initiatives. End the Prison Industrial Complex is a prison abolition group that challenges the ability of the Prison Industrial

Complex (PIC) to keep us safe and the notion that prison reforms can make the PIC just or effective. The Centre for Justice Exchange is a collective of academics, students, and community members who seek to share, create, and advance more inclusive understandings and practices of justice, which they contend is not only about being accountable to each other and to ourselves but about opportunities to live, grow, and create. Montréal Contre les Prisons is an online compilation of criminal justice and anti-capitalist events happening across Canada. Prison Justice is a resource in support of prisoners and prison justice activism in Canada. Prison Moratorium Action Coalition is an abolitionist Facebook group that demands that the government of Canada invest in eliminating poverty and its root causes, notably in disadvantaged communities, instead of prisons. Quakers Fostering Justice/ Canadian Friends Service Committee supports prisoners, with a long-term goal of abolishing prisons by developing responses that move beyond harm in relation to the justice system. Termite Collective is a group of creative and concerned people who expose the increasingly repressive nature of prison through writing, workshops, political parody, and criminal cabaret[6]. These are a few of the examples of the different groups across Canada actively contesting penal, carceral, and colonial regimes and working towards more inclusive models of justice.

More specific to women is the Canadian Association of Elizabeth Fry Societies (CAEFS)[7], an abolitionist not-for profit organisation that works for and with women and girls in the criminal justice system. CAEFS has successfully developed regional advocates for women's federal and provincial prisons who not only address the conditions of women's confinement but also advance the human rights of women by flagging systemic penal harms. From an abolitionist perspective, the ongoing documentation of rights violations highlights the overall problematic nature of the prison system while challenging its utility in addressing women's social needs. The Canadian Association of Elizabeth Fry Societies was originally involved in litigation to abolish of segregation, but from which it almost immediately withdrew, when the Canadian Civil Liberties Association, as well as all other parties engaging in similar litigation (i.e. B.C. Civil Liberties Association and the John Howard Society of Canada) refused to take a position that would argue for the abolition of segregation, as well as solitary confinement. Very very few groups in Canada, aside from the Canadian Association of Elisabeth Fry Societies Canada, Native Women's Association of Canada, DisAble Women's Action Network Ontario and Canadian Human Rights Commission, as well as individuals such as Louise Arbour C.C., G.O.Q. and Senator Kim Pate are taking an abolition position, while others or only advocating for limits or reforms. The organisation also petitions the state for resources to be allocated to entitlements and supports for women, such as employment, education, healthcare, childcare, housing, and social and financial support. Such advances are not only useful in terms of shifting responsibility for women's structural disadvantages onto the state but also in terms of promoting awareness of the conditions and struggles women experience more generally and challenging carceral logics specifically. As Emma Russell and Bree Carlton (2013) argue, the goal of abolition is not only offering critique but rather challenging the assumption that the prison is a viable solution to social harm. A penal abolitionist approach requires working outside corrective frames, discourses, and carceral systems from an anti-carceral and non-punitive perspective, with an ongoing concern for the immediate welfare of those in prison (Faith 2000; Mathiesen 2015).

Conclusion

After nearly thirty years of women-specific corrections, Canada's federal prisons for women remain 'ill-equipped' (OCI 2013b: 29). This failure persists despite the extant research on women in prison over the years, the widespread consultations in the implementation of the *Creating Choices* (1990) report, and the ongoing gendered management structure of women's corrections. Although feminist and social critique have provided profound understanding of the experiences of women in prison, this variant of critique and approach implicitly locates the prison as a milieu that can improve its practices and emancipate itself from its inherently despotic character. Although important, penal research and critique can become absorbed into even the most hidden carceral logics if incarceration is not identified as the fundamental problem. This is evident in the case of Ashley who, under a *Creating Choices* philosophy, experienced prolonged isolation, coerced programming, violent uses of force, and forced psychopharmaceutical compliance, resulting ultimately in a tragic death. Today, a women-centred carceral logic, although it recognises women's social disadvantage, creates gender-specific forms of correction that continue to enlist women within varying forms of control, segregation, and violence. This reflects Faith's (2000) contention that 'reformist reform' projects are easily absorbed into existing carceral logics that justify the continued use of imprisonment in response to social harm.

Social and feminist critique and penal research have reached a paradoxical dilemma. On the one hand, there is a need to research and develop knowledge about criminalised women in order to develop better and more humane responses to women's disadvantage and subsequent carceral experiences. On the other hand, this knowledge is used to constitute criminalised women as Others, which enjoins a carceral logic reinforcing a penal response to women's criminalisation. To this end, a penal abolitionist approach is fundamental to penal research and practice as it challenges, works through, breaks from, and partitions the lines of carceral power that marginalise and harm criminalised women.

Notes

1 The *Creating Choices* (1990) report led to the opening of five new regional federal women's prisons across Canada, centred around this correctional vision for women. The prisons were initially intended to be minimum-security, cottage-style houses with an environment of support and independence. They were all eventually adapted for maximum-security classification.

2 In the US, between 1980 and 2014, the number of incarcerated women increased by more than 700 per cent, rising from a total of 26,378 in 1980 to 215,332 in 2014 (Sentencing Project 2016). In England and Wales, between 2000 and 2010, the women's

prison population increased by 27 per cent, standing at 4,132 in England and 4,132 in Wales. In 1995, the female prison population in Ireland was 1,979 and increased to 3,355 in 2000 and again to 4,267 2010 (Prison Reform Trust 2012). In Australia, from 2005 to 2015, women's imprisonment rates increased by more than 50 per cent from 24 to 38 prisoners per 100,000 (Australian Bureau of Statistics 2016). In Canada, there are over 500 federally sentenced women incarcerated in the five multilevel regional women's facilities and one Aboriginal Healing Lodge. From 2005 to 2015, the number of federally incarcerated women increased by more than 50 per cent in comparison to less than 10 per cent for men (OCI 2015).

3 This research draws from a social and feminist critique, correctional documents, and other source literature, such as Commissions of Inquiry and reports of the Office of the Correctional Investigator. Data selection is not comprehensive but purposive and longitudinal, based on over 20 years of the authors' work experience and research in the area.

4 Faith (1993, 2011) coined the term 'victimization-criminalization continuum' to describe the complicated relationship between gendered violence and women's criminality (including violence). This continuum recognizes the power relations that flow from historical, cultural, economic, and sociopolitical practices that operate in tandem with dominant discourses and institutions (i.e. law, medicine, social welfare) and simultaneously contributes to women's endangerment and criminality. Faith notes that while much crime is rooted in victimisation, victimisation is not deterministic and cannot be named as the 'cause' of crime.

5 The 'WRAP' consists of applying multiple restraint belts to an individual sitting with their legs outstretched in front of them so as to prevent the possibility of any bodily movement; a hockey helmet is placed on the individual's head to prevent injury in the event that they topple over and to prevent the subject from biting or spitting. The Pinel Board involves strapping an individual on their back to a board in five point restraints (hands, feet, head, chest, hips, and legs) to cease bodily movement.

6 See https://justiceexchange.files.wordpress.com/2015/01/justice-resource-directory. pdf for more details.

7 Kim Pate, CAEFS' long-time Executive Director, was appointed to the Senate in 2016. This appointment brings an abolitionist voice directly into federal Canadian politics for the first time.

References

Adelberg, E. and Currie, C. (1987) *Too Few to Count: Canadian Women in Conflict with the Law*, Vancouver, BC: Press Gang Publishers.

Arbour, L. (1996) *Commission of Inquiry into Certain Events at the Prison for Women in Kingston*, Ottawa, ON: Canada Communication Group Publishing.

Armytage, P., Martyres, K. and Feiner, M. (2000) 'Women in Corrections: Getting the Balance Right', Paper presented at the Women in Corrections: Staff and Clients Conference, Australian Institute of Criminology and Department for Correctional Services SA, Adelaide, 31 October–1 November, 2000.

Aungles, A. (1994) *The Prison and the Home: A Study of the Relationship Between Domesticity and Penality*, Sydney: Institute of Criminology, University of Sydney Law School.

Australian Bureau of Statistics (2016) *Prisoners in Australia, 2016*, Canberra: ABS.

Baldry, E., McDonnell, D., Maplestone, P. and Peters, M. (2003) *Ex–Prisoners and Accommodation: What Bearing Do Different Forms of Housing Have on Social Reintegration?* Sydney: Australian Housing and Urban Research Institute.

Barton, A. (2004) 'Women and Community Punishment: The Probation Hostel as a Semi-Penal Institution for Female Offenders', *Howard Journal*, 43(2): 149–163.

Barton, A. (2005) *Fragile Moralities and Dangerous Sexualities: Two Centuries of Semi-Penal Institutionalisation for Women*, Burlington, VT: Ashgate.

Bloom, B., Owen, B. and Covington, S. (2004) 'Women Offenders and the Gendered Effects of Public Policy', *Review of Policy Research*, 21(1): 31–48.

Brown, A. P. (2004) 'Anti–Social Behaviour, Crime Control and Social Control', *Howard Journal*, 43(2): 203–211.

Butler, J. (1994) *Mending the Broken Road: The Post-Release Experience of Imprisoned Mothers*, Sydney: NSW Government Press.

Carlen, P. (1983) *Women's Imprisonment: A Study in Social Control*, London: Routledge & Kegan Paul.

Carlen, P. (2002) 'New Discourses of Justification and Reform for Women's Imprisonment in England', In P. Carlen (Ed.) *Women and Punishment: The Struggle for Justice* (pp. 220–236), Portland, OR: Willan Publishing.

Carlisle, J. (2013) *Inquest Touching the Death of Ashley Smith: Jury Verdict and Recommendations*, Toronto, ON: Office of the Chief Coroner. Retrieved 21 March 2014 at http://provincialadvocate.on.ca/documents/en/Ashley_Smith_Verdict.pdf.

Case, P., Fasenfest, D., Sarri, R. C. and Phillips, A. (2005) 'Providing Educational Support for Female Ex–Inmates: Project PROVE as a Model for Social Reintegration', *Journal of Correctional Education*, 56(2): 146–157.

Centre for Justice Exchange (2016) *Got Questions? We Have Answers*, Sherbrooke, QC: Bishops University.

Chartrand, V. (2014) 'Penal and Colonial Politics Over Life: Women and Penal Release Schemes in NSW Australia', *Settler Colonial Studies*, 4(3): 305–320.

Chartrand, V. (2015) 'Landscapes of Violence: Women and Canadian Prisons', *Champ pénal/Penal Field*, VII: 2–20.

Chartrand, V. (2017) 'Penal Tourism of the Carceral Other as Colonial Narrative', In J. Z. Wilson, S. Hodgkinson, J. Piché, and K. Walby (Eds.) *The Palgrave Handbook of Prison Tourism* (pp. 671–685). London: Palgrave Macmillan UK.

Chesney-Lind, M. (2006) 'Patriarchy, Crime, and Justice: Feminist Criminology in an Era of Backlash', *Feminist Criminology*, 1(1): 6–26.

Chesney-Lind, M. and Pasko, L. (2004) *Girls, Women, and Crime: Selected Readings*, London: Sage Publications.

Christie, N. (1977) 'Conflict as Property', *British Journal of Criminology*, 17(1): 1–15.

Chunn, D. and Gavigan, S. (2014) 'From Welfare Fraud to Welfare as Fraud: The Criminalization of Poverty', In G. Balfour and E. Comack (Eds.), *Criminalizing Women: Gender and Justice in Neoliberal Times*, 2nd Edition (pp. 217–232), Halifax, NS: Fernwood Press.

Comack, E. (2014) 'The Feminist Engagement with Criminology', In G. Balfour and E. Comack (Eds.), *Criminalizing Women: Gender and Justice in Neoliberal Times*, 2nd Edition (pp. 22–55), Halifax, NS: Fernwood Press.

Correctional Service Canada (CSC) (1990) *Creating Choices: The Taskforce on Federally Sentenced Women*, Ottawa, ON: Correctional Service of Canada.

Correctional Service Canada (CSC) (2003) *Secure Unit Operational Plan*, Ottawa, ON: CSC.

Correctional Service Canada (CSC) (2011) *Evaluation Report: Intensive Intervention Strategy for Women Offenders*, Ottawa, ON: CSC, Evaluation Branch, Policy Sector.

Correctional Service Canada (CSC) (2017) *Quick Facts: Women Offenders*, Ottawa, ON: Correctional Service Canada.

Corston, Baroness J. (2007) *The Corston Report: A Report of a Review of Women with Particular Vulnerabilities in the Criminal Justice System*, London: Home Office.

Covington, S. (1998) 'Women in Prison: Approaches in the Treatment of Our Most Invisible Population', *Women & Therapy*, 21(1): 141–156.

Daly, K. (1993) 'Class-Race-Gender: Sloganeering in Search of Meaning', *Social Justice*, 20(1/2): 56–66.

Damousi, J. (1997) *Depraved and Disorderly: Female Convicts, Sexuality and Gender in Colonial Australia*, Cambridge: Cambridge University Press.

Davies, S. and Cook, S. (1999) 'The Sex of Crime and Punishment', In S. Cook and S. Davies (Eds.), *Harsh Punishment: International Experiences of Women's Imprisonment* (pp. 53–78), Boston, MA: Northeastern University Press.

Dell, C. A., Fillmore, C. and Kilty, J. M. (2009) 'Looking Back 10 Years After the Arbour Inquiry: Ideology, Practice and the Misbehaved Federal Female Prisoner', *The Prison Journal*, 89(3): 286–308.

Dell, C. A., Gardipy, J., Kirlin, N., Naytowhow, V. and Nicol, J. J. (2014) 'Enhancing the Wellbeing of Criminalized Indigenous Women: A Contemporary Take on a Traditional Cultural Knowledge Form', In G. Balfour and E. Comack (Eds.), *Criminalizing Women: Gender and Justice in Neoliberal Times*, 2nd Edition (pp. 314–329), Halifax, NS: Fernwood Press.

Dobash, R. P., Dobash, E. R. and Gutteridge, S. (1986) *The Imprisonment of Women*, Oxford: Basil Blackwell Ltd.

Dodge, M. and Pogrebin, M. R. (2001) 'Collateral Costs of Imprisonment for Women: Implications of Reintegration', *The Prison Journal*, 81(1): 42–54.

Edwards, A. H. (1982) 'Women, Crime and Criminal Justice: The State of Current Theory and Research in Australia and New Zealand', *Australian and New Zealand Journal of Criminology*, 15(2): 69–89.

Faith, K. (2000) 'Reflections on Inside/Out Organizing', *Social Justice* 27(3): 158–167.

Faith, K. (1993, 2011) *Unruly Women: The Politics of Confinement & Resistance*, New York: Seven Stories Press.

Farrell, A. (2000) 'Women, Crime and Drugs: Testing the Effect of Therapeutic Communities', *Women & Criminal Justice*, 11(1): 21–27.

Freedman, E. B. (1981) *Their Sisters' Keepers: Women's Prison Reform in America, 1830–1930*, Ann Arbor, MI: University of Michigan Press.

Fox, K. (1999) 'Changing Violent Minds: Discursive Correction and Resistance in the Cognitive Treatment of Violent Offenders in Prison', *Social Problems*, 46(1): 88–43.

Frietas, M., McAuley, B. and Kish, N. (2014) 'Experiencing the Inside-Out Program in a Maximum-Security Prison', in G. Balfour and E. Comack (Eds.), *Criminalizing Women: Gender and Justice in Neoliberal Times*, 2nd Edition (pp. 303–313), Halifax, NS: Fernwood Press.

Galbraith, S. M. (2004) 'So Tell Me, Why Do Women Need Something Different?', *Journal of Religion & Spirituality in Social Work*, 23(1/2): 197–212.

Gelsthorpe, L. and Morris, A. (2002) 'Women's Imprisonment in England and Wales: A Penal Paradox, *Criminal Justice*, 2(3): 277–301.

Goulding, D. (2004) *Severed Connections: An Exploration of the Impact of Imprisonment on Women's Familial and Social Connectedness*, Perth: Murdoch University.

Guenther, L. (2013) *Solitary Confinement: Social Death and Its Afterlives*, Minneapolis, MN: University of Minnesota Press.

Haney, C. (2003) 'Mental Health Issues in Long-term Solitary and "Supermax" Confinement', *Crime & Delinquency*, 49: 124–156.

Haney, C. (2008) 'A Culture of Harm: Taming the Dynamics of Cruelty in Supermax Prisons', *Criminal Justice and Behavior*, 35(8): 956–984.

Hannah-Moffat, K. (2001) *Punishment in Disguise: Penal Governance and Canadian Federal Women's Imprisonment*, Toronto, ON: University of Toronto Press.

Hannah-Moffat, K. (2005) 'Criminogenic Needs and the Transformative Risk Subject: Hybridizations of Risk Need in Penality', *Punishment & Society*, 7(1): 29–51.

Hannah-Moffat, K. (2008) 'Re-Imagining Gendered Penalties: The Myth of Gender Responsivity', In P. Carlen (Ed.), *Imaginary Penalties* (pp. 193–217), Cullompton: Willan.

Hudson, B. (2002) 'Punishment and Control', In M. Maguire, R. Morgan and R. Reiner (Eds.), *The Oxford Handbook of Criminology* (pp. 233–261), Oxford: Oxford University Press.

Kendall, K. (2002) 'Time to Think About Cognitive Behaviour Programs', In P. Carlen (Ed.), *Women and Punishment: The Struggle for Justice* (pp. 182–198), Portland, OR: Willan Publishing.

Kilty, J. (2006) 'Under the Barred Umbrella: Is There Room for a Women-Centered Self-Injury Policy in Canadian Corrections?', *Criminology and Public Policy*, 5(1): 161–182.

Kilty, J. (2012) 'It's Like They Don't Want You to Get Better': Psy Control of Women in the Carceral Context', *Feminism & Psychology*, 22(2): 162–182.

Langner, N., Barton, J., McDonough, D., Noel, C. and Bouchard, F. (2002) 'Rates of Prescribed Medication Use by Women in Prison', *Forum on Corrections Research*, 4: 2.

Law, V. (2011) 'Where Abolition Meets Action: Women Organizing Against Gender Violence', Originally appeared in *Contemporary Justice Review*. Reprinted at: *New Clear Vision*. At: www.newclearvision.com/2011/03/04/where-abolition-meets-action/. Accessed 24 August 2017.

LeBaron, G. and Roberts, A. (2010) 'Toward a Feminist Political Economy of Capitalism and Carcerality', *Signs: Journal of Women in Culture and Society*, 36(1): 19–44.

Maidment, M. R. (2006) 'We're Not All That Criminal: Getting Beyond the Pathologizing and Individualizing of Women's Crime', *Women & Therapy*, 29(3/4): 35–56.

Mathiesen, T. (2015) *The Politics of Abolition Revisited*, New York: Routledge.

McCorkel, J. (2003) 'Embodied Surveillance and the Gendering of Punishment', *Journal of Contemporary Ethnography*, 32(1): 41–76.

McCorkel, J. (2004) 'Criminally Dependent? Gender, Punishment, and the Rhetoric of Welfare Reform', *Social Politics*, 11(3): 386–410.

Messina, N. P., Burdon, W. M. and Prendergast, M. L. (2003) 'Assessing the Needs of Women in Institutional Therapeutic Communities', *Journal of Offender Rehabilitation*, 37(2): 89–106.

Miller, J. G. (1991) *Last One Over the Wall: The Massachusetts Experiment in Closing Reform Schools* (p. 8), Columbus, OH: Ohio State University Press.

Moore, L. and Scraton, P. (2013) *The Incarceration of Women Punishing: Bodies, Breaking Spirits*, Basingstoke: Palgrave Macmillan.

Naffine, N. (1997) *Feminism and Criminology*, St Leonards: Allen & Unwin.

O'Brien, P. (2001) 'Just Like Baking a Cake: Women Describe the Necessary Ingredients for Successful Re-entry after Incarceration', *Families in Society*, 82(3): 287–295.

O'Brien, P. and Harm, N. (2002) 'Women's Recidivism and Reintegration: Two Sides of the Same Coin', In J. Figueira-McDonough and R. C. Sarri (Eds.), *Women at the Margins: Neglect, Punishment, & Resistance* (pp. 295–318), New York: Haworth Press.

O'Connor, B. (1996) 'Creating Choices or Just Softening the Blow? The Contradictions of Reform: Inmate Mothers and Their Children', *Current Issues in Criminal Justice*, 8(2): 144–151.

Office of the Correctional Investigator [OCI] (2013a) *Annual Report of the Office of the Correctional Investigator 2012–2013*, Ottawa, ON: The Correctional Investigator Canada.

Office of the Correctional Investigator [OCI] (2013b) *Risky Business: An Investigation of the Treatment of Chronic Self-Injury Among Federally Sentenced Women*, Ottawa, ON: The Correctional Investigator Canada.

Office of the Correctional Investigator [OCI] (2014). *Annual Report of the Office of the Correctional Investigator 2013–2014*, Ottawa, ON: The Correctional Investigator Canada.

Office of the Correctional Investigator [OCI] (2015) *Annual Report of the Office of the Correctional Investigator 2014–2015*, Ottawa, ON: The Correctional Investigator Canada.

Parkes, D. and Pate, K. (2006) 'Time for Accountability: Effective Oversight of Women's Prisons', *Canadian Journal of Criminology and Criminal Justice*, 8: 251–285.

Pate, K. (2014) *Guest Presentation: Women in the Penal System*, Sherbrooke QC: Bishop's University, 3 April.

Petersilia, J. (2003) *When Prisoners Come Home: Parole and Prisoner Re-entry*, New York: Oxford University Press.

Phillips, S. D. and Harm, N. J. (1998) 'Women Prisoners: A Contextual Framework', In J. Harden and M. Hill (Eds.), *Breaking the Rules: Women in Prison and Feminist Therapy* (pp. 1–9), New York: Harrington Park Press.

Pogrebin, M. R. and Dodge, M. (2001) 'Women's Accounts of Their Prison Experiences: A Retrospective View of Their Subjective Realities', *Journal of Criminal Justice*, 29(1): 531–541.

Pollack, S. (2014) 'Rattling Assumptions and Building Bridges: Community Engaged Education and Action in a Women's Prison', In G. Balfour and E. Comack (Eds.), *Criminalizing Women: Gender and Justice in Neoliberal Times*, 2nd Edition (pp. 290–302). Halifax, NS: Fernwood Press.

Pollack, S. and Kendall, K. (2005) 'Taming the Shrew: Regulating Prisoners through Women-Centred Mental Health Programming', *Critical Criminology*, 13: 79–87.

Power, J. and Brown, S. L. (2010) *Self-Injurious Behaviour: A Review of the Literature and Implications for Corrections*, Ottawa, ON: Correctional Service Canada.

Prison Reform Trust (2012) *Women in Prison*, London: Bromley Trust, Retrieved 11 March at www.prisonreformtrust.org.uk/Portals/0/Documents/WomenbriefingAug12small.pdf.

Rafter, N. H. (1983) 'Prisons for Women, 1790–1980', *Crime and Justice*, 5: 129–181.

Rhodes, L. (2004) *Total Confinement: Madness and Reason in the Maximum-Security Prison*, Berkeley, CA: University of California Press.

Richie, B. E. (2004) 'Challenges Incarcerated Women Face as They Return to Their Communities: Findings from Life Histories Interviews', In M. Chesney-Lind and L. Pasko (Eds.), *Girls, Women and Crime: Selected Readings* (pp. 231–245), London: Sage Publications.

Russell, E. and Carlton, B. (2013) 'Pathways, Race and Gender Responsive Reform: Through an Abolitionist Lens', *Theoretical Criminology*, 17(4): 474–492.

Sapers, H. (2008) *A Preventable Death*, Ottawa, ON: Office of the Correctional Investigator.

Sentencing Project (2016) *Fact Sheet: Incarcerated Women and Girls*, Washington DC. Retrieved 11 March at www.sentencingproject.org/wp-content/uploads/2016/02/Incarcerated-Women-and-Girls.pdf.

Severance, T. A. (2004) 'Concerns and Coping Strategies of Women Inmates Concerning Release: 'It's Going to Take Somebody in My Corner', *Journal of Offender Rehabilitation*, 38(4): 73–97.

Schrader, T. (2005) 'Close Your Eyes and Throw Away the Key: Mental Health of Female Prisoners', *New Doctor*, 83(1): 4–8.

Shalev, S. (2009) *Supermax: Controlling Risk through Solitary Confinement*. Collumpton: Willan.

Smart, C. (1977) *Women, Crime and Criminology: A Feminist Critique*, London: Routledge & Kegan Paul Ltd.

Smiley, M. (2001) 'Welfare Dependence: The Power of a Concept', *Thesis Eleven*, 64(1): 21–38.

Snider, L. (2003) 'Constituting the Punishable Woman: Atavistic Man Incarcerates Postmodern Woman', *British Journal of Criminology*, 43: 354–378.

Strange, C. (1985) 'The Criminal and Fallen of Their Sex: The Establishment of Canada's First Women's Prison, 1874–1901', *Canadian Journal of Women & the Law*, 1(1): 79–92.

Thuma, E. (2015) 'Lessons in Self-Defense: Gender Violence, Racial Criminalization, and Anticarceral Feminism', *Women's Studies Quarterly*, 43(3): 52–71.

Wacquant, L. (2009) *Punishing the Poor: The Neoliberal Government of Social Insecurity*, Durham, NC: Duke University Press.

Yúdice, G. (1989) 'Marginality and the Ethics of Survival', *Social Text*, 21: 214–236.

Zakaria, D., Thompson, J. M. and Borgatta, F. (2010) *Rates of Reported HIV and HCV Infections since Admission to Canadian Federal Prison and Associated Incarceration Characteristics and Drug-Related Risk-Behaviours*, Ottawa, ON: Correctional Service Canada.

7

IN PURSUIT OF FUNDAMENTAL CHANGE WITHIN THE AUSTRALIAN PENAL LANDSCAPE

Taking inspiration from the Corston Report

Julie Stubbs and Eileen Baldry

Introduction

The Corston Report, commissioned by the British Labour Government and published in 2007, identified the need for a radically different approach to criminalised disadvantaged women, aiming to reduce significantly the numbers cycling in and out of prison in the United Kingdom (UK). Internationally, Baroness Jean Corston's report spurred a revisiting of women-specific correctional agendas focussed on decarceration in states including Australia, the United States (US), Canada and New Zealand.

Some Australian states and territories, particularly New South Wales (NSW), Queensland and Victoria have a strong history of prison activism, focussing on women's criminalisation and imprisonment. This provided the foundations and context for advocates, anti-discrimination campaigners and some correctional officials to use Corston to renew political pressure to address women's criminalisation. Nevertheless, increasing rates of imprisonment of women in Australia, particularly of Indigenous women, indicate that the core issues highlighted by Corston – the factors that render women vulnerable to criminalisation and incarceration – have not been tackled with conviction.

This chapter briefly introduces women's imprisonment in Australia. It examines the history of activism challenging women's criminalisation and imprisonment, focussing on NSW, before outlining and discussing post-Corston reform developments. Inspired by Corston's recommendations for the expansion of women's community justice centres in the UK, the NSW Women's Correctional Services Advisory Committee, the Community Restorative Centre and an independent group of committed women in the community have embarked on the Miranda Project. This is comprised of initiatives, outlined below, to reduce criminalisation and prevent women's imprisonment. We consider the potential of this project in the Australian context, given the contrary significant investment by most states and territories in dramatically increasing the women's penal estate, often via public-private partnerships. This investment contradicts the approach endorsed by Corston.

Women's imprisonment in Australia

Under the Australian federal system, each state and territory has specific criminal laws, criminal courts and a prison system.[1] In some states, women are held exclusively in women-only prisons. Elsewhere, women are held in prisons operated for both men and women. Some women are held in men's prisons, specifically in regions of NSW and Western Australia (WA) (Australian Bureau of Statistics (ABS) 2016: Table 33). Unsentenced prisoners are often held in prison alongside those who have been sentenced. According to the 2016 prison census, there were 3,094 women in prisons across Australia with a rate of 32.6 per 100,000. That figure masks the much higher number of women who pass through prisons in any year. It also conceals substantial differences in women's imprisonment rates across Australia, ranging from a low of 17.8 per 100,000 in Victoria to a high of 147.6 per 100,000 in Northern Territory (NT). Further, it fails to identify the gross over-representation of Indigenous women, who represent less than 3 per cent of the population but 35 per cent of Australian women prisoners. Three states – NSW, WA and Queensland – account for 73 per cent of all women prisoners in Australia (ABS 2016: Tables 13, 14). The most populous Australian state, NSW, accounts for approximately one-third of the Australian prisoner population.

History of reform and activism in Australia

As Corston (2007: i) states in the UK context, 'many of the recommendations I make have been made before'. Her comment applies also in the Australian context, where recommendations aimed at the decarceration of women prisoners have been repeated over many decades, encompassing elements based on abolition and reform.

Activism on behalf of Australian prisoners has been characterised as a 'diffuse patchwork' of approaches shaped by local politics and conditions (Baldry, Carlton and Cunneen 2015) that cannot be described adequately by the conventional dichotomy of abolitionism versus reform. As Bree Carlton (2016) has noted, and as demonstrated by the examples provided below, Australian prison activists and campaigns, including those with an explicit abolitionist stance, have forged links with broader social movements and drawn connections between criminalisation, prison-based oppression and other forms of structural injustice. This is particularly evident in campaigns and advocacy regarding criminalised women.

Bree Carlton (2016: 3) contrasts abolitionist approaches that, while diverse, have traditionally focussed on 'institutional punishment and criminal justice', with anti-carceral feminist critiques that 'target strategies and campaigns to resist what they see as a clear continuum between intersectional structures of subordination, oppression and violence and their institutional manifestation'. Reform strategies used by anti-carceral feminists have the potential to 'subvert official discourses about reform and centre women's experiences and voices' (Carlton 2016: 12). Carlton is careful neither to romanticise the possible gains nor to overlook 'carceral clawback' (Carlen 2002) and the tendency for reformist strategies to feed into prison expansion (Hannah-Moffat 2002; Cunneen et al. 2013). However, she notes the possibility for reform strategies mobilised by anti-carceral feminist activism to 'consolidat[e] cross movement solidarities in the struggle for structural and social change' (Carlton 2016: 19) and 'generat[e] public literacy for abolitionist critiques' (Carlton 2016: 20).

It is possible to read the Corston Report through an anti-carceral feminist lens and to identify in the analysis and recommendations strategies aligned with anti-carceral feminist approaches. In developing what she describes as a radically different approach, Corston (2007: 2–3) framed her inquiry in terms of substantive equality and recognised underlying structural, relational and personal circumstances that generate vulnerabilities for women, put women at risk of offending and often result in imprisonment. Her recommendations were not focussed narrowly on criminal justice and had the potential to decentre prisons, although subsequent political decisions stymied that possibility in England and Wales (Hedderman 2011). Corston's support for expanding women's centres into a substantial network of community-based services, offering holistic support to offenders and non-offenders using a one-stop shop model appropriate to the needs of local women, including minorities (Corston 2007: 10), has been widely endorsed (Plechowizc 2015). As this chapter demonstrates, her intervention continues to inspire feminist activism.

An understanding and analysis of activism, ideology, government reforms and reversal of reforms assists in positioning and contextualising the most recent activism regarding women's criminalisation and imprisonment in Australia. From the mid-twentieth century, there has been prisoner-led activism and coalitions between prisoners and former prisoners alongside outside groups, such as trade unions, lawyers and community legal centres, academics and Aboriginal rights groups. Throughout the 1970s and 1980s, heightened action developed, initiated by small groups of prisoners, ex-prisoners and broader community members, particularly in NSW (Zdenkowski and Brown 1982) and Victoria (Carlton 2007). These developments were a response to brutal prison regimes and, nationally, a response to Aboriginal deaths in custody. Eileen Baldry and Tony Vinson (1991) document several community-led campaigns in the 1980s, including the Campaign for the Prevention of Custodial Death (Searcy 1991) as well as the instigation of the Royal Commission into Aboriginal Deaths in Custody (Corbett and Vinson 1991). These campaigns were inspired by, and allied to, broader international social movements demanding rights for women and minority groups. The Fairlea Research Group in Victoria (George 1999; Carlton 2016) and the Prisoners' Action Group (PAG) and Women Behind Bars

(WBB) in NSW are further examples of community-based action including both abolition and reform elements demanding changes to criminal justice policy and practice in Australia. The tensions between abolition and reform were clearly evident for groups involved in these coalitions. For instance, the PAG and WBB, together with the Council for Civil Liberties and other community-based organisations, campaigned for a royal commission into the NSW prison system. This followed the beatings and systemic (often racist) abuse meted out by officers to prisoners, prisoner riots and the burning of a prison. Yet having achieved the establishment of the commission in 1976, led by Justice Nagle,[2] activists debated whether participation in the inquiry would compromise their position. This was amid concerns that the inquiry would be a 'whitewash' or that their participation would be interpreted as endorsing official accounts (Zdenkowski and Brown 1982: 166–8).

Women's prison action groups

Activism focussing on women's prisons in Australia has long been situated within wider feminist politics, founded in women's experiences, contributing to and shaped by feminist legal theory and praxis. WBB was established in 1972 by student activist Wendy Bacon, drawing on her experience of incarceration and disillusionment with libertarianism, alongside Jeune Pritchard, Liz Fell and others involved in grassroots feminist campaigns and the 'New left legal community'. Initially, the group was associated with the PAG, sharing 'a commitment to pluralism across theoretical and activist lines' while developing a more women-centred activism with 'a reformist agenda inscribed on an anarchist foundation' (Genovese 2010: 61, 65). WBB challenged the 'unequal and discriminatory effects of law' and 'the gendered embodiment' of the treatment of women within prison, whereby violence and coercion were enacted through withholding services (Genovese 2010: 60). The group obtained legal aid to make representations to the Nagle Royal Commission and held demonstrations outside Mulawa Training and Detention Centre (now Silverwater Women's Correctional Centre and, at the time, the only women's prison in NSW), including the display of a banner reading, 'Mulawa Jail makes women sick' (Genovese 2010: 61). They recognised the limits of liberal reform and the need 'to confront law'. Wendy Bacon and Robyn Lansdowne (1982) from WBB subsequently undertook research and activist work with the Feminist Legal Action Group (FLAG), particularly on behalf of women prisoners convicted of homicide offences who had killed in response to domestic violence. They 'knowingly combined reformist and activist skills and practical legal and theoretical positions on law reform', demonstrating that 'a specifically feminist critical approach to law reform was possible' (Genovese 2010: 65). They achieved the release of Violet Roberts, and her son Bruce, and the reform of provocation law to better accommodate the circumstances in which battered women kill an intimate partner.[3] WBB provided inspiration and a theoretical and practical underpinning for much subsequent activism regarding criminalised women in NSW.

While Nagle's inquiry had limited focus on women (Baldry 2004), it substantiated long-standing concerns about the treatment of women prisoners, including inadequate medical care, overuse of tranquilisers, the poor standard of largely dormitory accommodation, 'primitive' punishment cells and the lack of educational and work opportunities (Nagle 1978: Chapter 27). Nagle made over 250 recommendations, including improvements in staff training, management and systems of accountability, and although relatively few were gender-specific, he recommended improving medical care and other conditions for women and increased contact between mothers and infants. The reformist NSW Commissioner of Corrective Services Dr Tony Vinson (1979–1981), appointed by a progressive Labour Government, initiated the majority of the reforms recommended by Nagle, including changes in the women's prison (Vinson 1982), but was frustrated by opposition and lack of support from government and elements within the prison service.[4] Many reforms were not continued or were reversed by ideologically punitive government regimes (Baldry 2004). It was not until 1984 that a major inquiry into women's prisons, the NSW Women in Prison Task Force, was established. One impetus for the establishment of the Task Force was the campaign by WBB and others against a proposal to build a new women's prison.

When the Task Force began its work, there were two women's prisons in NSW. Prison conditions had deteriorated since the Nagle report, and WBB had conducted numerous campaigns, drawing attention to the plight of women prisoners. It also called for Mulawa Training and Detention Centre to be 'emptied'. Mulawa was overcrowded, with substandard accommodation. Many women were held in dormitories, and most were subjected to a higher degree of security than necessary. There had been seven suicides in 10 years. At the minimum-security Norma Parker Centre, opened after the Nagle Report, women were subjected to petty and inconsistent rules and demeaning treatment. At both prisons, medical care, educational and other programmes were seriously inadequate. During the inquiry, women began to be transferred to men's prisons, held in wings redesignated for women (Brown, Kramer and Quinn 1988: 286–7).

The Task Force had a broad membership, including a woman prisoner, representatives from WBB and the Children of Prisoners Support Group. Members included Pat O'Shane, who was to become the first Aboriginal magistrate in NSW and represented the Ministry of Aboriginal Affairs, and Virginia Bell (now Justice Bell of the High Court of Australia), who was a representative from the community legal sector. The Task Force prioritised women's experiences as reflected in its methodology: interviews with 84 per cent of sentenced women; group discussions with women prisoners; pre- and post-release interviews with women leaving prison; and interviews with custodial, executive and professional staff throughout the women's prisons (NSW Women in Prison Task Force 1985: iv–v).

At the time, the number of women in prison in NSW had more than doubled in just two years. NSW women's rate of imprisonment was 10.1 per 100,000, more than twice that of Victoria (NSW Women in Prison Task Force 1985: 40). There had been pressure to build a new women's prison, but plans were halted, pending the outcome of the Task Force's work. The Task Force adopted a critical approach and a strong reductionist stance. It recognised that imprisonment rates were the result of 'mediating definitions, political, police and legal processes' and that reductions in imprisonment could be achieved by changes within these processes and other areas of social policy (NSW Women in Prison Task Force 1985: 40). It concluded that building a new prison for women would 'in all probability be counter-productive' (NSW Women in Prison Task Force 1985: 47) and urged immediate government action to reduce women's incarceration in NSW (NSW Task Force 1985: 40). The Task Force also noted the savings that could be achieved by providing alternatives to incarceration and argued that savings should be 're-invested to improve conditions and services for those for whom no alternatives can be found' (NSW Women in Prison Task Force 1985: 44).

The Task Force report was comprehensive and remains a key document with continuing relevance. It demonstrated the neglect of women prisoners, 'unacceptable prison conditions' and 'severe discrimination in terms of the range of programmes, activities, educational courses and work available', paying 'scant attention to their special problems and needs'. There had been no evident improvement in healthcare for women prisoners (NSW Women in Prison Task Force 1985: 44), despite the criticisms made by the Nagle Royal Commission (1978).

The Task Force observed that despite their marked over-representation, Aboriginal women were given little consideration in the criminal justice process or in academic research. It noted that Aboriginal women's imprisonment needed to be understood with reference to their dispossession, urging for the political recognition of Aboriginal people (NSW Women in Prison Task Force 1985: Chapter 6).

Many of the issues identified by the Task Force regarding the profile of women prisoners have persisted over time, particularly the high number of women on remand. Compared with men, a greater proportion of women serve short sentences or are imprisoned for drug offences, and the overwhelming majority of women have been imprisoned previously (Corben 2014). The Task Force's findings and recommendations resonate with those of subsequent inquiries in NSW and elsewhere, including the Corston Report (2007). As Corston did later, the Task Force recognised the structural factors beyond the prison that make some women, and racialised women in particular, vulnerable to criminalisation and incarceration. It advocated penal reduction and reforms intended to improve prison conditions. Its recommendations extended beyond the criminal justice system to other areas of social policy and service provision within the community, identifying the need for a Women's Council to be established to monitor and implement the programme. While its vision for penal reduction and penal reform was resisted, some recommendations were not implemented and many of its proposed reforms were undermined (Brown et al. 1988), like the Nagle Royal Commission, the Task Force substantiated many activist claims and, for a time at least, reshaped discourses about imprisonment. It remains a touchstone for, and has informed, all subsequent reports and inquiries into women's imprisonment in NSW.

Aboriginal women were, and remain, the most severely disadvantaged and over-represented group among women prisoners. The over-representation of Indigenous[5] Australians in prison became a national scandal in the late 1980s, following campaigns that exposed the high number of deaths of Aboriginal people in custody. Concerted lobbying by Indigenous organisations and their supporters (Corbett and Vinson 1991) led to the establishment of a national inquiry in 1987: the Royal Commission into Aboriginal Deaths in Custody (RCIADIC). The Royal Commission documented the substantial over-representation of Indigenous people in prison and police custody, investigated custodial deaths and analysed the underlying factors (Johnston 1991). That work was significant and was intended to lay the foundation for thorough change in the criminal justice system and beyond to redress those factors. Yet again, recommendations were only partially implemented, with the most important, regarding Indigenous self-determination, redressing inequality and strategies to reduce the criminalisation of Indigenous Australians, largely ignored. The RCIADIC report remains significant but gave limited attention to Indigenous women prisoners (Howe 1988; Marchetti 2007), a neglect that continued for over a decade.

Given the disproportionate number of Indigenous women in prison, in 2002, the NSW Aboriginal Justice Advisory Council initiated a study, resulting in a landmark report by Aboriginal researcher Rowena Lawrie (2003) entitled *Speak Out Speak Strong*. In 2003, Indigenous women constituted 31 per cent of women prisoners in NSW (in 2016, it is 35 per cent). The study took a critical approach, relying on information provided by Indigenous women prisoners themselves. It was directed towards identifying 'causes for imprisonment of Aboriginal women, the experiences of Aboriginal women in the criminal justice system and to identify their needs once incarcerated' (Lawrie 2003). Lawrie identified high rates of prior sexual and physical abuse, high levels of drug addiction, substantial prior contact with the criminal justice system, low educational attainment, and the women's status as primary carers within their communities: factors contributing to incarceration and therefore relevant to addressing the needs of Indigenous women prisoners. Despite this powerful report, Aboriginal women continued to be incarcerated in increasing numbers in NSW.

Campaigns against new women's prisons

Resisting the building of new prisons has been a consistent focus of activism. In Victoria, the tensions and paradoxes faced by anti-carceral activists were writ large in the 'save Fairlea campaign'. Faced with a proposal to close the only women's prison and move women into a men's prison, activists launched a campaign to save Fairlea Prison. While aware of the potential contradictions this raised, they maintained an abolitionist approach: 'our campaign to save the prison never minimised the problems of Fairlea or the futility of incarceration' (Amanda George, cited in Carlton 2016: 13). The Fairlea Women's Prison campaign, entitled *The Wring Outs*, lasted for six weeks, culminating in over 1,000 people encircling the prison (George 1999: 194–5).

In the late 1990s, a proposal to build a new women's prison returned to the agenda in NSW. A NSW Parliamentary Committee was set up following agitation by the No New Women's Prison Campaign, comprising activists emerging from various penal reform groups in the 1990s in NSW. Again, the tension between penal abolition, decarceration, reduction and reform was evident. The Committee was tasked with enquiring into factors driving the rise in imprisonment in NSW and reporting on the increase in women's imprisonment and whether this warranted the construction of a new women's prison. The Committee received 138 submissions. The only support for the building of a new prison came from the Department of Corrective Services. The interim report on women's imprisonment (NSW Legislative Council Select Committee on the Increase in Prisoner Population 2000; Brown 2002) included recommendations to suspend the planned new prison and a moratorium on expanding the number of places for women in prison aligned with a focus on prison reduction (Brown 2002; Australian Prisons Project 2012). It also included unanimous recommendations for wider use of bail and probation hostels, transitional centres, rehabilitation facilities and residential programmes; measures to meet the special needs of Indigenous prisoners; and improved liaison between corrective and community services. Despite these recommendations, within 20 minutes of the Committee's report being tabled, the government announced that the new women's prison would go ahead (O'Gorman 2000). The No New Women's Prison Campaign demonstrated against the new prison by setting up camp in a caravan outside the site of the prison at Windsor, with support from trade unions, ex-prisoners, church groups, parliamentarians, academics and women's groups. The protest was to no avail.

As in comparable states, women prisoners, former prisoners and activists in Australia have used a range of tactics to educate the public about experiences of incarceration, to challenge sentencing and punishment policies and practices and to highlight the inequities faced by women prisoners. These have included graffiti, postcards, posters, magazines and other publications produced within prisons and performances by theatre groups such as Somebody's Daughter (www.somebodysdaughtertheatre.com). Services have been established, such as Flat Out (www.flatout.org.au), an advocacy and homelessness service for women who have had contact with the criminal justice system in Victoria, and Sisters Inside Inc. (www.sistersinside.com.au) in Queensland, which works with women in prison, advocates on their behalf and provides a range of services to women and their families during imprisonment and on release. The NSW Women in Prison Advocacy Network, now called the Women's Justice Network

(WJN, https://womensjusticenetwork.net.au), formed in 2008, was inspired by the work of Sisters Inside. WJN provides mentoring, support and advocacy for women and girls involved in the criminal justice system.

Using rights and anti-discrimination mechanisms

The introduction of anti-discrimination laws provided another strategy adopted by Australian activists to challenge the treatment of women in prison. In the early 1980s, with the threat of the transfer of women to men's prisons, the Fairlea Research Group lodged a complaint with the Equal Opportunity Commission on behalf of women prisoners (George 1999). More recently, inspired by Canadian initiatives, Australian activists again turned to anti-discrimination provisions (Armstrong, Baldry and Chartrand 2007). This was another example of drawing together 'reformist and activist skills and practical legal and theoretical positions on law reform' (Genovese 2010: 65). These interventions have been informed by intersectional (Crenshaw 2012) and critical (Baldry and Cunneen 2014) theory and practice and demands for substantive equality (Armstrong et al. 2007).

In 2001, the Canadian Association of Elizabeth Fry Societies (CAEFS) and the Native Women's Association of Canada, in coalition with other activists, lodged a complaint to the Canadian Human Rights Commission (CHRC), identifying systemic discrimination against women in federal prisons. The grounds included the inadequacy of community-based release options, particularly for Aboriginal women, the inappropriate classification system used and inadequate and inappropriate placements of women with cognitive and mental disabilities (Kilroy and Pate 2010). The CHRC found that 'the Canadian government is breaching the human rights of women prisoners by discrimination on the grounds of sex, race and disability' (Kilroy and Pate 2010: 331). It made recommendations directed towards ensuring that the Correctional Service of Canada was compliant with the *Canadian Human Rights Act* (CHRC 2003).

Following suit in Australia, the independent community organisation Sisters Inside lodged a formal complaint with the Anti-Discrimination Commission Queensland (ADCQ) on the basis 'that women prisoners experience direct and indirect discrimination on the grounds of sex, race, religion and impairment' (Kilroy and Pate 2010: 332). The ADCQ found 'a strong possibility of *systemic* discrimination occurring in the classification of female prisoners, particularly, those who are Indigenous' (ADCQ 2006: 45) and concluded that the 'absence of a community custody facility in North Queensland... is a *prima facie* instance of *direct* discrimination' (ADCQ 2006: 110). Indigenous women were regularly in prison for shorter sentences but were over-represented in secure custody and less likely to receive release-to-work, home detention or parole and have higher recidivism rates (ADCQ 2006: 32, 108). The report also questioned the validity of a 'risk assessment tool' in use, concluding that based on the tool, Indigenous women were likely to be assessed as high risk (ADCQ 2006: 51).

In concert with the Queensland complaint, in 2005, the Beyond Bars Alliance in NSW submitted a complaint to the Anti-Discrimination Board (ADB), alleging 'race', sex and disability discrimination against female prisoners under federal anti-discrimination legislation and human rights conventions. The areas covered in the submission included policing, courts and issues specific to custodial corrections, such as access to work opportunities, community corrections and post-release matters. Specific examples of gender discrimination included strip-searching; the unmet needs of women with cognitive and mental disabilities; inappropriate risk classification and assessments (thereby discriminating against women, Aboriginal women and women with disabilities in particular); lack of low security correctional facilities for women in NSW; lack of accessible information for women from culturally and linguistically diverse backgrounds; and inadequate provision of post-release support places for women (Armstrong et al. 2007). The ADB declined to investigate.

The Ombudsman for the NT (2008: 4) also found systemic discrimination and cited

> [a] lack of resources, poor planning, outdated and inappropriate procedures and a failure to consider women as a distinct group with specific needs. This had resulted in a profound lack of services, discriminatory practices, inadequate safeguards against abuse and very little in the way of opportunities to assist women to escape cycles of crime, poverty, substance abuse and family violence.

These findings are in stark contrast to the *Standard Guidelines for Corrections in Australia*, which then, as now, require that 'the management and placement of female prisoners should reflect their generally lower security needs but their higher needs for health and welfare services and for contact with their children'.

Despite the range of detailed findings and recommendations made by the numerous inquiries, committees and commissions, the rates of women in prisons across Australian jurisdictions, particularly Indigenous Australian women, continued to rise and at a more rapid rate than did the male prisoner population (Baldry and Cunneen 2014). There remains a gulf between the reports and recommendations of parliamentary, government agency, NGO and community activist inquiries over the past five decades and the policies and practices of criminal justice agencies and successive governments.

The present Australian context

Women constitute a larger proportion of the prisoner population in Australia (8 per cent in 2015, ABS 2016) than in England and Wales (5 per cent in 2015, Ministry of Justice 2016: 109). Patterns in Australia also differ from those in England and Wales in other respects. There has been a significant increase in women's imprisonment throughout Australia, especially for remandees and among Aboriginal and Torres Strait Islander women. Unsentenced women now account for around 32 per cent of women prisoners in Australia (ABS 2016). In contrast, following a period of marked increase, the number of women in prison in England and Wales fell during the last decade (by 14 per cent) and then plateaued, with the decrease greater among Black, Asian and minority ethnic (BAME) women prisoners and for remandees (Ministry of Justice 2016: 109, 111).

In Australia in 2016, the national rate of incarceration for non-Indigenous women was 21.9 per 100,000 (ABS 2016: Table 20) as compared with a shocking rate of 464.8 per 100,000 for Indigenous women. Between 2000 and 2015, the incarceration rate for all women increased by 55 per cent (ABS 2001, 2016). During this period, rates for Indigenous women increased by 118 per cent and for Indigenous men by 50 per cent (Overcoming Indigenous Disadvantage 2016: Table 4A, 13.4). Even in the formerly low incarceration state of Victoria, the number of women imprisoned has increased substantially and at twice the rate of increase for men. Indigenous incarceration has increased faster than in any other state or territory (Victorian Ombudsman 2015: 32, 73).

Indigenous women are criminalised through high rates of arrests and court appearances for vehicle and traffic matters, justice offences and shoplifting, leading in some jurisdictions to their incarceration for lesser offences than their non-Indigenous peers (Bartels 2012; MacGillivray and Baldry 2015). Eileen Baldry and Chris Cunneen (2014) have argued that the ongoing and long-term negative impacts of patriarchal colonialism and its particular manifestation in the twenty first century across Australia, which are implicated in the criminalisation of Indigenous women, must be exposed and challenged to understand, explain and change this extraordinary over-representation. They also argue that much of the rapid growth in women's rates of imprisonment in Australia can be accounted for by the explosion in Indigenous women's incarceration. Yet there remains an 'apparent invisibility of Indigenous women to policy makers and programme designers in a criminal justice context, with very little attention devoted to their specific needs and circumstances' (Social Justice Commissioner 2005: 15; Stubbs 2013). There are few specific preventive or rehabilitative programmes, either in the community or in criminal justice settings, for Indigenous women and little data on women's participation in programmes (Baldry and McCausland 2009).

While there have been some improvements in the provision of women's health services, and while the number of deaths in custody has declined since the RCI-ADIC, it remains that women in prison have poor health and complex support needs, and the level of mortality among women released from prison is a significant concern (Carlton and Segrave 2015). The growth in the women's prison population throughout Australia has resulted in deterioration in conditions, less access to services and supports and more women being incarcerated in men's facilities. The Brisbane Women's Correctional Centre is the most overcrowded prison in Queensland, and women are often required to sleep on mattresses on the floor. The Queensland Ombudsman (2016) found that services and facilities are worse for women than men, thus constituting discrimination. In WA, a quarter of women prisoners are held in regional prisons that predominantly hold male prisoners, and they have limited access to health and other services (Inspector of Custodial Services 2014a: 8, 18). Boronia Women's Prison in WA, a pre-release centre for women deemed to be low risk, has attracted positive attention for its gender-responsive design and programs (Bartels and Gaffney 2011), although the programs have not been evaluated. However, the prison is now overcrowded, and education and other programmes have failed to meet the needs of the expanding women's population (Inspector of Custodial Services 2015).

While across Australia there are now multiple plans, policies and strategies for women prisoners, some of which expressly use the language of gender responsiveness, few programmes have been evaluated (Bartels and Gaffney 2011), and often, there is a marked disconnect between policy and practice. For instance, the Inspector of Custodial Services in WA (2014a: 16) noted that three new policy documents on women contained some useful elements but had no measurable outcomes or targets and were 'not operationally relevant' as staff were unaware of their existence. He was scathing in his criticisms of the male-dominated culture within the Department of Corrections, the removal of key personnel who had been driving more gender-responsive developments and the failure to plan for growth in the women's estate. He noted that institutionally, the response to growth in women's incarceration had been to adapt or redeploy units and other resources intended for male prisoners.

The abject failure to identify and meet the needs of women prisoners in WA is made starkly evident in a review of Bandyup Women's Prison (Inspector of Custodial Services 2014b). The Inspector found the prison to be the most crowded in the State, where more than 300 women with lesser security classifications are held unnecessarily in maximum security. There were 'piecemeal attempts to rectify the shortage of beds with leftovers from the male estate…female prisoners at Bandyup are still in the undignified position of having to sleep on mattresses on the floor of cells designed for a single occupant' (Inspector of Custodial Services 2014b: 1). Moreover, there was 'a racial divide, with the 'best' parts of the prison dominated by non-Aboriginal women and the more decrepit parts dominated by Aboriginal women' (Inspector of Custodial Services 2014b: vii).

Prison expansion is underway across Australia, driven by law and order rhetoric. There is an unquestioning acceptance by governments that rising prisoner numbers indicates a safer community. Imprisonment becomes justified through employing rehabilitation and programmes claiming to meet prisoners' needs. For example, a new private prison for women in WA, the Melaleuca Remand and Reintegration facility, opened in December 2016 on the site of a men's prison, expanding capacity by 254 'beds'. It is operated by the international company Sodexo in conjunction with community partners. Part of its funding is based on a payment-by-results scheme. It has been justified by the government on the grounds that it provides women with 'culturally appropriate services which respond to their unique needs and experiences', aligned with a 'rehabilitative philosophy… to deliver international best-practice' at a 20 per cent reduction in cost

(Government of Western Australia 2016: 14, 15). Like the new Ravenhall Prison for men in Victoria, which also involves a private prison operator and a payment by results funding model, such developments are inspired by UK examples, such as Peterborough Prison, and contested assumptions that payment-by-results schemes generate innovation and reduce recidivism (Fox and Albertson 2012). Other scholars have noted concerns that the payment-by-results frameworks are poorly suited for women offenders (Gelsthorpe and Hedderman 2012).

Increasingly, Australia is shifting towards a mixed penal economy with more public-private prisons and privatised services. Community groups are drawn into new arrangements for programme and service delivery in partnership with private-sector providers fearful that they will be excluded from future-funded community service provision and support for prisoners and ex-prisoners if they fail to partner with private corporations. Such arrangements can be highly prescriptive. They raise new dilemmas for activist organisations and groups that have been providing services to criminalised women, such as whether they should participate on adverse terms or be excluded from funding. There are parallels between these developments and those in the UK, where charities and others in the voluntary sector have been drawn into a mixed penal economy and deliver services under contract. There is debate about how such developments are 'shaping voluntary sector agents to the demands of the penal marketplace' (Corcoran 2011a: 45), and there is a need to recognise diversity within the voluntary sector and the importance of the specific local context (Tomczak 2017). Such developments, however, are novel in Australia, offering new challenges for activists and reformers, especially those wanting to support women in the community as recommended by Corston.

Women's imprisonment in NSW

NSW is the jurisdiction in Australia with the most women prisoners (944 in 2016) at a rate of 31.0 per 100,000. This is slightly below the national rate (ABS 2016). During the period of 2001 to 2015, the number of women imprisoned in NSW increased by 555. However, the trends differed by offence. The number of women imprisoned for theft, robbery and unlawful entry decreased, while those imprisoned for justice offences (e.g. breach of suspended sentences or community based orders) increased substantially, and imprisonment for acts intended to cause injury, illicit drugs and traffic and regulatory offences also increased. We suggest this reflects increases in criminalisation with harsher law enforcement and greater scrutiny of those on conditional bail or community-based sanctions. During this time, in most categories, the proportion of women sentenced to imprisonment rather than other penalties increased, especially for offences against justice, fraud, theft and public order offences (data supplied by the NSW Bureau of Crime Statistics and Research).[6] Despite marked *decreases* in arrests of Indigenous women for property offences and violent offences from 2001 to 2015 (Weatherburn and Ramsey 2016a), the increase in the incarceration of Indigenous women was proportionately greater than it was for other groups (Baldry and Cunneen 2014). Research points to an increase in the refusal of bail, harsher law enforcement and an increased commitment by courts to impose prison sentences as factors driving the increase in Indigenous incarceration (Weatherburn and Ramsey 2016b).

The NSW prison system is overcrowded, operating at 122 per cent of design capacity in 2015–16, and there has been a consequent decline in prisoner access to services and facilities. Out-of-cell times have been reduced to an average of 7.8 hours per day, and the ratio of nursing staff to prisoners as well as waiting times have deteriorated. Remand receptions have increased, and periods on remand have become longer due to court delays, while remandees have poor access to programmes (Auditor General 2016: Chapter 6).[7] Moreover, the government recently amended public health regulations to exempt prison facilities from minimum standards, giving the Commissioner of Corrective Services greater discretion to determine cell sizes and permitting further doubling and tripling of cell occupancy (Timms 2016). Media reports indicate that many prisoners are sleeping on mattresses on floors in prisons across NSW and that in some prisons, industrial and recreation areas are being repurposed as cells (Harris 2016).

The NSW government has responded to these conditions by accepting prison growth and allocating $3.8 billion to building new prisons. Corrective Services NSW has implemented a new program, *Better Prisons*, using 'market testing' to generate competition between government and private suppliers, who are compelled to demonstrate 'value for money' in 'the delivery of standards'. Corrective Services NSW claims that *Better Prisons* will deliver a prison system that accommodates more prisoners, operates more efficiently and has a greater focus on rehabilitation without compromising safety and security (Corrective Services NSW 2016). Currently, one male prison is being 'market tested' with the possibility of others to follow. Educational programmes and vocational training in NSW are being outsourced. Thus, NSW is following the UK, where prison-building spending is relatively unconstrained, while operating costs are reduced through competition between public and private suppliers (Corcoran 2014).

It is unclear what a strong focus on rehabilitation means within the *Better Prisons* programme, but activities geared to rehabilitation have been set as performance measures. Further, all prisons will have benchmarks set to determine budgets within which performance targets must be met. In publicly available documents, there is no reference regarding planning targeted to the needs of women. However, prison expansion will include a new 300-bed maximum-security unit for women on the same site as a men's prison at Grafton, the 're-purposing' of a juvenile detention centre as a 90-bed maximum-security remand centre for women, additional beds for women (and men) at the North Coast Correctional Centre and, possibly, additional beds for women at Wellington Correctional Centre, where temporary dormitory-style accommodation is under construction (Corrective Services NSW website).

Explicit commitment to penal reduction, along with careful consideration of prison design, gender-appropriate programmes and services, as evident in the

NSW Women in Prison Task Force report (1985) and the report of the Inquiry into the Increase in Prisoner Population, seem long forgotten in NSW, having entered an era of prison expansion demanding 'value for money'. Even more remote is a commitment to address either the drivers of incarceration or initiatives to reduce criminalisation and pull back from the heavy reliance on incarceration. The paucity of preventive and reductionist policies on the part of the government has lead Australian activists to look to other jurisdictions for potential game-changing community-based initiatives, such as the Corston Report (2007). These have provided both inspiration and cautionary tales (Corcoran 2011b).

Beyond government – the Miranda Project

The publication of the Corston Report (2007) and the expansion of Women's Centres, networked through Women's Breakout (www.womensbreakout. org.uk), together with positive evaluations (New Economic Foundation 2012), prompted Australian activists (including the second author of this chapter, Eileen Baldry) to visit centres in England, such as Tomorrow's Women Wirral in Liverpool (www.tomorrowswomen.org.uk). These centres, with others like those in Scotland ('218' in Glasgow and the Willow Project in Edinburgh), inspired the development of a similar project in Sydney.

The Miranda Project (www.crcnsw.org.au/miranda-project) was created by the Women's Advisory Council of NSW Corrections and activists alongside dedicated individuals who personally financed its development. This group consulted with Women's Breakout, Corston and other organisations in the UK. The Miranda Project has been developed under the auspices of the Community Restorative Centre, an NGO supporting people involved in the criminal justice system and their families. The project's primary aim is to ensure criminalised women, and those at risk of criminalisation, are kept out of the criminal justice system. The project develops partnerships with women's health and other community-based centres that already provide services and trains staff to deliver programmes designed to assist women to remain in the community and desist from offending. It is proposed that the Miranda Project will function as a pre-sentence option for women on bail, a community-based sentencing option, a condition of parole and provider of ongoing support on the completion of a sentence. A drop-in centre and employment initiatives are also planned. A trial is underway at a number of sites, and more than a dozen women are already involved on a voluntary basis during the trial. As in the UK, the project has the support of local criminal justice agencies. However, it is intended that the Miranda Project will be situated in the community, thus avoiding enmeshment with the criminal justice system. It is focussed on the prevention of women's criminalisation, a reduction in women's imprisonment and promotion of decarceration. Whether in the current climate of massive prison expansion, with its public-private penal estate development, it is possible for community-based, non-government organisations to maintain such a focus remains to be seen.

The ongoing challenge

Kimberlé Crenshaw (2012: 1428–9) has observed that in the US, '[p]roblems that were once debated within political discourse as the product of illegitimate social power are now less controversially seen as individual pathologies and cultural deficits' (p. 1451), de-emphasising structural and historical causes (p. 1452). In Australia too, we see 'the weakened capacity of social justice discourse to resist the neo-liberal ideologies that underwrite the expansion of social punishment and mass incarceration' (pp. 1428–9). The clear message of the Corston Report (2007), other government inquiries and numerous NGO reports into women's incarceration – that prisons are an expensive and ineffective means to deal with most women who offend – has little purchase in contemporary Australia.

The extreme injustices and prison over-representation experienced by Indigenous Australian women, outlined earlier, require urgent attention. Although the Miranda Project is working with Indigenous Australian women and organisations to develop Indigenous women's community programmes, it will require more than a community programme to resolve the inequities embedded in white Australian institutions and culture that underpin the criminalisation of disadvantaged Indigenous women.

The developing shift towards a mixed penal economy in Australia poses complex questions and challenges for activists. It signals an acceptance by governments of penal expansionism while ignoring the apparent tensions between market forces and social justice (Players 2013). The ideological commitment to payment-by-results schemes as a means to provide incentives to private operators to reduce recidivism sidesteps the significance of criminalisation. Also, it is at odds with research (NEF 2012) demonstrating that effective, reintegrative re-entry schemes can be undertaken by community organisations with strong local connections. We acknowledge, however, the need for

> qualitative-driven approaches that can produce context-rich accounts of women's post-release support and survival…[and] a deeper systemic account of support structures and programs in action to shed light on the various roles correctional systems and community support agencies play in determining women's post-release trajectories.
>
> *(Carlton and Segrave 2015: 296)*

Yet there remains a risk that community organisations are vulnerable to being reshaped by these new arrangements reflecting government agendas that are not necessarily aligned with the experiences of women with first-hand experience of prison or those who work with them.

Despite challenges and setbacks, anti-carceral feminists and their partners in allied community-based organisations continue to strive to change the terms of the debate and to shape practice, within and beyond the criminal justice system. In Australia, in the face of government intransigence, activists have developed and delivered their visions of women-centred initiatives informed by experience and have shared knowledge about what is meaningful and relevant to women. They have also moved beyond the abolition/reform binary to embrace strategies aimed at greater equity, decarceration and reducing criminalisation. The Miranda Project is one promising example.

Notes

1 There are also federal criminal laws, for instance, dealing with terrorism-related offences, drug importation and welfare fraud. People imprisoned for federal offences are held in state/territory prisons. There were 95 prisons in Australia in mid-2016, plus 4 transitional centres, 1 periodic detention centre and 12 court cell complexes operated by state and territory corrective services (Productivity Commission 2017: 8.3), but several new prisons have opened since that time, and others are under construction.

2 The report by Justice Nagle found that in the aftermath of a 'riot' and the burning of Bathurst Gaol in February 1974, more than 50 prisoners were injured by batons and gunfire, 'mostly inflicted by prison officers illegally using unreasonable and unnecessary force' (Nagle 1978: 19). The inquiry also documented other evidence of the brutality of the NSW prison regime, including systematic floggings of a large number of prisoners by prison officers under the control of the Superintendent at Bathurst Gaol in 1970; a 33-year-long regime at Grafton Gaol of 'brutal, savage and sometimes sadistic violence' against prisoners who were labelled intractable (p. 108); and the fact that Katingal, a special security unit, was an 'electronic zoo' that should be closed because it exacted too high a cost in human terms (p. 199). However, despite finding evidence of illegal assaults by prison officers, no recommendations were made for action against officers (Zdenkowski and Brown 1982).

3 Violet and Bruce Roberts received life sentences for the murder of Eric Roberts, Violet's brutal husband and Bruce's father (*R v Violet Roberts, Bruce Roberts*, unreported Supreme Court of NSW, Newcastle 15 March 1976). Activism by WBB, FLAG and others secured their release and influenced law reform (Genovese 2010); in 1982, in NSW, the mandatory life sentence for murder was replaced, allowing greater sentencing discretion and the partial defence of provocation, which reduces murder to manslaughter, was broadened to better accommodate battered women by recognising 'cumulative' provocation and removing the requirement that provocation must occur immediately before the killing.

4 Vinson (1982: 130–134) recounts how his attempts to provide more humane treatment to women in the segregation unit at Mulawa Prison were resisted by officers who failed to act on his instructions to provide basic facilities, such as furniture so that women had somewhere to eat, access to exercise yards and art supplies.

5 Within Australia, the term 'Indigenous' includes Aboriginal people and Torres Strait Islanders.

6 The percentage receiving sentences for homicide-related offences and sexual assault also increased, but the numbers were very small.

7 The Audit Office of NSW reported on the prison system in general and not specifically on women's prisons.

References

Anti-Discrimination Commission Queensland ('ADCQ') (2006) *Women in Prison: A Report by the Anti-Discrimination Commission Queensland*, www.adcq.qld.gov.au/pubs/WIP_report.pdf.

Armstrong, K., E. Baldry and V. Chartrand (2007) 'Human rights abuses and discrimination against women in the criminal justice system in New South Wales', *Australian Journal of Human Rights*, 12(2): 203–227.

Auditor-General (2016) *Report to Parliament, Volume 7 Report on Justice*, Sydney: Audit Office of NSW, www.audit.nsw.gov.au/publications/latest-reports/financial/volume-seven-2016-justice/service-delivery.

Australian Bureau of Statistics (2001) *Prisoners in Australia, 2000* (Cat. 4517.0), Melbourne: Australian Bureau of Statistics.

Australian Bureau of Statistics (2016) *Australian Prisoners, 2015* (Cat. 4517.0), Canberra: Australian Bureau of Statistics.

Australian Prisons Project (2012) *Women prisoners*, http://cypp.unsw.edu.au/women-prisoners.

Bacon, W. and R. Lansdowne (1982) 'Women who kill husbands: The battered wife on trial', in O'Donnell, C. and Craney, J. (eds) *Family Violence in Australia*, Melbourne: Longman Cheshire.

Baldry, E. (2004) 'Women in prison 25 years after Nagle', *Current Issues in Criminal Justice*, 16(1): 101–105.

Baldry, E., B. Carlton and C. Cunneen (2015) 'Abolitionism and the paradox of penal reform in Australia: colonialism, context, cultures and cooption', *Social Justice: A Journal of Crime, Conflict and World Order*, 41: 168–189.

Baldry, E. and C. Cunneen (2014) 'Imprisoned Indigenous women and the shadow of colonial patriarchy', *ANZ Journal of Criminology*, 47: 276–298.

Baldry, E. and R. McCausland (2009) 'Mother seeking safe home: Aboriginal women post-release', *Current Issues in Criminal Justice*, 21(2): 288–301.

Baldry, E. and T. Vinson (eds) (1991) *Actions Speak: Strategies and Lessons from Australian Social and Community Action*, Melbourne: Longman Cheshire.

Bartels, L. (2012) 'Sentencing of Indigenous women', *Research Brief* 14, Sydney: Indigenous Justice Clearinghouse.

Bartels, L. and A. Gaffney (2011) *Good practice in women's prisons: A literature review* (AIC Report no. 41), Canberra: Australian Institute of Criminology.

Brown, D. (2002) 'Legislative council select committee on the increase in prisoner population, interim report, July 2000; final report, November 2001: A review', *Current Issues in Criminal Justice*, 14(1) 112–118.

Brown, D., H. Kramer and M. Quinn (1988) 'Women in prison: Task force reform', in M. Findlay and R. Hogg (eds) *Understanding Crime and Criminal Justice*, Sydney: Law Book Co., 273–308.

Canadian Human Rights Act (1985) Legislation *Canadian Human Rights Act* Revised Statutes of Canada, 1985, c. H-6.

Canadian Human Rights Commission (CHRC) (2003) *Protecting their Rights: A Systemic Review of Human Rights in Correctional Services for Federally Sentenced Women*, Submission to Parliament, Canada, preface, www.chrc-ccdp.ca/legislation_policies/consultation_report-eng.aspx.

Carlen, P. (2002) 'New discourses of justification and reform for women's imprisonment in England', in P. Carlen (ed) *Women and Punishment: The Struggle for Justice*, Cullompton: Willan Publishing, 220–236.

Carlton, B. (2007) *Imprisoning Resistance: Life and Death in an Australian Supermax*, Sydney: Sydney Institute of Criminology Series & Federation Press.

Carlton, B. (2016) 'Penal reform, anti-carceral feminist campaigns and the politics of change in women's prisons, Victoria, Australia', *Punishment & Society*. First published date: November-24-2016. doi:10.1177/1462474516680205.

Carlton, B. and M. Segrave (2015) 'Rethinking women's post-release reintegration and 'success'', *Australian & New Zealand Journal of Criminology*, 49(2): 281–299.

Corben, S. (2014) *NSW Inmate Census 2014* Corrective Services NSW www.corrective services.justice.nsw.gov.au/Documents/SP42-NSW-Inmate-Census-2014.pdf.

Corbett, H. and T. Vinson (1991) 'Black deaths in custody: Instigating the royal commission', in E. Baldry and T. Vinson (eds) *Actions Speak: Strategies and Lessons from Australian Social and Community Action*, Melbourne: Longman Cheshire, 95–104.

Corcoran, M. (2011a) 'Dilemmas of institutionalisation in the penal voluntary sector', *Critical Social Policy*, 31(1): 30–52.

Corcoran, M. (2011b) 'Snakes and ladders: Women's imprisonment and official reform discourse under New Labour', *Current Issues in Criminal Justice*, 22(3): 233–251.

Corcoran, M. (2014) 'The trajectory of penal markets in a period of austerity: The case of england and wales', in M. Deflem (ed.) *Punishment and Incarceration: A Global Perspective* (Sociology of Crime, Law and Deviance, Volume 19) Bingley, UK: Emerald Group Publishing Limited, 53–74.

Corrective Services NSW (2015) 'Classification of Female Inmates; Offender Classification & Case Management', *Policy & Procedures Manual*, 12.2, www.correctiveservices. justice.nsw.gov.au/Documents/Related%20Links/open-access-information/offender-classification/12.2-Classification-Procedures-for-Female-Inmates.pdf.

Corrective Services NSW (2016) *Better prisons overview: Factsheet #1*, Sydney: Corrective Services NSW, www.correctiveservices.justice.nsw.gov.au/Documents/ CSNSW%20Fact%20Sheets/better%20prisons/Better_Factsheet_1_The_project_ INTERNET_171116_ACCESSIBLE.pdf.

Corston, J. (2007) *The Corston Report*, London: Home Office.

Crenshaw, K. (2012) 'From private violence to mass incarceration: Thinking intersectionally about women, race and social control', *UCLA Law Review*, 59(6): 1418–1472.

Cunneen, C., E. Baldry, D. Brown, M. Brown, M. Schwartz and A. Steel (2013) *Penal Culture and Hyperincarceration: The Revival of the Prison*, Farnham: Ashgate.

Fox, C. and K. Albertson (2012) 'Is payment by results the most efficient way to address the challenges faced by the criminal justice sector?', *Probation Journal*, 59(4): 355–373.

Gelsthorpe, L. and C. Hedderman (2012) 'Providing for women offenders: The risks of adopting a payment by results approach', *Probation Journal*, 59(4): 374–390.

Genovese, A. (2010) 'A radical prequel: Historicising the construct of gendered law in Australia', in M. Thornton (ed) *Sex Discrimination in Uncertain Times*, Canberra: ANUE Press, 47–73.

George, A. (1999) 'The new prison culture: Making millions from misery', in S. Cook and S. Davies (eds) *Harsh Punishment: International Experiences of Women's Imprisonment*, Boston, MA: Northeastern University Press, 189–210.

Government of Western Australia, Department of Corrective Services (2016) *Project Summary: The Melaleuca Remand and Reintegration Facility*, Department of Corrective Services, Perth. www.parliament.wa.gov.au/publications/tabledpapers.nsf/displaypaper/ 3914458a655f89b8815dc96c4825801800591715/$file/4458.pdf.

Hannah-Moffat, K. (2002) 'Creating choices: Reflecting on choices', in P. Carlen (ed) *Women and Punishment: The Struggle for Justice*, Cullompton: Willan Publishing, 199–219.

Harris, L. (2016) 'The big squeeze is on in jails', *The Sunday Telegraph*, December 18: 7.

Hedderman, C. (2011) 'Policy developments in England and Wales', in R. Sheehan, G. McIvor and C. Trotter (eds) *Working with Women Offenders in the Community*, Abingdon: Willan, 26–44.

Howe, A. (1988) 'Aboriginal women in custody: A footnote to the royal commission', *Aboriginal Law Bulletin*, 30: 5–7.

Inspector of Custodial Services (WA) (2014a) *Female Prisons in Western Australia and the Greenough Women's Precinct* (No. 91), Perth: Office of the Inspector of Custodial Services, http://oics.wa.gov.au/wp-content/uploads/2014/10/91-Greenough-Women.pdf.

Inspector of Custodial Services (WA) (2014b) *Report of an Announced Inspection of Bandyup Women's Prison* (No. 93), Perth: Office of the Inspector of Custodial Services, http://www.oics.wa.gov.au/reports/93-report-announced-inspection-bandyup-womens-prison/.

Inspector of Custodial Services (WA) (2015) *Report of an Announced Inspection of Boronia Pre-release Centre for Women*, www.oics.wa.gov.au/wp-content/uploads/2015/10/OIC-Boronia-Report-100.pdf.

Johnston, E. (1991) *Royal Commission into Aboriginal Deaths in Custody, National Report* (Vols 1–5), Canberra: AGPS.

Kilroy, D. and K. Pate (2010) 'Activism around gendered penal practices', *Current Issues in Criminal Justice* 22: 325–343.

Lawrie, R (2003) *Speak Out Speak Strong*, Aboriginal Justice Advisory Council NSW http://nla.gov.au/nla.arc-38089.

MacGillivray, P. and E. Baldry (2015) 'Australian indigenous women's offending patterns' *Research Brief* 19, Sydney: Indigenous Justice Clearinghouse, pp. 1–12.

Marchetti, E. (2007) 'Indigenous women and the RCIADIC: Part I', *Indigenous Law Bulletin* 7(1): 6–9.

Ministry of Justice (UK) (2016) *Statistics on Women and the Criminal Justice System 2015*, London: Ministry of Justice.

Nagle, J. (Justice) (1978) *Report of the Royal Commission into New South Wales Prisons* Sydney: Government Printer.

New Economics Foundation (2012) *Women's Community Services: A Wise Commission* London: New Economics Foundation.

NSW Legislative Council Select Committee on the Increase in Prisoner Population (2000) *Interim Report: Issues Relating to Women*, Sydney: NSW Parliamentary Papers.

NSW Women in Prison Taskforce (1985) *Report of the NSW Taskforce on Women in Prison,* Sydney: Government Printer.

O'Gorman, K. (2000) 'Campaign against Windsor Women's Prison', *Green Left Weekly*, September 13, www.greenleft.org.au/content/campaign-against-windsor-womens-prison.

Ombudsman for the NT (2008) *Report of the Investigation into complaints from women prisoners at Darwin Correctional Centre*. At: www.ombudsman.nt.gov.au/publications/report-investigation-complaints-women-prisoners-darwin-correctional-centre.

Players, E. (2013) 'Prisons and privatisation: Policy, practice and evaluation', in A. Dockley and I. Loader (eds) *The Penal Landscape: The Howard League Guide to Criminal Justice in England and Wales*, Milton Park: Routledge, 26–48.

Plechowizc, L. (2015) 'Women's centres', in J. Annison, J. Bradford and J. Deering (eds) *Women and Criminal Justice: From the Corston Report to Transforming Rehabilitation*, Bristol: Policy Press, 119–135.

Productivity Commission (2017) *Report on Government Services 2016*, Canberra: Productivity Commission.

Queensland Ombudsman (2016) *Overcrowding at Brisbane Women's Correctional Centre*, Brisbane: Queensland Ombudsman.

Searcy, J. (1991) 'Prison deaths: Campaign and reform', in E. Baldry and T. Vinson (eds), *Actions Speak: Strategies and Lessons from Australian Social and Community Action*, Melbourne: Longman Cheshire, 203–214.

Social Justice Commissioner (2005) *Social Justice Report 2004*, Sydney: Human Rights and Equal Opportunity Commission.

Standard Guidelines for Corrections in Australia (2012) www.aic.gov.au/media_library/aic/research/corrections/standards/aust-stand_2012.pdf.

Stubbs, J. (2013) 'Indigenous women and penal discourse', in K. Carrington, M. Ball, E. O'Brien, E. and J. Tauri (eds) *Crime, Justice and Social Democracy*, Houndmills: Palgrave Macmillan, 248–266.

Timms, P. (2016) 'NSW Government accused of sneaking through changes to prison cell sizes 'in the deep of the night'', *ABC Radio*, PM, 8 October 2016.

Tomczak, P. (2017) *The Penal Voluntary Sector*, Milton Park: Routledge.

Victorian Ombudsman (2015) *Investigation into the Rehabilitation and Reintegration of Prisoners in Victoria*, Report to Parliament, Melbourne: Victorian Ombudsman, www.ombudsman.vic.gov.au.

Vinson, T. (1982) *Wilful Obstruction: The Frustration of Prison Reform*, Sydney: Methuen.

Weatherburn, D. and S. Ramsey (2016a) *Trends in Indigenous Offending NSW: 2001–2015* (Bureau Brief No. 117), Sydney: NSW Bureau of Crime Statistics and Research.

Weatherburn, D. and S. Ramsey (2016b) *What's Causing the Growth in Indigenous Imprisonment in NSW?* (Bureau Brief No. 118), Sydney: NSW Bureau of Crime Statistics and Research.

Zdenkowski, G. and D. Brown (1982) *The Prison Struggle*, Ringwood Vic: Penguin.

8

'UKHOHLIWE'

A South African perspective on the Corston Report[1]

Lillian Artz

Introduction

There is an undeniable universality reflected in the Corston Report's (2007) observations on the particular vulnerabilities of women in prisons, including the heightened prevalence of mental illness and substance abuse, self-harm and deaths in custody; the pervasive histories of violence and abuse; and the marginalisation of women-specific needs in relation to health and hygiene, mental health services, parenting and childcare, privacy, rehabilitation and transitional opportunities post-release. Stemming from Baroness Jean Corston's observations of the conditions and effects of imprisonment are, from some perspectives, ambitious proposals for reform. These proposals assume: particular structural 'spaces', a common law framework, the existence or accessibility of public service institutions and basic social services, inside and outside prison, for sentenced offenders and the general population, certain perceptions of 'community', and political will. Corston's approach does not necessarily take into account the diverse structural realities of imprisonment in non-Western or developing contexts. In this sense, the radical (re)visioning of women's imprisonment seems far removed from the interminable efforts in post-conflict, transitional and emerging democratic contexts to secure even rudimentary conditions for safe and humane detention.

In analysing the conditions of the imprisonment of women in Africa, Lisa Vetten (2008: 134) revealed that it is not only the unique political histories of African states but

> the culturally specific nature of imprisonment as a form of punishment as well as the diverse legal systems to which women in Africa are subject (including indigenous African law, religious law such as *shari'a*, and colonial systems inherited from the British, Germans, French and Portuguese)

that both complicate the ability to compare contexts and the capacity to easily adopt Western approaches and paradigms in the analysis and reform of women's prisons. Women in Africa are prosecuted for a range of 'offences', based on gender, sexuality, entrenched poverty, sex outside of marriage, abortions, HIV transmission, same-sex relationships (Todd-Gher 2014), 'witchcraft' (UNICEF 2012), adultery (even after a reported rape), livestock and produce theft and the inability to post bail or fines, resulting in high rates of pretrial detention (UNODC 2007). Arbitrary detention and the lack of any legal representation compound already deep inequalities in the imprisonment of African women (Ackermann 2016). The conditions of detention, described by the African Commission's Special Rapporteur on Prisons and Conditions of Detention in Africa (2012: 10, 12) provide a picture of African constraints:

> [...] Africa's prison populations have risen by 71 per cent since 2009 meaning an escalating prison population that aggravates associated problems of overcrowding – central to innumerable problems – and depleted resources, leading to poor prison control, inadequate operation, and ongoing failure to protect inmates' rights. The 2010 figures estimate that almost all African prisons are dangerously above capacity. Around 50 per cent of prisoners are on remand, possibly for crimes as minor as stealing a pen knife or a chicken. A shortage of lawyers and the inmates' lack of means can greatly extend remand periods. [...] Women in African prisons are overwhelmingly poor and uneducated. They are frequently incarcerated for crimes such as murder and attempted murder, infanticide, abortion, theft and alcohol brewing (Sudan). Sexism is apparent in the criminalization and sentencing of certain conducts. For example, in many countries abortion – which only women can obtain – is punished by life sentence. Once in prison, discrimination against women persists. Vocational and recreational programs are more often than not inadequate. Prisons often lack appropriate supplies to accommodate menstruating women.

The Corston Report was not intended in its reach for a global audience, but many of the transformative recommendations Corston proposes are promising practices in any context. Corston's references to integrated, holistic and women-centred strategies, combined with the preferment of non-custodial and alternative sentencing, are well-respected principles that should be applied in sentencing practices and prison reform. However, while many African states have signed or ratified a number of progressive international treaties on the rights of prisoners, and the human rights of women more generally, there are indisputable structural obstacles to the application of these norms and principles in practice, at least in this moment of Africa's penal history. This is not to say that Corston's recommendations are not desirable nor that her motivation for 'radical' reform is not compelling. It is the absence of any analysis of 'contexts' – some with seemingly intractable structural conditions – that makes the realisation of these recommendations challenging to advocate for at this juncture. Corston's unambiguous critique of prison conditions, her conceptual concerns about the overuse of custody and her call for a more strategic and better-articulated approach to psychosocial support services are certainly global concerns. There are still penal contexts, however, with almost implausible levels of overcrowding: antediluvian facilities located within severely economically deprived geographies, where the implementation of her recommendations would be extremely challenging. The question is whether one sees Corston's reimagining of women's imprisonment – towards more communal, less institutionalised spaces – as aspirational for 'justice' systems or whether it forces a further vision for penal reform in diverse geopolitical contexts.

As there are only a handful of studies and regional human rights reports on women in prison in Africa, the experiences and conditions of women in prison in South Africa will be used to analyse the extent to which Corston's recommendations can be considered and redefined in other, developmental settings. South Africa is an example of how the complex colonial and apartheid systems have left a legacy of a deeply fractured state and society. The management of offenders, who are seen as creating further insecurity in an already fragile sociopolitical context, makes advocacy for alternative sentencing and the improvement of prison conditions particularly challenging. Since the dismantling of apartheid and the emergence of a new democratic state, South Africa has undergone, and continues to undergo, massive political, social, legal and economic redress. This is within a context of continued economic and racial inequalities, challenges with basic service delivery, contested leadership, high crime rates and corruption. Within this, is a fractured and overburdened criminal justice system.

In Corston's (2007: i) Foreword, she writes,

> There are some crimes for which custody is the only resort in the interests of justice and public protection, but I was dismayed to see so many women frequently sentenced for short periods of time for very minor offences, causing chaos and disruption to their lives and families, without any realistic chance of addressing the causes of their criminality.

It is the disproportionate, and sometimes arbitrary, sentencing and punishment regimes, coupled with deplorable conditions of incarceration, that remain the biggest challenges for prison reform advocates in developing countries. South Africa's mandatory minimum sentencing regime, and the absence of endorsed noncustodial options, has resulted in the over-utilisation of custodial sentencing. Disparities based on race, gender and financial status (particularly the ability to secure private legal counsel) continue to characterise sentencing outcomes. While South Africa is not representative of countries in Africa, being generally better resourced and arguably more advanced in terms of general infrastructure, it does share some fundamental features regarding conditions of imprisonment with other African and developing states. It is from this position that this chapter will reflect on the feasibility of Corston's recommendations.

An enabling legal context

Since 1994, the year of the democratic elections, South Africa has established a strong legal framework and a progressive body of jurisprudence that promote fundamental human rights and protect vulnerable persons from violence and ill treatment. It has signed and/or ratified a number of important international and regional human rights conventions,[2] many of which have been judiciously integrated into domestic laws and policies – such as the South African Constitution and Bill of Rights (108 of 1996), which has been internationally acclaimed for its progressive principles on equality – and has powerfully reinforced these rights within legal jurisprudence and case law. Lukas Muntingh (2012: 266) has argued that South African courts have been particularly eager to adopt 'a progressive and expansive interpretation of prisoners' rights, especially where their conditions of detention and the actions of the [Department of Correctional Services] have posed a threat to, or already violated, the right to dignity'. He further argued that when one considers the rights enshrined in the 1996 Constitution and the successive case law, there are clearly articulated and, by international standards, progressive human rights obligations that promote and reinforce prisoners' rights, including with regard to the conditions under which they are detained. Muntingh (2012) cites examples of this emerging jurisprudence on conditions of detention to include the right to dignity, solitary confinement, access to medical care, access to electricity, transfers to maximum-security prisons and the transfer of children sentenced to a reform school from prison to reform schools. However, even with ongoing pressure from human rights organisations, it took 15 years after ratifying the *UN Convention against Torture and Other Cruel, Inhuman or Degrading Treatment or Punishment* (UNCAT 1984) for the South African government to enact the *Prevention and Combatting of Torture of Persons Act* (No. 13 of 2013), a law that created the specific offence of torture in places of detention. The reference in the Act's Preamble to South Africa's 'shameful history of gross human rights abuses, including the torture of many of its citizens' is of symbolic importance to a country early in its democracy.

While well reinforced on paper, South African human rights and harm prevention laws suffer from partially promulgated legislation, widespread implementation and compliance challenges as well as a sustained absence of specifically designated state budgets to support implementation (Artz 2017). The actualisation of human rights, particularly of the rights of prisoners, is far from that powerfully articulated in the Constitution through case law or in prison policy. For example, findings of the South African-based Article 5 Initiative[3] maintain that there is significant disparity between what the law provides in terms of safeguards for persons deprived of their liberty and what occurs in practice, with reports of torture and other ill treatment of persons deprived of their liberty.[4] As key challenges to the promotion of human rights in prison settings, the Article 5 Initiative also highlights overcrowding and a growing prison population; increasing sentence lengths and a rapid increase in prisoners serving life imprisonment; a high mortality rate amongst prisoners, presumably due to HIV/AIDS and other chronic disease; high levels of inter-prisoner violence; the assault of prisoners by officials, often with fatal consequences, and an increasingly youthful prison population (Artz et al. 2013).

Corston's specific recommendation for government(s) to take a more proactive, gender-centred approach to the treatment of prisoners, an approach that has been well articulated through the 2010 *United Nations Rules for the Treatment of Women Prisoners and Non-Custodial Measures for Women Offenders* (the *Bangkok Rules*), has yet to take any noticeable effect in South African prisons. This is largely as a result of these principles and rules having gone unnoticed, or disregarded, by policymakers and independent judicial oversight and monitoring bodies.[5] The governance and transformation of the South African prison system is guided by two 'White Papers' published by the Department of Correctional Services (DCS) in 1994 and 2005, the Correctional Services Act (1998; as amended 2011) and the White Paper on Remand Detention Management (2014). Although the White Papers recognise the poor conditions of DCS facilities, overcrowding and the needs of special categories of offenders, including women, little has been done to address these. Only a few paragraphs are devoted to the needs of women in the White Paper (2005) as a 'special category of offenders', and two of these relate to the needs of mothers of children. Although the White Paper notes that 'rehabilitation processes must also be responsive to the special needs of women' (DCS 2005: 4) and that the DCS's 'approach to gender will inform the management of female offenders' (DCS 2005: 68), it provides no insight as to what those special needs are, apart from the obligation to incarcerate women as close to their homes as possible and the obligation to provide women with development opportunities on a non-discriminatory basis (DCS 2005). No further guidance is given about what these 'non-discriminatory opportunities' should entail. For mothers of young children, the DCS recognises the need to provide appropriate crèche facilities and mother-child units as well as an appropriate environment for visitation for those children not living with their mothers (DCS 2005).

A disabling social context: South African demographic data

To better understand the complexities of prison reform, including the challenges of advocating, at least in part, for abolitionism and the promotion of non-custodial sentencing in South Africa, the socio-demographics of the country must be presented. This context is important, not only because South Africa has been referred to as one of the 'most crime-ridden and unequal countries' in the world but also because the amalgam of pressing developmental needs in South Africa makes advocating for the social and institutional security of prisons particularly challenging. With less than 4 per cent of the South African prison population composed of women (DCS 2016), (re)prioritising state resources to focus on 'women in prison', given the already staggering levels of violence against women in the country, makes this quest seem even further out of reach.

Statistics South Africa's last census publication was in 2012 (Statistics South Africa-Revised 2012). For general context, it reports the population of South Africa to be 51.7 million, of which 52 per cent is female. The population is categorised into four main racial groups: 79.2 per cent of the population is classified as African (Black), 8.9 per cent as White, 8.9 per cent as Coloured[6] and 2.5 per cent as Indian (Statistics South Africa 2012). Life expectancy at birth is estimated at 54.9 years for males and 59.1 years for females. In terms of levels of education, the census reports that 23.2 per cent of African females and 16.7 per cent of Coloured females older than 20 years are still functionally illiterate, compared to 11.3 per cent of Indian/Asian women and 2 per cent of White women. Functionally illiterate is defined as a person 'who had no education or a highest level of education of less than Grade 7' (Statistics South Africa-Revised 2012: 40). As expected, female unemployment rates are higher: Where the official unemployment rate among men is 25.6 per cent, among women, it is 34.6 per cent.[7] Based on the 'expanded definition' of unemployment, the rate among men is 34.2 per cent, while among women, it is 46 per cent.[8] The estimated HIV prevalence rate is approximately 11.2 per cent of the total South African population, and the total number of people living with HIV is estimated at approximately 6.19 million (Statistical Services of South Africa, 2015). The main causes of death of South Africans are as follows: 47,219 by non-natural causes (accidents, violence) and 411,714 by natural causes, with tuberculosis (TB) as the leading cause of death (8.8 per cent), followed by influenza and pneumonia (5.2 per cent) and HIV (5.1 per cent) (Statistics South Africa-Revised 2012) – all preventable diseases.

Criminal justice statistics not only reveal the extent of violent crime in South Africa but the context in which the criminal justice system is responding to crime through proactive arrest, prosecution, sentencing and custodial measures. The most recent South African Police Annual Report of 2015/16 reported that there were 18,673 cases of murder – 34 per 100,000 (AfricaCheck 2016) – which is 51 murders a day, five times higher than the global average. In terms of other forms of interpersonal violence, the police also reported 18,127 attempted murders (49.7 attempts per day), 51,895 sexual offences (an average of 142.2 per day), 182,933 assaults with the intent to inflict grievous bodily harm (501 per day) and 164,958 common assaults (452 per day) in the 2015/16 reporting year (AfricaCheck 2016).

Within this context of persistent poverty and inequality; high rates of interpersonal violence; escalating levels of mortality and morbidity due to HIV and tuberculosis; violence and injury; chronic disease; and maternal, neonatal, and child mortality (Chopra et al. 2009; Statistics SA 2014), the health, mental health and personal development needs of prisoners are low on a long list of national development priorities. The lack of basic services and high crime rates means that public opinion, encouraged by political and community leaders, is steeply inclined towards 'getting tough on crime and throwing away the key' rather than the safety, support and rehabilitation of offenders.

South African prisons

In her analysis of visible leadership and the development of strategic approaches required to meet the needs of women prisoners, Corston (2007: 10) recommends a 'central repository for information for and about women who offend or are at risk of offending and to promote its use by others'. Implicit in this recommendation is the need for reasonably detailed prison population data and evidence-led interventions and the premise that data means more than just numbers, where data is crucial for policy development, budgeting and resource allocation, monitoring and accountability of the state. At present, the South African prison system has yet to publish prisoner-related data that goes beyond rudimentary rates and profiles of detention. Although correctional services policies in theory have recognised the distinct needs of male and female offenders, data on offenders remains disaggregated only according to the number of sentenced versus pretrial women, and even this data is inconsistently presented in the DCS's annual reports.

The limitations of accessible and accurate biographical and demographic data do not only pertain to female prisoners. While the South African prison system is known to take general admissions and health data once a prisoner enters the system, the collation, analysis and dissemination of detailed offender data is not presented in the annual reports of the DCS. Despite commitments set out in the DCS White Paper (2005) – which refers to itself as 'the principal strategic document aimed at directing the management and service provision of the department and the official policy framework for the operations of DCS' – prisoner demographics are still inadequately presented in the DCS key annual and strategic reports (Artz 2017). There is varying information on the number of correctional services facilities in South Africa, but the most frequently cited number is 240. Of these, nine are female-only facilities, 13 are youth correctional facilities, 130 are male-only facilities and 86 accommodate both male and female offenders (there is no information on the remaining two). The DCS annual reports provide only a few key indicators of imprisonment. These are mainly incarceration rates and sometimes include offence profiles. Mostly, they focus on 'achievements and challenges', of the DCS in terms of its own administrative, financial and human resource operations.

The DCS Annual Report of 2015/16 stated that there were 161,984 offenders in South African prisons, of whom 4193 were women. Of the total population of women in prison, 3,036 were sentenced prisoners and 1,157 were unsentenced. This is a 5 per cent increase from previous year ($n = 3,915$ in 2014/15) and 18 per cent from three years earlier ($n = 3,380$ in 2012/13), a sign that custodial sentencing of women will not soon find relief. The most recent and publicly accessible data from the DCS on the offences for which women are most likely to receive a custodial sentence comes from the 2013/14 Annual Report (the 2015/16 report does not contain this breakdown). It notes that most crimes committed by women were 'economically related' (45 per cent) – though this term is not defined – with 'aggressive crimes' being the second most prevalent type for which women are incarcerated (38 per cent). There is no other official South African data on women in prison. The most detailed sentencing and prisoner profile data emanates from a few key studies.

For example, the National Institute for Crime Prevention and the Reintegration of Offenders (NICRO 2014) found that since 1994, the year of the first South African democratic elections, the number of sentenced prisons has increased by 22 per cent, with a peak of incarceration in 2004, 10 years into democracy. At the time, one-third of prisoners (32 per cent) were serving less than 6 months to 5 years, 20 per cent were serving 5–10 years, 29 per cent were serving 10–20 years (one-third of which were serving 15–20 years), 10 per cent were serving over 20 years and 9 per cent were serving life sentences. Increases in sentences from 2004 to 2010 were also analysed by NICRO (2014): The number of offenders serving 10–15 years increased 238 per cent from 2004 to 2010, with those serving 15–20 years and more than 20 years increasing 335 per cent and 443 per cent, respectively. Life imprisonment during this period increased by a staggering 2,197 per cent (NICRO 2014).

There is no empirical evidence that explains increases in sentences and the use of custodial sentencing during this period, but it is an unsettling trend, particularly when contemplating advocating for alternative sentencing and noncustodial measures. Some attribute this pattern of sentencing to the *Criminal Law Amendment Act 105, 1997*, which made provision for mandatory minimum sentences.[9] Section 51 of the Act lists a range of offences (i.e. murder, robbery and rape) and prescribes mandatory sentences. This includes life imprisonment for murder and rape except where 'substantial and compelling' circumstances can be found by the courts to justify a lesser sentence. There are a range of aggravating factors that the Act requires the court to consider, including whether the offender is a first or repeat offender, whether the offence was committed with 'common purpose' and the age and mental capacity of the victim, among others. The term 'substantial compelling circumstances' is not defined and therefore has been subject to wide interpretation despite the extent to which it has limited the discretion of Magistrates and Judges in sentencing.[10]

Information about women in prison is even more difficult to locate. The lack of disaggregated data by the DCS and the Office of the Judicial Inspectorate in their annual reports to parliament, poor documentation systems and no ascertainable prisoner information 'upstreaming' system, combined with the highly dispersed population of women prisoners over a vast geographical region (91 facilities throughout the country), mean there is no repository or substantive analysis of information about women in South African prisons that can be consulted in efforts to initiate reform. Small-scale, prison-specific studies have gone some way towards providing a socio-demographic picture of women in prison, their pathways to imprisonment and their experiences within and after prison (Africa 2015; Artz et al. 2012; Haffejee et al. 2005; Luyt and du Preez 2010).

Together, these studies reveal the complex lives of women in prison. Louis Luyt and Max du Preez (2010) and Lillian Artz et al. (2012) found that the average South African female offender is in her mid- to late thirties, is likely to be single or divorced, has children (78 per cent in Luyt and du Preez, 75 per cent in Artz et al.), is very unlikely to have completed secondary school (30 per cent in Luyt and du Preez, and 9 per cent in Artz et al. matriculated), had her first children between the ages of 16–19 years old and was incarcerated for the first time at the time that these studies were undertaken (57 per cent in Luyt and du Preez, 74 per cent in Artz et al.). South African women prisoners are much less likely than men to be serial offenders or recidivists, and their age of first convictions is about 10 years older than that of men. 47 per cent reported having had, or having, a male member of the family in prison. Male siblings constituted a third of these incarcerations (28 per cent). Just over a quarter (27 per cent) of women had a 'few friends' with previous incarcerations.

Contrary to international literature, which suggests that the offences that women engage in are typically 'less serious, violent, and profitable' (Becker and McCorkel 2011: 79), leading feminist criminologists argue that certain offences are expressly gender-related (Belknap et al., 1997). Artz et al.'s (2012) study found that South African women were sentenced mainly for violent offences such as murder (32 per cent) and armed robbery (11 per cent), constituting almost half of the female prison population. Similar to Anglo-American research, this research found that most of those women who committed murder did so against someone they knew or had an intimate relationship with.

The Artz et al. (2012) study also reflected burdens that many women in South Africa face: 75 per cent reported having children, 45 per cent of whom had their first child between the ages of 16–19. Most received no support from the fathers of their children. Only 50 per cent reported having a 'regular' income prior to incarceration. Disclosures of experiences of abuse revealed the multiple victimisations experienced by women, committed by perpetrators with different levels of responsibility and attachment to them over the course of their lifetimes. Experiences of physical abuse as a child were disclosed by 38 per cent; 29 per cent reported childhood sexual abuse, and 67 per cent had experienced physical or sexual abuse as adults. Haffejee et al. (2005), who surveyed 569 female prisoners, found disturbing levels of trauma and mental health issues. Self-harm was reported by 11 per cent of the women in their study; 23 per cent had suffered suicidal ideation, and 16 per cent attempted suicide.

Regrettably, deaths in custody due to natural or unnatural causes are an issue not reported in a gender-disaggregated form by the DCS. In 2015/16 DCS Annual Report, 62 deaths in custody were reported, but there is no public record of how many were women or children. The main causes of unnatural deaths in South African prisons are suicides 'due to hangings and overdoses' (DCS 2016: 53). Also absent in these reports are records of injuries or violence against prisoners – by other prisoners or staff – though incidents against DCS personnel are reported.

Of particular concern are cases of reported deaths (and other human rights violations) in police custody. These are reported annually by the Independent Police Investigative Directorate, an arm of the South African Police Services, and other municipal policing services, that is responsible for investigating complaints against the police. This service also does not disaggregate cases of deaths in custody in terms of gender or age or, for that matter, make reference to persons with mental health issues or psycho-social disabilities, undocumented migrants/refugees, foreign nationals or any other marginalised or vulnerable groups. In the last period under review (2015/16), there were 216 deaths in police custody (of which 66 were due to suicide/hanging), 366 deaths as a result of police action (of which 109 were in police cells), 112 reported rapes by a police officer (46 per cent by an officer on duty) and 23 reported rapes while in police custody, 145 cases of torture of detainees and 3,509 cases of assault against arrestees/accused persons. It can be assumed that the majority of cases of rape were committed against women. In other contexts, these matters would go unreported – such as the case of incommunicado detention or under authoritarian regimes – or be met with public outrage or the establishment of Commissions of Inquiry. In South Africa, these annual rates of deaths in custody are met with administrative reviews and disciplinary actions.

The indignity of imprisonment in South Africa

Oppler (1998) explains that, historically, the one distinguishing feature of South African prisons was its resemblance to apartheid state mining compounds that housed mine workers in large communal cells filled with rows and rows of metal bunk beds. This 'design' has hardly changed. Documented and publicly available accounts of prison conditions are scarce and mainly biographical, reported through investigative media or documented covertly. This is because the DCS has generally been reluctant to allow external researchers to document these conditions or has not permitted these conditions to be published in the public domain. The first post-apartheid report on prison conditions in South Africa was undertaken by the Jali Commission in 2001, appointed by the President of South Africa (Thabo Mbkei) to investigate incidents of maladministration, violence and corruption. The findings were candid and unprecedented and exposed frequent abuses of power by DCS officials, including the rape of female prisoners in their cells, coerced sex and 'sexual favours' with prison officials in exchange for work privileges and the overlooking of extensive abuse of transgendered prisoners by other prisoners and officials (Stone 2015).

While progress has been made in terms of the administration of prisons since the Jali Commission, with the establishment of monitoring and reporting mechanisms for violations against prisoners, little has been revealed about the improvement of structural conditions of detention. In 2015, Constitutional Court

Justice Edwin Cameron wrote a candid report on the remand and women's sections of Pollsmoor Prison (Cape Town) (Cameron 2015: 13–15). His detailed observations capture inhumane and deplorable conditions:

> Entering cells in the remand detention centre proved to be a shocking experience. The conditions we witnessed can, with deliberate understatement, only be described as appalling. The overcrowding is extreme. To know, statistically, that there is 300% overcrowding does not prepare the outsider for the practical reality. Again, with understatement, it can only be described as horrendous. There is an average of 65 inmates per cell. The overcrowding is practically, undoubtedly and daily degrading and hazardous for every detainee subjected to it. The cells were filthy and cramped. Detainees are forced to share single mattresses, often on triple bunk beds. Those who are unable to secure a bed have to sleep on the floor. In one of the cells, we noted 60 inmates with 24 beds. There are no sheets on the beds. Inmates reported that bedding and mattresses have never been washed. Consistently with [the prison doctor's] reports, they complained of skin boils, scabies and severe itchiness. Some detainees displayed rashes, boils, wounds and sores to us. The ablution facilities we saw were deplorable. 50 to 60 people are forced to use one toilet and one shower. The toilets we saw had no seats, and the showers lacked shower heads. No privacy is possible. The drains in the first three cells we visited were blocked. And the toilets did not flush. Inmates are forced to flush the toilet with buckets. They are also forced to use the sink to bathe. And it appears they are also forced to use it to urinate. It appeared to leak and smelt of urine. Uniform reports to us suggested there is no hot water for the shower. Even in the middle of the day, the cells were dark, dingy and cold. There is hardly any natural light. And artificial lighting in the cells is inadequate. Several windows are also broken. The thickness of the air and lack of ventilation was palpable.

With specific reference to the women's section in the prison, Judge Cameron reports,

> The remand cell visited was in as poor a condition as the male remand cells. 94 women were crowded into a poorly aerated room. The women shared beds or slept on the floor on thin mattresses. The mattresses were stinking. There was no working toilet, a clogged sink drain and only cold water. They showed us tattered and torn sheets and blankets, which were infested with lice. They noted that the cell was also infested with cockroaches. Finally, the women complained that as remand detainees they were not afforded library books or magazines to read. Fights often broke out. They attribute this to extreme boredom.
>
> *(Cameron 2015: 25)*

TABLE 8.1 Bed Capacity and Overcrowding in Three South African Prisons

Prison	Approved bed capacity	Number of inmates	Excess number of inmates	Overcrowding
Pollsmoor (Cape Town)	329	744	415	126%
Durban	244	443	199	82%
Kgosi Mampuru II (Pretoria)	166	267	101	61%

Source: Figures derived from PSC (2016), Table 1, p. 4. Available at: www.psc.gov.za/documents/reports/2016/Consolidated%20report%20on%20service%20delivery%20inspections%20conducted%20in%20the%20department%20of%20correctional%20service.pdf. Accessed 24 August 2017.

In 2016, the Public Service Commission (PSC) of South Africa provided prison capacity and overcrowding data in women's sections from three prisons as shown in Table 8.1.

The PSC's Report (2016) also found that Pollsmoor's Admission Centre (remand section) was 180 per cent overcrowded, with 4,538 prisoners in the bed capacity of 1,619. Cells meant to accommodate 20 prisoners had 72 prisoners sharing the space, and those with medical conditions such as TB and mental health issues were forced to share cells with other prisoners. The conditions of cells at the Female Centre at the Kgosi Mampuru II Prison were 'untenable', 'highly congested and cluttered' and 'untidy and not fit for human habitation' (PSC 2016: 5). The environment was unhygienic, posing serious health risk as cells had open toilets that were filthy due to overcrowding (PSC 2016: 10). Artz et al.'s (2012) research found similar conditions, with large communal cells having only two showers, two sinks and two toilets (at least one of which was often not working) for 30 or more women. Many women reported waking at 2 or 3 a.m. in order to shower and be ready for 6:30 a.m. parade.

These findings have been presented to provide a picture of prison spaces and the contours of crime and imprisonment in South Africa. They constitute a clear and deliberate depiction of social 'context', of legal practices and of institutional realities and fill the critical gaps about women in prison that should be included in official reports. Yet this data, as compelling as it is, does not provide the complete picture. It does not wholly support the contention that, in these contexts, Corston's reimagining of women's imprisonment is something (or a series of somethings) that can be easily, or even usefully, adopted, due to vastly diverse social, geopolitical and institutional contexts. To take this further, what follows focusses on women's health and mental health in South African prisons. It explores representations of justice, equality and security and questions notions of 'community-based and non-custodial sentencing' and abolitionism. This does not mean that the philosophical foundations of these positions are rejected but rather that the context poses particular challenges.

Health, mental health and well-being: the contradictions of women's imprisonment in South Africa

The South African DCS is mandated by domestic and international law to provide a humane environment for its prisoners, including the provision of healthcare services. The South African Constitution (1996), the bedrock of prisoners' rights, is explicit about the rights of arrested, detained and accused persons. These rights require that

> everyone who is detained, including every sentenced prisoner, has the right to conditions of detention that are consistent with human dignity, including at least exercise and the provision, at the state expense, of adequate accommodation, nutrition, reading material and medical treatment.
>
> *(Section 35(2)(e))*

Human dignity is a non-derogable right. The White Paper on Corrections (2005: 78) has taken the concept of medical treatment a little further and refers to prisoners' healthcare as requiring more than the simple addressing of specific medical problems, stating that the DCS must also 'provide conditions that promote the well-being of prisoners and correctional officials'. The concept of 'well-being' is cited in several places in the White Paper to include 'mental', 'psychological' and 'spiritual' well-being and includes the rights of prisoners to access social and psychological services (DCS 2005: 7, 13, 64, 65, 75, 78). International literature has shown that prison populations are often made up of individuals who, prior to incarceration, lived on the margins of society with poor health and healthcare access (Niveau 2006; Wilper et al. 2009). While the DCS White Paper (2005: 77) recognises that the number of offenders with health issues and communicable diseases entering correctional centres is higher than the national average and acknowledges that 'cramped and inadequate living conditions' make prisoners 'even more vulnerable to disease and infection', it fails to consider the impact of these issues in housing prisoners. Even less attention has been paid to the unique and differentiating health and mental health issues affecting incarcerated women.

The Corston Report (2007) acknowledges the health and mental needs of women prisoners throughout. Corston's recommendations, focussing largely on the role of the NHS, provide few substantive offerings in terms of *prison*-based legal obligations for reform and offer little guidance about the range of services to address the distinct needs of incarcerated women. The *Bangkok Rules* (2010), on the other hand, pay special attention to the heightened vulnerabilities of women in prison, including mental health, family, pregnancy and childcare, reduced access to justice as a result of economic and social disadvantage as well as specific healthcare and hygiene needs. Rules 6 and 7 provide the following guidance:

> *Rule 6*: The health screening of women prisoners shall include comprehensive screening to determine primary health care needs, and also shall

determine: (a) The presence of sexually transmitted diseases or blood-borne diseases; and, depending on risk factors, women prisoners may also be offered testing for HIV, with pre- and post-test counselling; (b) Mental health care needs, including post-traumatic stress disorder and risk of suicide and self-harm; (c) The reproductive health history of the woman prisoner, including current or recent pregnancies, childbirth and any related reproductive health issues; (d) The existence of drug dependency; (e) Sexual abuse and other forms of violence that may have been suffered prior to admission.

Rule 7: If the existence of sexual abuse or other forms of violence before or during detention is diagnosed, the woman prisoner shall be informed of her right to seek recourse from judicial authorities. The woman prisoner should be fully informed of the procedures and steps involved. If the woman prisoner agrees to take legal action, appropriate staff shall be informed and immediately refer the case to the competent authority for investigation. Prison authorities shall help such women to access legal assistance.

In light of prison overcrowding and the transfer of prisoners after sentencing or by request of prisoners to be closer to family, the admissions process is an important opportunity to assess health and mental health needs, as instructed by the *Bangkok Rules*. In South Africa, DCS case officers should complete an admission risk and needs assessment document within six hours of a prisoner's admission (DCS Comprehensive Risk and Needs Assessment (G303); n.d.). Artz et al. (2012) explain that, in theory, the admissions process should involve a comprehensive risk and needs assessment, which must be completed within 21 days of admission in order to develop a more complete picture of the woman's history, needs and interests. However, when discussing the admissions procedures with women in prison, Artz et al. (2012) were told that

> At the store they are searched,[11] all their belongings are handed over to 'property', they are given uniforms, sent to the 'sister' (nurse). The sister asks them questions about their history of illnesses and allergies, takes blood pressure, weight but "doesn't even like to touch you". One participant reported that in Pollsmoor Prison the sister did not give her medication for her high blood pressure but said "When you were doing your crime you weren't thinking of your high blood pressure". Inmates are not asked anything about their reproductive history or mental health. They are not informed of the rules and regulations. This is a problem as it is only when something happens/goes wrong, they are asked why they do not know the rules, or when activities or freedoms are revoked, that they are informed that they were 'privileges' in the first place, so may be removed.
> *(Transcript, Focus group with women in prison; 12th June 2011)*

In Artz et al.'s (2012) study, women prisoners also reported that they do not receive annual general medical check-ups, routine Pap smears or mammograms and that healthcare is reported to be periodic (as opposed to 'routine') and usually provided on the basis of a request by the prisoner. Women had to request sanitary towels from officers and were only issued two pads for every day while menstruating; they were rarely provided with painkillers for menstrual cramps when requested. Again, the *Bangkok Rules* have been instrumental in advocating for basic reproductive health services. Rule 5 stipulates that women's prisons must have appropriate 'facilities and materials required to meet women's specific hygiene needs including sanitary towels provided free of charge'.

Abuse histories

Childhood and adult experience of abuse is probably the single most important factor that distinguishes women prisoners from men. In the in-depth, life story interviews conducted by Artz et al. (2012), 38 per cent of women discussed their experiences with childhood physical abuse, with one-third of women (29 per cent) discussing their experiences of childhood sexual abuse or rape. 67 per cent had experienced domestic violence and/or rape sometime during their adulthood, three times the rate of abuse reported in the general population of South Africa.[12] The average age of victimisation by sexual assault and/or rape was seven years old, with the earliest age of victimisation being three years old and the highest (of those under the age of 18) being 16 years old. Many women interviewed had been sexually assaulted over a period of time during their childhood, with several being sexually assaulted by different men over the course of their childhoods. 62 per cent of those that experienced child sexual abuse were abused by a father figure, while the remaining 38 per cent were sexually assaulted by someone other than a father figure but typically someone trusted or known well to the family. Of those who experienced sexual assault and rape during their childhood, 56 per cent were convicted of murder.

In South Africa, the rates of violence against women and children are among the highest in the world, and the exposure to violence occurs at multiple phases over their lifetimes. The challenge for both sentencing and imprisonment is the recognition of the impact of abuse and the systems that fail women over their lifetimes.

THE STORY OF MELLY – WHEN SYSTEMS FAIL

Despite taking the bold step to protect herself from further violence, Melly's life story features prepubescent (consensual) sexual intercourse, early drug and alcohol abuse (at 13), years of working as a sex worker, and the birth of her first child at the age of 14:

I was sitting in front of the social worker's office up until nine o'clock when they open. She came there, she asked me, 'What are you doing here so early?' I told her, 'No, I know my mother is alive and I want to go to my mother, I'm not staying there [foster care] a day longer.' She asked me why. Then I took off my shirt and I showed her the marks on my body, the bruises and stuff. She asked me, um 'For how long has this been going on?' And I just, I was just looking at her, I couldn't answer her. She took me to the car, she got back into the car and she took me back to the foster parents. She asked them, um 'What is this? For how long is this, this abuse been going on?' Because as far as she know there never were complaints of them and this is the first time this stuff like that. And the men tried to cover up so I told them, 'No, it's been going, it's been going on for a couple of years now. And if I'm right it's been going on ever since we've been living here because that is one of the reasons all of the other children left.' And that was the first time that a social worker found out that none of the seven children were living there anymore.

(Transcript excerpt from Artz et al., 2012)

Corston (2007) argues persuasively for more individualised, women-centred mental healthcare and rehabilitation services. Yet, again, little guidance is offered for minimum standards of care. One could argue that in the South African context, these services 'exist'. Women in South African prisons have access to a psychologist on request, but one psychologist serves approximately 200 sentenced prisoners and is only available twice a week. Social workers are also available but also attend to the needs of hundreds of prisoners, which includes making assessments on admission, providing individual counselling services and running 're-habilitation' groups. Some women, however, reported that prison does provide an opportunity to seek counselling and psychological and psychiatric services that they were unable to access in their communities (Artz 2012). Those able to maintain an ongoing relationship with a mental health professional – either a prison-appointed psychologist or a private practitioner – emphasise the significance of these relationships, particularly as a major form of support in prison. Prison-appointed psychologists and social workers have also been credited with assisting with addiction, depression and anxiety, dealing with childhood trauma and abuse as well as preparing women for family visits and contact with children and court cases over access or custody, services they would have never had access to on 'the outside' (Artz 2012). Yet the nature, accessibility and regularity of these services is not prescribed in any correctional services' policies.

The notion that psychosocial services in prisons are reported by women as being life-changing leads us to the irony of imprisonment of women in South Africa. Our research with women in prison (Artz 2012) forced our research team to (re)consider the concept of prison as place of rehabilitation, not in the conventional, prisoner reform sense of the term but somewhere where women, exposed to intolerable levels of violence and persistent poverty, found 'a place of safety'. While women discussed at length the horrors of incarceration, overcrowding, violence and theft of personal items, invasive cell checks, grossly unhygienic quarters and lack of freedom, some also spoke of the order and routine of prison life as somehow 'comforting', giving their lives structure and stability, where 'there are no decisions to make' and no daily strategies for basic subsistence. The research team tried to put this perplexing notion into some perspective:

> These findings are contradictory to what we *know* about incarceration. The deprivation of liberty, the overcrowding, the lack of privacy, the endless hours and days spent idle seem nothing but undesirable. It mostly is, and the women are clear about this. But there are – and we have our own inherent reservations about stating this – some positive aspects to imprisonment. Or at least, the women that we have interviewed have found something about imprisonment to be 'valuable' in their lives. Although no women reported actively enjoying being in prison, several said that they were glad that they were in prison, or that they had learned valuable lessons while in prison; "I would either have been much worse off, or dead, if I didn't end up here" was a popular response. Several women felt that they have become 'better' people, by learning to control their anger, to be calmer, to be patient, to be disciplined, to respect others, to respect people's boundaries, to be honest, to communicate, to be assertive, and to appreciate the small things in life. Others mentioned that since coming to prison, they were struck by the realisation that the relationships they were in had been bad for them, or that they will no longer tolerate abuse, and have ended or plan to end the relationships. Being in prison removed them from their (often violent) situations, and they were subsequently able to see that those relationships had been unhealthy. For others, prison was a straightforward method of escaping abusive relationships.
>
> *(Artz et al. 2012: 66–67)*

South African psychologist Adelene Africa (2015: 125), who interviewed 24 women convicted of violent crime using a life narrative method, also found women 'focused quite strongly on the transformative role of their incarceration experiences'. She found that women considered incarceration as having prevented them from engaging in any further violent behaviour and protecting them from further victimisation, even death. Other women interviewed by Artz et al. (2012) spoke of 'the outside', their 'communities', as being dangerous places that they did not ever want to return to: places where drugs and alcoholism are endemic, where they are vulnerable and face ostracisation, where support is scarce and poverty a tenacious feature of their lives. When hearing these narratives, it becomes clear that noncustodial alternatives for women in contexts like

South Africa should not be assumed to be a more sensible and proportionate alternative to incarceration. 'Community spaces' are not necessarily ideal places for women. It raises the vexed question about where one begins in providing women-centred, individualised health, mental health and other social development services in the context of national concerns regarding pervasive structural inequalities within South Africa.

Contextualising Corston

More than any concrete recommendation, the Corston Report offers a vision. This vision sees a route (pathway) for how female offenders should be 'managed' within the criminal justice process. It is important to read between the lines of Corston's review, to acknowledge the similarities in institutional conditions for incarcerated women and common individual experiences with violence and vulnerabilities and to tease out minimum standards of care. The vision 'does not lie in abolishing prisons because they are failed institutions, but rather to use them selectively, judiciously and with a clear understanding of their purpose and what they can realistically achieve' (Muntingh 2008: 8). South Africa, and other African states, have not been without guidance from international bodies and instruments as well as African-centric declarations and guidelines that support state parties in establishing monitoring mechanisms, drafting laws and creating guidelines for the implementation of international norms and minimum standards.

The adoption of the *Bangkok Rules* (2010), for instance, concentrates on 'women's health and safety' procedures and promotes 'documentation'. African states have an opportunity to begin a concerted process of screening, recording and reporting on the profile and conditions of women in prisons, not to mention applying the most basic (gender-relevant) admissions and prisoner management procedures in a manner that is compliant with basic international norms. There are many other guiding documents, including the *2015 Doha Declaration*, which proposes that states promote gender-specific measures as an integral part of policies on criminal justice and the treatment of offenders, and other specific regional instruments that have been created by and for African states. The *African Charter on Human and People's Rights* (1986), the *Protocol to the African Charter on Human and People's Rights on the Rights of Women in Africa* (the 'Maputo Protocol' 2003), the *Robben Island Guidelines* (2003) and the *Luanda Guidelines on the Conditions of Arrest, Police Custody and Pre-Trial Detention in Africa* (2014) have substantive provisions relating to the fundamental rights of prisoners and the treatment of prisoners in all places of custody and detention. The *Ouagadougou Declaration and Plan of Action on Accelerating Prison and Penal Reform in Africa* (2003) even calls members states of the African Union to reduce the size of prison populations and to decriminalise antiquated offences that, in effect, criminalise poverty, homelessness and unemployment and result in arbitrary arrests and detention of vulnerable populations. Acknowledging the range of substantive laws and implementation guidelines within the region for minimum standards of care in prisons, the African Commission's Special Rapporteur on Prisons and Conditions of Detention in Africa (2012: 18) has critiqued the lack of progress:

> Whilst governments claim reform and rehabilitation as the aim of criminal justice, in practice, prison systems fail to deliver as expected and recent reports have shown that prison systems in most African countries are in crisis, burdened with overcrowding and an inability to satisfy basic human rights standards, despite states' ratification of regional and international protocols and conventions. Addressing this crisis demands action not only in better resourcing and support of prison systems but in challenging practices throughout the justice system – such as inappropriate sentencing policies – that are responsible for high rates of imprisonment.

It is therefore neither a lack of policy, a lack of vision nor a misguided understanding of the causes and impacts of imprisonment that inhibits prison reform in South Africa and the Africa continent. There are structural barriers and institutional 'spaces' that inhibit (re)visioning of prisons, their purpose and what can be done – however incrementally – to achieve basic minimum standards of care and a more deliberate approach to justice and the rehabilitation of offenders. The challenge for South Africa is to move beyond commitments on paper and to use resources to implement measures that address the increasing levels of imprisonment through sentencing practices, to better understand the purpose and impact of sentencing, particularly of women, in developing contexts and to (re)define the scope and intentions of custodial 'rehabilitation'. An informed and critical engagement of the limitations of the current structural conditions of institutions, together with a challenge to the systemic barriers that lead to overcrowding and the inability to provide basic and humane conditions and services to women in prison, will go some way towards addressing these constraints. This means working towards a more pragmatic, perhaps less ambitious, prison reform agenda that translates 'paper promises' into 'women-centred' practices.

Notes

1 Ukhohliwe is roughly translated from Zulu as 'forgotten' or 'the forgotten'.
2 International instruments include *UN Convention on the Elimination of All Forms of Discrimination against Women* (CEDAW) 1979 (ratified 15 December 1995), the *UN Optional Protocol to the Convention on the Elimination of All Forms of Discrimination against Women* (CEDAW-OP) 1999 (ratified 18 October 2005), the *UN Convention on the Rights of the Child* (UNCRC) on 16 June 1995, the *UN Convention against Torture and Other Cruel, Inhuman or Degrading Treatment or Punishment* (UNCAT) on 10 December 1998. Important regional (African) human rights instruments include the *SADC Protocol on Gender and Development* (signed 17 August 2008) and the *Protocol to the African Charter on Human and Peoples' Rights on the Rights of Women in Africa* 2003, also known as the 'Maputo Protocol' (ratified 17 December 2004), and the *African [Banjul] Charter on Human and People's Rights*, ratified on 9 June 1996.
3 The author's research unit (The Gender, Health & Justice Research Unit, UCT), along with three other organisations, including the University of the Western Cape

(Civil Society Prison Reform Initiative, Community Law Centre), The African Policing Civilian Oversight Forum and the University of Bristol (Human Rights Implementation Centre), established the Article 5 Initiative or A5I. The project aim is to promote the prevention and eradication of torture and other ill treatment in Africa by supporting relevant institutions to improve domestic compliance with both the international and regional human rights obligations under UNCAT, OPCAT and the African Charter on Human and Peoples' Rights (African Charter).

4 See The UN Committee against Torture Consideration of Reports submitted by States Parties under Article 19 of the Convention, Conclusions and Recommendations of the Committee against Torture – South Africa CAT/C/ZAF/CO/1 6–24 November 2006; UN Human Rights Council Summary prepared by the OHCHR A/HRC/WG.6/1/ZAF/3 11 March 2008, paras 5–13; Judicial Inspectorate of Correctional Services 2010 Annual Report 2009–2010 Pretoria, Chapter Three & pp. 59–76; Independent Complaints Directorate 2011 Annual Report 2010–2011 Pretoria.

5 The *Bangkok Rules* provide guidelines for admission procedures (including rules related to family contact, legal advice and the receipt of information on prison rules and the prison regime, and provisions related to caretaking arrangements for children); personal hygiene; healthcare; safety and security; contact with the outside world; prison staff; classification of inmates; prison regimes; prison visits; reintegration upon release; minority needs; and noncustodial measures. The *Bangkok Rules* require state parties to organise and promote research on female criminality, including the reasons that trigger women's confrontation with the criminal justice system, and on programming designed to reduce recidivism. States are further mandated to publicise this research with the aim of reducing stigma and facilitating the social reintegration of female offenders in order to reduce the negative impact of incarceration on them and their children.

6 'Coloured' is a widely accepted but contentious label that refers to people of mixed lineage, often descended from slaves brought to the country from East and Central Africa, the indigenous Khoi and San peoples, and various indigenised Black and White inhabitants. The majority speak Afrikaans (A5I South African Baseline Study, to be published).

7 The Census defines unemployed (official definition) as 'persons who did not work, but who looked for work and were available to work in the reference period' (2012: 48).

8 The Census defines unemployed (expanded definition) as 'persons who did not work, but were available to work in the reference period' (2012: 48).

9 Criminal Law (Sentencing) Amendment Act 38 of 2007.

10 See cases such as *S v Mofokeng and Another* 1999 (1) SACR 502 (W); *S v Malgas* 2001 (1) SACR 469 (2001 (1) SA 1222); *S v Dodo* 2001 (3) SA 382 (CC).

11 There is a *Guide to the Rights of Inmates as Described in the Correctional Services Act and Regulations* that outlines the conditions for bodily searches of inmates. In terms of these guidelines, searchers must be authorised, conducted in private and only a registered nurse or medical practitioner may conduct them. A registered nurse or medical practitioner must also supervise searches involving the taking body of tissue and the detention of a prisoner for the recovery of objects by the normal excretory process.

12 It is estimated that one in five women are victims of domestic violence and that one in four women have been victims of a sexual assault/violation over their lifetime.

References

Ackermann, M. (2016) 'Women in detention in Africa: A review of the literature'. *AGENDA: Empowering Women for Gender Equity*, 106: 80–91.

Africa, A. (2015) 'Bad girls to good women – women offenders' narratives of redemption'. *AGENDA: Empowering Women for Gender Equity*, 196(29): 120–128.

AfricaCheck (2016) FACTSHEET: South Africa's 2015/16 crime statistics. Available at: https://africacheck.org/factsheets/factsheet-south-africas-201516-crime-statistics/. Accessed 2 May 2017.

African Commission on Human and Peoples' Rights (2003) *ACHPR /Res.64 (XXXIV) 03: Resolution on the adoption of the 'Ouagadougou Declaration and plan of action on accelerating prison and penal reform in Africa'*, African Commission.

Artz, L. (2017) 'Women in prison: An African perspective on the implementation of the Bangkok Rules'. In P. H. van Kempen (ed) *Women in Prison – The Bangkok Rules and Beyond*, UK: Intersentia Publishers.

Artz, L., Aschman, G., Dereymaeker, G., Edwards, L., Long, D., Lorizzo, T., Muntingh, L. and Tait, S. (2013) *Practical Monitoring Tools to Promote Freedom from Torture*, South Africa: An Article 5 Initiative Publication funded by the EIDHR Instrument of European Union.

Artz, L., Hoffman-Wanderer, Y., and Moult, K. (2012) *Hard Time(s): Women's Pathways to Crime and Incarceration*, South Africa: UCT/European Union and the Office of the Presidency.

Becker, S., and McCorkel, J. A. (2011) 'The gender of criminal opportunity: The impact of male co-offenders on women's crime', *Feminist Criminology*, 6(2): 79–110.

Belknap, J., Holsinger, K., and Dunn, M. (1997) 'Understanding incarcerated girls: The results of a focus group study, *Prison Journal*, 77: 381–404.

Cameron, E. (2015) *Pollsmoor Correctional Centre – Remand Centre and Women's Centre*, Constitutional Court of South Africa Report.

Chopra, M., Lawn, J. E., Sanders, D., Barron, P., Karim, S., Bradshaw, D., and Jewkes, R. (2009) 'Achieving the health Millennium Development Goals for South Africa: Challenges and priorities', *The Lancet*, 374(9694): 1023–1031.

Constitution of the Republic of South Africa, No 108 of 1996, Pretoria: Government Printer. Available at: www.ilo.org/dyn/natlex/natlex4.detail?p_lang=en&p_isn=45811. Accessed 25 August 2017.

Correctional Services Act (111 of 1998), South Africa: Department of Correctional Services. Available at: www.dcs.gov.za/Publications/Legislation.aspx. Accessed 25 August 2017.

Corston, J. (2007) *The Corston Report: A Review of Women with Particular Vulnerabilities in the Criminal Justice System*, London: Home Office.

Department of Correctional Services (1994) *White Paper on Corrections in South Africa*, Pretoria, South Africa: Department of Correctional Services.

Department of Correctional Services (2005) *White Paper on Corrections in South Africa*, Pretoria, South Africa: Department of Correctional Services.

Department of Correctional Services (2014) *Incarceration Levels 2011*. Available at: www.dcs.gov.za/AboutUs/StatisticalInformation.aspx. Accessed 8 March 2017.

Department of Correctional Services (2014) *2013/2014 Annual Report*, Pretoria, South Africa: Department of Correctional Services.

Department of Correctional Services (2016) *2015/2016 Annual Report*, Pretoria, South Africa: Department of Correctional Services.

Haffejee, S., Vetten, L., and Greyling, M. (2005) 'Exploring violence in the lives of women and girls incarcerated at three prisons in Gauteng Province, South Africa', *AGENDA: Empowering Women for Gender Equity*, 66: 40–47.

Luyt, W. F. M., and du Preez, N. (2010) 'A case study of female incarceration in South Africa', *Acta Criminologica*, 23(3): 88–114.

Muntingh, L. (2008) 'Punishment and deterrence: Don't expect prisons to reduce crime', South Africa: NICRO. *South African Crime Quarterly*, 26: 309.

Muntingh, M. (2012) 'Human rights standards', in *An Analytical Study of South African Prison Reform after 1994*, Thesis submitted in fulfilment of the requirements for the degree of Doctor of Law in the Faculty of Law of the University of the Western Cape.

National Institute for Crime Prevention and the Reintegration of Offenders (NICRO) (2014) *The State of South African Prisons*, 1st edition: South Africa: NICRO Public Education Series.

Niveau, G. (2006) 'Prevention of infectious disease transmission in correctional settings: A review', *Journal of the Royal Institute of Public Health*, 120(1): 33–41.

Oppler, S. (1998) *Correcting Corrections: Prospects for South Africa's Prisons*, Monograph No 29 of October 1998, Pretoria, South Africa: Institute for Security Studies.

Prevention and Combatting of Torture of Persons Act (2013), Republic of South Africa, *Government Gazette*. Available at: www.justice.gov.za/legislation/acts/2013-013.pdf. Accessed 25 August 2017.

Public Service Commission (2016) *Consolidated Report on Service Delivery Inspections Conducted in the Department of Correctional Services*, South Africa: Public Service Commission.

Report of The Special Rapporteur on Prisons and Conditions of Detention in Africa (2012) 52nd Ordinary Session of the African Commission on Human and Peoples' Rights, Côte d'Ivoire, 9–22 October 2012, Available at: www.achpr.org/sessions/52nd/intersession-activity-reports/prisons-and-conditions-of-detention/. Accessed 8 March 2017.

Statistics South Africa (2012-Revised) *Census 2011 Statistical Release, 2012*, Available at: www.statssa.gov.za/publications/P03014/P030142011.pdf. Accessed 8 March 2017.

Statistics South Africa (2014) *Mortality and causes of death in South Africa, 2013: Findings from death notification*, Available at: www.statssa.gov.za/publications/P03093/P030932013.pdf. Accessed 24 August 2017.

Stone, K. (2015) 'The right to privacy for women in detention: Contestations of power in South Africa's penal systems', *AGENDA*, 106(29): 14–23.

Thirteenth Congress on Crime Prevention and Criminal Justice (2015) *Doha Declaration on Integrating Crime Prevention and Criminal Justice into the Wider United Nations Agenda to Address Social and Economic Challenges and to Promote the Rule of Law at the National and International Levels, and Public Participation*, Doha, 12–19 April 2015.

Todd-Gher, J. (2014) 'Policing bodies, punishing lives: The African Women's Protocol as a tool for resistance of illegitimate criminalisation of women's sexualities and reproduction', *African Human Rights Law Journal*, 14: 725–756.

UN General Assembly (1984) *Convention against Torture and Other Cruel, Inhuman or Degrading Treatment or Punishment*. Entered into force 26 June 1987.

UN General Assembly (2010) *United Nations Rules for the Treatment of Women Prisoners and Non-Custodial Measures for Women Offenders*, A/C.3/65/L.5.

UNICEF (2012) *Children Accused of Witchcraft: An Anthropological Study of Contemporary Practices in Africa*, Dakar: UNICEF.

United Nations Office on Drugs and Crime (2007) *Handbook of Basic Principles and Promising Practices on Alternatives to Imprisonment*. Available at: www.unodc.org/pdf/criminal_justice/Handbook_of_Basic_Principles_and_Promising_Practices_on_Alternatives_to_Imprisonment.pdf. Accessed 14 March 2017.

Vetten, L. (2008) 'The imprisonment of women in Africa', in Sarkin, J. (ed.) *Human Rights in African Prisons*, Cape Town: HSRC Press.

Wilper, A. P., Woolhandler, S., Boyd, J. W., Lasser, K. E., McCormick, D., Bor, D. H., and Himmelstein, D. U. (2009) 'The health and health care of US prisoners: results of a nationwide survey', *American Journal of Public Health*, 99(4): 666–672.

9

BEYOND CORSTON

The politics of decarceration and abolition in a punitive climate

Phil Scraton and Bree Carlton

Introduction

The Corston Review (2007) revealed starkly the debilitating consequences directly attributable to the institutionalised neglect of women's and girls' incarceration. Throughout the previous two decades, feminist studies conducted across diverse jurisdictions had demonstrated the impact of gender-specific criminalisation and punishment on women, girls and their families. As discussed in earlier chapters, comparatively low rates of women's incarceration had deflected attention away from the conditions and regimes to which they were subjected, concentrating resources and initiatives on men's prisons. This profound lack of public and political interest in, and commitment to, the development of gender-appropriate regimes stood in marked contrast to the gratuitous, voyeuristic obsession with rare serious crimes committed by women whose profiles were, and continue to be, exploited by the tabloid media. As prison staff have profited from side deals with journalists eager to write the 'latest exposé' of well-known women prisoners, in popular discourse the less sensationalist but more compelling story regarding the pains of incarceration has remained untold.

Jean Corston's 43 recommendations were directed towards penal reform that would improve prison conditions for women while affirming the importance of keeping them out of prison through gender-appropriate alternatives. Conceptually, Corston emphasised distinctiveness, proportionality, holism and integration as fundamental to interventions for women and girls in conflict with the law. Her recommendations endorsed community-based women's centres where women could have their complex needs addressed alongside national diversion initiatives promoting necessary localised support focussing particularly on mental ill health. Alternatives to custody, she argued, required appropriate, affordable and safe housing supported by local community services. Clearly, such wide-ranging alternatives to custody could be realised only through inter-agency cooperation and collaboration. The success of this latter objective, underpinned by several recommendations, demanded a move beyond the boundaries of criminal justice to include housing, education and health services – specifically, mental health and community support initiatives.

In a comprehensive 10-year review of developments post-Corston, Women in Prison (2017) records that of the 43 recommendations, only two, one partially, had been realised. Limited progress had been made on two-thirds of the recommendations, but there had been no progress on 19. This raises profound concerns regarding the United Kingdom (UK) government's commitment to penal reform. Corston's recommendation that a 'clear strategy' be presented within six months of her report's publication, directed towards the replacement of women's prisons with appropriate custodial centres, specifically for 'high risk' prisoners, was rejected.

Other key recommendations for policy and practice reform remain unaddressed. These include reviews of conditions under which foreign national women are held; funding for bereaved families, with appropriate legal representation following a death in custody; immediate establishment of an interdepartmental ministerial group for women offenders; supported accommodation in the community; restriction of custodial sentences to serious and violent offences; the end of prison as a place of retribution or 'safety' or for detoxification; the introduction of community services to replace prison sentences for non-violent offences (84 per cent of women sentenced to prison are convicted of a non-violent offence); immediate access to psychiatric reports to reduce remands; and women-only day centres in all health authorities.

This concluding chapter reflects critically on the limited transformative potential of penal reform within a climate of penal expansionism. It draws on recent studies within the USA and Australia, revealing the inter-sections of class, race and gender underpinning the inexorable rise of women's imprisonment. This brings into stark relief the significance of and tension between decarceration, a clear commitment within Corston, and a renewed politics of abolition rejected out of hand by Corston. Revealing persistent deficits within penal reformism, the chapter interrogates the decarceration: abolition agendas and their theoretical foundations, recent advances and future potential.

Contextualising Corston

On 25 May 1895, in highly publicised and controversial circumstances, the playwright and author Oscar Wilde was found guilty of 'gross indecency' and sentenced to two years' hard labour. The appalling conditions he suffered in Pentonville and Wandsworth prisons, including hard labour, a starvation diet and sleeping without a mattress, broke his health but not his intellect. Following release he wrote *The Ballad of Reading Gaol*, exposing the 'bricks of shame' within which men, women and children endured extremities of violent incarceration – 'a foul and dark latrine', where 'some grow mad, and all grow bad, and none a word may say' (Wilde, n.d.). Calibrated pain was inflicted purposefully and callously within the prison under the 'hard, pitiless' gaze of captors whose brutality was commonplace. Recounting the irreversible damage perpetrated on the body alongside destruction of the human spirit, Wilde captured the immediacy of the personal within the routine of the institutional. The damage to prisoners was profound and enduring: 'on their release [they] carry their prison about with them into the air... hid[ing] it as a secret disgrace in their hearts'. Outside the gates, the prisoner experienced abandonment 'at the very moment when its [the State's] highest duty towards him begins'.

The so-called new prison era of 19th-century incarceration was laid bare by Wilde's account, as it was again almost two decades later when women protesting for suffrage were imprisoned under the 1913 Prisoners (Temporary Discharge for Ill-Health) Act – known as the 'Cat and Mouse' Act. Following violent arrests, in gaol and on hunger strike, prisoners were fed forcibly. They experienced 'great suffering', were 'reduced to a dangerous state of illness', were released and, following recovery, returned to gaol (Cole and Postgate 1961: 490). In prison, a letter from Sylvia Pankhurst recalled that

> Twice every day, four, five or six wardresses come in as well as the two doctors. I am fed by a stomach tube. They prise open my mouth with a steel gag, pressing it in where there is a gap in my teeth.

The vindictive, cruel punishment endured by suffragettes clearly demonstrated the limits of penal reform. Throughout the 20th century, the deprivations of women's incarceration persisted, including standing naked on entry; restricted access to underwear and basic necessities; the isolation of lockdowns; institutionalised violence; restricted visits; inadequate healthcare; mental ill heath, self-harm and suicide; vindictive and violent guards; mind-numbing boredom ... the list goes on.

Reflecting on penal reform in early capitalist societies transitioning from feudalism, Michael Ignatieff (1978) establishes that political debate had centred on achieving a balance in the public consciousness: the seriousness of the crime committed matched to the severity of the punishment administered. The principle being that the 'pain' inflicted should be proportionate and therefore 'just'. This shift in emphasis suggested an emerging political commitment to transition prisons from hopeless places of severe punishment to processes of calibrated containment and rehabilitation. The contemporary prison system, as noted by Michel Foucault (1977), originated ideologically not in 'punishing less' but in 'punishing better'.

The contrasting theoretical contexts underpinning such transition are well summarised by Michael Cavadino and James Dignan (2007). The principle of *retributivism* committed the state to assessing the seriousness of the offence and administering a sentence accordingly (now popularly represented as 'payback').

Alongside this, *reductivism* addressed habitual offending, the prison sentence being directed towards *deterrence* via incapacitation and towards *reform* of the individual. The assumption being that prison sentences and their harsh conditions were calibrated to reflect public admonition and encourage crime prevention while providing regimes based on personal reflection, generating mindful restoration and enabling the prisoner's eventual *reintegration* into 'society'. In practice, these contradictory perspectives were, and remain, in permanent tension.

This tension prevails throughout all forms of contemporary incarceration: the control of the prisoner set against care, imposed security set against freedom of movement and association and institutional priorities elevated above personal needs and development. As Joe Sim (2009) demonstrates, contemporary penal regulation – solitary confinement, the use of force and persistent surveillance – has a long history. Arguing that prison regimes reflect continuity rather than discontinuity, he challenges the suggestion that 'rehabilitative discourses have *ever* been an institutionalised presence in the everyday, working lives of prison officers or landing culture that legitimates and sustains their often regressive ideologies and punitive practices' (Sim 2009: 4). Jails are 'invisible places of physical hardship and psychological shredding' in which punishment is administered routinely 'by non-accountable power of prison officer discretion'.

More than any other criminal justice institution, the prison is the most pernicious in disguising its true purpose and operation behind what Nils Christie (1981: 13) argues is a 'shield of words'. Thus, incarceration becomes 'humane containment', the 'person to be punished' becomes the 'client', the prisoner becomes the 'inmate', the cell becomes a 'room' and solitary confinement, euphemistically, becomes 'single-cell containment'. Increasingly in the UK, prison guards are recruited with diploma or degree qualifications. This reflects a climate in which processing and punishing crime adopts a professional veneer through which the debilitation of incarceration and the pains of confinement are 'vanished from the text-books'. As Christie concludes, incarceration strips away all dignity and self-worth, leaving the prisoner 'scared, ashamed, unhappy'.

Every moment of the prisoner's day is routinised: work, healthcare, meals, time out of cell, exercise, visits. Association with other prisoners and access to facilities, even the act of walking freely, are reconstituted as 'privileges' awarded at the discretion of guards and managers whose power is absolute, manifested by imposing penalties for the mildest institutional infractions. A slight breach of prison rules, such as alleged insubordination, leads to the loss of 'privileges' as instant punishment. The jailers' default position is total lockdown, with prisoners individually or collectively confined to their cells for 23 hours a day. Half a century has passed since Erving Goffman (1968: 47) described the inhumanity of the penitentiary: a place where 'self-determination, autonomy and freedom of action' are removed from the prisoner with the purpose of breaking her/his personal will.

Writing on prisoners' 'agency', Mary Bosworth (1999: 3) suggests that prisoners remain 'independent actors whose actions help to determine the meanings and effects of punishment'. Yet the negotiation of institutional power and arbitrary control to which they are subjected, in terms of 'choice, autonomy and responsibility' central to adult agency, is severely curtailed. Bosworth remains optimistic that women prisoners retain the capacity to 'assert themselves as agents'. Undoubtedly, there are spontaneous, even orchestrated, moments of opposition and resistance. But they are contained, regulated and punished within the confines of the closed institution and at the discretion of its guards and managers. Negotiating that discretion on a daily basis is particularly difficult for mothers, who fear that questioning the regime and its routine administration might restrict their access to their children (Moore and Scraton 2014). The extent of regulation imposed routinely on prisoners, the explicit denial of agency even at the most mundane levels, is dehumanising.

Ruth Wilson Gilmore (2007: 243) argues powerfully that 'if the twentieth century was the age of genocide on a planetary scale, then in order to avoid repeating history, we ought to prioritize coming to grips with dehumanization'. In effect, this means establishing and naming the 'deliberate, as well as mob-frenzied, ideological displacements central to any group's ability to annihilate another in the name of territory, wealth, ethnicity, religion'. Further, dehumanisation is a 'necessary factor in the acceptance that millions of people should spend part or all of their lives in cages'. While Gilmore concentrates specifically on racism as the 'ordinary means through which dehumanization achieves ideological normality', the political-economic creation and ideological representation of an underclass within advanced capitalist societies is not determined exclusively by 'race'. Persistent poverty and exclusion reproduce the conditions of working-class marginalisation – a social and structural location that is gendered.

Analysing the impact of mass incarceration in the USA, Drew Leder (2004: 61) provides a graphic account of fundamental restrictions on freedom of movement, right to privacy and mundane choices concerning 'location, dress and actions largely dictated by the state'. Within jail the 'imprisoned body' becomes 'associated with violence and deficit, objectified by a fearful gaze, appropriated by hostile others'. As Leder demonstrates, prison regimes function via regimes of physical and psychological regulation. It is no surprise, therefore, that women in conflict with their jailers face the ultimate sanctions of strip-searches, full lockdown and solitary confinement. Reflecting on women's imprisonment in Australia, Jude McCulloch and Amanda George (2009: 122) conclude, 'coercive removal of prisoners' clothes' constitutes, 'a symbolic enactment of the stripping of rights that accompanies imprisonment ... particularly resonant as an identity-stripping and negating act for women who so often have their identities and rights stripped through sexual assault outside the prison'. Enforced isolation, a 'prison within a prison', constitutes the 'ultimate regulation of the female body' (Shaylor 1998: 386).

The harsh punishments of solitary confinement and strip-searching, alongside less cruel but routine gender-specific regulations imposed on women, demonstrate the persistent, institutionalised failure of unreconstructed penal regimes that purposefully adopt the language and clichés of desistance and rehabilitation. Not only do they impose regimes and routines that undermine and incapacitate, they condemn already troubled, traumatised and vulnerable women and girls to inhumane, degrading and permanently damaging isolation.

Yet policy commitments and mission statements adorning prison corridors and landings offer quasi-evangelical declarations alongside photographs of wildlife and remote places, illustrated by capitalised keywords: 'Hope', 'Motivation', 'Commitment', 'Leadership'. They proclaim human rights standards, warn against bullying and extortion and publicise complaints procedures. The message to the uninitiated is that old regimes have been consigned to history, replaced by a comprehensive, institutional commitment to a duty of care. In this vision, managers and guards, doctors and nurses, psychiatrists and psychologists and all who administer the 'healthy prison' are 'rights compliant', transparent in their dealings with prisoners and accountable through inspection and monitoring.

On the surface, such developments suggest that penal regimes can be transformative, encouraging prisoners to desist from repeat offending. In practice, however, operational regimes mitigate against positive outcomes. For prisoners, 'all reference points to their regular worlds are suspended ... time has no meaning beyond the opening and closing of the spy-hole, keys are turned at another's whim, and weekly visits with loved ones are programmed without consultation' (Scraton 2016: 9). Women prisoners interviewed following arrival in prison for the first time – transport, strip-search, shower, keys, lockdown, noise, stale air, sleeplessness – all recount profound, destructive experiences of hopelessness, loss, guilt and fear (Scraton and Moore 2007).

In their in-depth study of the long-term incarceration of women, considered comparatively with men's experiences, Ben Crewe, Susie Hulley and Serena Wright (2017: 18) state, 'there is no necessary contradiction between recognizing the multiple victimization experienced by the majority of female prisoners, while attributing them with agency, rationality and voice'. The issue, however, is not that prison eradicates totally those three key elements but that it sets severe limits on each, experienced differentially by women, not least in the context of their personal histories. As Crewe, Hulley and Wright conclude, most women prisoners' 'deprivations and debasements' are 'more acutely painful and problematic' than those endured by most men.

For women and men, incarceration is a damaging, alienating and dehumanising process that retains ideological traction derived in the (mis)representation of prison within popular discourse. Consistently defended as subject to democratic accountability via formal processes of 'independent' inspection and monitoring, the persistence of prisons reflects an institutionalised reluctance to challenge 'an apparently intractable culture of casual cruelty' (Medlicott 2009: 259). Moving beyond Diana Medlicott's implicit reformism, David Scott and Helen Codd (2010: 212) demonstrate that prison regimes and practices are 'inherently harmful ... undermin[ing] human dignity', while Richard Quinney (2006: 270) argues eloquently that the social and psychological harm inflicted within prison walls is 'shared by all … anything done to others is done to ourselves'.

In their review of the persistent increase in the prison population in England and Wales, doubling between 1990 and 2010, Mick Ryan and Tony Ward (2015: 107) note that despite a significant reduction in crime rates, 'delivering pain' through incarceration had become 'big business in liberal market economies'. Mick Ryan and Joe Sim (2016: 713) propose that what has been created is 'an edifice of punishment which appears unshakeable in the ongoing conflict to restore law, maintain order and reduce risk to communities beleaguered by feral atavists who are either unwilling or unable to responsibilize themselves'.

Fundamental to the political economy of criminalisation, prison constitutes part of what Christie (1994) identifies as the 'industry' of 'crime control'. Yet, as analysed throughout the preceding chapters, incarcerating women, men and children comes at a high price – material and human. The material opportunities are vast as giant corporations ruthlessly exploit cheap labour offered by captive populations. Eye-watering profits are guaranteed by the opportunism afforded in the commodification and supply of confinement's processes – transporting, feeding, watering, medicalising, visiting, 'educating', working, releasing.

Beyond the profit margins imbedded in private and public institutions, and their broad array of eager goods and services providers, is the less visible human cost. The Hippocratic Oath, taken by medical professionals and paraphrased as 'first, do no harm', obliges medical workers to 'use treatments for the benefit of the ill in accordance with my ability and my judgment, but from what is to their harm and injustice I will keep them'. It establishes a primary 'duty of care', one that should extend beyond medicine to all state institutions that have responsibility for personal health and welfare. This includes the daily routines and interactions within penal institutions where 'reform', 'rehabilitation' and 'desistance' are proclaimed within mission statements. Operational policies, priorities and practices, however, present a different reality. The harms done in the collective name of citizens whose taxes contribute significantly to the process are not restricted to the prisoners confined by reinforced walls, electrified fences and intrusive surveillance.

Richard Quinney (2006: 270) comments that incarceration 'creates populations of incomplete and wounded lives', choreographing 'the dance of the slave and slaveholder, inmate and captor, prisoner and non-prisoner'. Within society, 'no-one escapes' the 'pervasive' harm of the prison 'on all levels, economic, social, psychological, and, ultimately, spiritual'. Accepting that there are 'real and consequential differences' between the 'lives of those in prison and the lives of those outside the prison', the 'damage' and 'injuries' endured by prisoners impact all citizens, most forcefully, the prisoners' families.

Writing nearly two decades earlier, Thomas Mathiesen exposed the illusion that prisons could offer rehabilitation. Penal expansionism was, he argued, no more than a 'fiasco' sustained by contrasting political ideologies and by an uncritical mass media (Mathiesen 1990: 193). Yet, within the 'narrower public sphere' of criminal justice, crime prevention and burgeoning university criminology programmes, minimal attention was paid to abolitionism. The failures of penal reform, the persistence of recidivism and the deceit of rehabilitation were ignored as politicians in the UK and Europe, following their USA counterparts, demanded harsh and lengthy sentences. This 'wave' of 'penal populism', encouraged by 'media panics', reinforced a punitive climate so severe that even penal reform campaigns for more humane regimes were marginalised (Mathiesen 2008: 58). As progressive reform was consigned to history, the prison industrial complex entered a new phase of expansion. It has produced a worldwide 'carceral chill', underpinned by highly emotional demands for 'retribution, incapacitation, and determinate sentencing' that 'purge individualization and resocialization from the practice of punishment' (Whitman 2005: 69). It is a reactionary response born in the USA.

Mass incarceration in the USA: the sharp end of the continuum

Whatever measure is used to assess the level and intensity of imprisonment in advanced democratic states, mass incarceration across the USA is exceptional. During a period when penal reformism throughout Western Europe was exploring potential alternatives to custody, the USA embarked on a programme of unprecedented penal expansion, sacrificing the historically progressive, liberal commitment to rehabilitation on the altar of increasingly punitive incarceration. No longer was the penitentiary portrayed as a site of penitence and hope but as one of condemnation and rejection: a 'space of pure custody, a human warehouse' operating as a 'kind of human waste management' (Simon 2007: 142). What informed this apparent transformation?

The Richard Nixon-Ronald Reagan-George W. Bush Republican presidential dynasty reversed what their administrations perceived as a liberal, 'soft on crime' direction of travel, 'reject[ing] the possibility, and perhaps even the desirability, of rehabilitation' (Western 2006: 60). This reactive intensification of incarceration 'repudiated the philosophy of rehabilitation and its accompanying methods of individualised sentencing' (Western 2006: 61). Incarceration was presented in public discourse as necessary to mobilise and fight the 'war on crime', to incapacitate 'social predators', thereby reaffirming social order. Its legitimacy was secured in political and popular discourse. Locking up felons, whatever the social and economic long-term costs, was 'common-sense'.

As Elliott Currie (1998: 185–186) demonstrates, what followed was an uncompromising commitment to increasingly severe prison sentences. Three offences, regardless of severity, resulted in a prison sentence ('three strikes and you're out'), encouraging a populist, vote-catching and reactionary enthusiasm for incarceration as an antidote to political-economic crisis. Cynically, compelling evidence that violent crimes had roots in 'social exclusion', 'poverty', 'besieged families' and economic marginalization was dismissed. Deploying the rhetoric of Armageddon, 'bursting prisons' were built and filled, worsening the plight of 'devastated cities and a violent crime rate still unmatched in the developed world'.

The exponential growth in the USA prison population removed the 'invisible poor' from plain sight. Their citizenship was revoked through voter deregistration and their unemployed status expunged from unemployment figures. Through this political sleight of hand, the 'disadvantaged' were rendered 'literally invisible', warehoused 'behind the walls of America's prisons and jails' (Western 2006: 87). According to Christian Parenti (1999: 48), during Reagan's presidency the federal judiciary was replete with 'mean spirited, anti-crime, anti-drug zealots'. A profoundly reactionary political and religious backlash was directed against the poor, reflecting the ideological construction of a threatening 'underclass'. Its soft targets were 'idlers', 'loafers', 'scroungers', 'beggars' and 'squeegee merchants', allegedly opting for a 'dysfunctional' lifestyle. They were condemned as marginal by choice rather than circumstance.

Clinton inherited the authoritarian mantle, heralding the Violent Crime Control and Law Enforcement Act as an 'unprecedented federal venture into crime-fighting'. Billions of dollars were invested into the Crime Trust Fund, policing expansion, state prison-building, increasing mandatory sentences and placing severe limitations on parole, extending federal capital punishment, prosecuting juveniles as adults, hiring new border patrol agents, providing advanced surveillance initiatives and streamlining the asylum and deportation processes. Within this context, mass imprisonment became 'self-sustaining', operating 'as an engine of social inequality' and reflecting the political-economic marginalisation that characterised the 'landscape of American poverty and race relations' (Western 2006: 198). For women, as partners of incarcerated men and as the fastest-growing section of the prison population the shift to mass imprisonment had catastrophic consequences on their lives, their families and their communities.

By the late 2000s, both conceptually and politically, mass incarceration in the USA was justified politically and economically as *the* most effective weapon in 'fighting crime', specifically in the 'war on drugs'. Popularised particularly in cities broken by a collapsed industrial base and heralding a seemingly irreversible escalation in poverty, doing time in prison became a 'new normal'. The helplessness experienced within housing schemes riven by unemployment and easily accessible drugs was matched by the vindictiveness of harsh penalties, incorporating 'aggressive incapacitation' and 'containment' (Fleury-Steiner and Longazel 2014: 8). Alongside the 'war on drugs', the 'war on terror' added a further dimension to USA incarceration.

As Avery Gordon (2009: 172–173) notes in her detailed analysis of the rise of the 'military prison', prison guards' 'exceptional brutality' became normalised with the rise of super-maximum imprisonment at the 'cutting edge in carceral technology', providing 'the prototype for the retooling of the military prison'. A century on from Wilde's fierce portrayal of Victorian gaols built on 'bricks of shame', the 'forward march of a more retributive, denunciatory and mortifying discourse of punishment, fuelled by the new right's economic, social and cultural ascendancy' (Sim 2009: 2) in the USA and the UK reversed dramatically any gains achieved by penal reformism.

In the USA, the correlation between 'race', unemployment and poverty consolidated in the 1970s and 1980s. Structural unemployment among Black blue-collar workers rose from an already high figure of 30 per cent to 72 per cent. In poor Black neighbourhoods demoralised by a deepening sense of hopelessness, impoverishment was accompanied by an overwhelming tide of drugs – legal and illegal, particularly crack. Heavy and often unlawful policing, mandatory minimum prison sentences and housing evictions followed. What was popularised as a 'war on drugs' in reality was a 'war' waged against the poor and destitute in economically and politically marginalised communities. Neighbourhood conflicts, reflecting identity and territoriality, contributed to an escalating death toll on the streets. In this context, Dylan Rodriguez (2009: 200) argues, 'the prison regime is the organic descendant of durable and gender-specific mobilisations of anti-Black geopolitical and socioeconomic containment ... and programmatic state terror vis-á-vis domestic police ground wars' (see Gilmore (2007) for a full analysis of USA penal expansionism).

Michelle Alexander (2010) is unequivocal in naming racially targeted hardline policing, the deaths of young Black men and exemplary harsh sentences as the birth of the 'New Jim Crow', exposing a universal deficit in rights within Black neighbourhoods across the USA. As the 20th century dawned, Black people's incarceration, particularly for drug-related offences, had increased exponentially during the previous two decades. Driven by increasingly strident legislation, 'doing time' for drug-related offences extended beyond the served sentence to a state of 'permanent exile' within but apart from the community.

While accepting the significance of Alexander's compelling analysis in revealing the extreme consequences of economic deprivation and political exclusion, James Forman (2017) argues that the relationship between drugs and violence within Black communities remains intrinsically predatory and devastating in its consequences. He considers the 'war on drugs', resulting in escalating sentences, to be a class as well as a 'race' issue, reflected within Black communities by internal economic and territorial divisions. What this debate illustrates is the significance of the interlocking inequalities of class, 'race' and gender as structural determinants of political and economic marginalisation. The consequences are multiple: persistent poverty, inadequate housing, deficient schooling, poor health, punitive welfare and low life expectancy. The intersection of these prevailing structural inequalities is the context in which harsh policing and mass incarceration consolidated as the front line in the 'war'. If this epithet was ever appropriate, it was as an orchestrated war waged against the poor and marginalised.

As Victoria Law (2009: 169) demonstrates in her detailed and moving analysis of women's resistance in USA jails, 'prisons act not only as sites of social control' but also constitute 'sites of violence against women, particularly women of color, poor women who transgress social norms'. The 'war on crime' became cemented as a mantra adopted by the leading political parties in the USA, triggering an intensification and expansion of criminalisation: 'higher rates of arrest, prosecution and incarceration while shifting money and resources away from education, housing, health care, drug treatment, and other societal supports' (Law 2009: 169). This reactionary cross-party political agenda generated an unswerving commitment to the fast-expanding prison industrial complex and its supply pipeline, fuelled by breadline poverty, institutionalised racism and gendered victimisation.

It is a commitment that has been realised but not without opposition. Founded in 1997, the abolitionist organisation Critical Resistance has developed an international movement with the primary objective of ending the prison industrial complex. Based within marginalised communities, Critical Resistance challenges the orthodoxy that prisons are a fundamental necessity in preventing crime and making communities safe. It proposes that those actions defined, prioritised and policed as crimes are the direct consequence of economic marginalisation, political exclusion and structural deprivation. Central to its work is the 'creation of genuinely healthy, stable communities' alongside the eventual abolition of prisons (Critical Resistance 2017).

Justice Now is also a USA abolitionist organisation condemning incarceration as a 'form of violence' directed particularly at women. Rejecting the 'gender responsive project' adopted increasingly in USA women's prisons, Cassandra Shaylor (2009: 159) dismisses Corston's commitment to women-centred imprisonment and proposes a 'radical alternative': 'Platform for Gender Justice'. Its key objective is 'decarceration', comprising 'the closure of prisons and parole reform' and extending to 'moratoria on prison construction'. This includes 'speciality prisons' (for example, gender-responsive facilities, geriatric units and prison hospices) that are 'often sites of more egregious human rights abuses than traditional prisons'.

Institutionalised racism and resistance in Australian prisons

Three decades on from the profoundly disturbing findings of the 1990 Royal Commission into Aboriginal Deaths in Custody (RCIADIC), carceral violence and neglect remain cornerstones of institutional and racialised injustice in Australia (see Cunneen et al. 2013; Johnson 1991). Despite the political and public debate arising from the Commission, national government reform has failed to redress the structural disadvantages and injustices that underpin the disproportionate imprisonment of Aboriginal and Torres Strait Islander people and their high rates of death in custody (Anthony 2016). This includes multiple deficiencies within programmes aimed at reforming the conditions and causes underpinning the deaths in custody of Indigenous women (Porter 2016). Ethan Blue (2016: 3) notes their 'massive over-representation' within the Australian prison population as a consequence of 'colonial patriarchal dominance and, moreover, of the failure of the Royal Commission into Aboriginal Deaths in Custody, to adequately address Indigenous women's experiences with the carceral colonial state' (see also Baldry and Cunneen 2014).

Historically, while penal reform in Australia has achieved some minimisation of harm, it has also been central to penal expansion (Carlton 2016; Russell and Carlton 2013). The administration and targeting of neocolonial criminal justice has proliferated in each State and Territory (see Baldry et al. 2015; Cunneen et al. 2013). It also has driven strong, anti-carceral resistance and campaigns (Carlton 2016). The complex historical and political contexts of proliferation reflect institutionalised control, punishment and genocide perpetrated against Aboriginal and Torres Strait Island people. Colonial settler capitalism continues to exploit Aboriginal land and resources, supported by ideological discourses derived in eugenicist polemics that promote a discourse of racial inferiority (Birch 2007; Wolfe 2001).

In this political context, punitive and reformist ideologies became codependent, generating and implementing harmful, systemic practices targeting Indigenous communities. Consequently, Indigenous people experience markedly lower life expectancy, ill health and poverty, together with over-policing and incarceration at disproportionately higher rates than non-Indigenous Australians (Anthony 2016). Black deaths in prison custody have increased, and prisons have become repositories that neglect or deny the complex structural oppression and deeply imbedded injustices of neocolonialism (Davis 2003).

Institutionalised racism has met with strong resistance and a range of initiatives, including protests spearheaded by women and men surviving increasingly harsh conditions in prison. Strong visions for change have emerged and consolidated, mobilised by the determined action of anti-carceral feminist coalitions (see Carlton 2016). Across several States, anti-discrimination campaigns arose from women prisoners' resistance to being held in regimes and conditions designed for men (see Baldry et al. 2015). Anti-carceral feminists in the community supported rooftop protests, sit-ins, public education campaigns and hunger strikes inside prisons. This collective resistance has led to short-term reforms while remaining committed to decarceration and abolition (see Carlton 2016; Carlton and Russell 2015).

In South Eastern Australia, however, penal reform rooted in anti-discrimination campaigns has contributed to the consolidation and expansion of women's incarceration. This includes increased governance, regulation and control derived in gender-specific responses to risk and need assessed within prisons at the discretion of guards and managers. These unintended outcomes highlight the paradoxical relationship between reform and abolition. While opposition to incarceration from feminist organisations remains resolute, penal reforms have been incorporated within the relentless expansion and violence of incarceration. Adopting the guise of welfare reform, this harsh penal expansionism reflects an alliance of conservative punitive and liberal therapeutic ideologies.

In Australia, the mantra of reform, therefore, ideologically and politically has become integral to the proliferation and expansion of imprisonment as well as conceptualising, developing and delivering physical structures, regimes and cultures that define modern punishment. As Angela Davis (2016: 22) concludes,

> the site of the jail or prison is not only material and objective, it's ideological and psychic as well. We internalize the notion of a place to put bad people. That's precisely one of the reasons we have to imagine the abolitionist movement as addressing those ideological and psychic issues as well. Not just the process of removing material institutions.

Australian abolitionists have adopted a necessarily pragmatic approach in working towards dismantling the established processes of institutionalised criminal justice while, in the short term, continuing to address the excesses and failures of reformist policies and program initiatives. Their primary intention is to minimise harm while progressing the eventual eradication of a system that continues to expand to the detriment of the daily lives of criminalised people and their families (Carlton 2016). While penal reform is necessary, it carries risks and consequences.

Consistently, Aboriginal and Torres Strait Islander campaigners have named, challenged and resisted the continua of structural violence, domination, exploitation, oppression and control rooted in the racism, heteropatriarchy and imperialism on which the colonial carceral complex was founded and has been reproduced. The campaign of resistance has been complemented by activist organisations, including Queensland's Sisters Inside, Victoria's Flat Out Inc. and New South Wales' Women in Prison Advocacy Network. These collectives have established international solidarity with imprisoned women, advocates and activists in the USA, Canada, New Zealand and the UK. Such transnational coalitions facilitate the sharing of activist knowledge, strategies, mutual support and visions towards realising the abolitionist agenda.

Towards abolition

> Judge Carter, of Ohio … favoured the abolishment of prisons and the use of greater efforts for the prevention of crime … Any system of imprisonment or punishment was degradation, and could not reform a man. He would abolish all prison walls, and release all confined within them.
>
> *(Minutes of the Congress of the American Prison Association/American Correctional Association, 1870)*

> There ought to be no jails; and if it were not for the fact that people on the outside are so grasping and heartless in their dealings with the people on the inside, there would be no such institutions as jails … abolish the big ones and the little ones together … they do not accomplish what they pretend to accomplish.
>
> *(Clarence Darrow, Address in Cook County Jail, Chicago, 1902)*

We must destroy the prison, root and branch ... almost anything would be an improvement. It cannot be worse. It cannot be more brutal and useless.

(Frank Tannenbaum, Crime and Community, 1938)

One of the most difficult and ignored of our social problems is prisons – a problem that cannot be ameliorated thru drastic prison reform, but can be solved only through the abolition of prisons ... The advocacy of prison abolition implies simply that other courses of action, including sometimes doing nothing at all, are preferable to imprisonment.

(David S. Greenberg, The Problem of Prisons, 1970)

Four quotes, spanning a century, introduce a handbook first published in 1976 by the Prisoner Education Advocacy Project and republished by Critical Resistance (2005). Presented alongside extensive quotes from a range of academic researchers and policy commentators, these quotes demonstrate that from its inception, the 'modern' prison has been the focus of abolitionist critique, consistently challenging the ever-expanding prison industrial complex.

'Abolish Prison!' 'No More Prison!' – a mantra, a plea, a movement – are exhortations that generate incredulity throughout societies in which prison, as the primary site of punishment, has become locked into the national psyche, inherited as 'common sense'. Angela Davis, pre-eminent abolitionist and former political prisoner, considers in public discourse, 'the prison is considered an inevitable and permanent feature of our social lives', that 'abolition is simply unthinkable and implausible' (Davis 2003: 9). Consequently, abolitionists

are dismissed as utopians and idealists ... a measure of how difficult it is to envision a social order that does not rely on the threat of sequestering people in dreadful places designed to separate them from their communities and families.

(Davis 2003: 10)

In taking incarceration 'for granted', the spectre emerges; it has become 'an inevitable fact of life, like birth and death' (Davis 2003: 15).

Introducing her report, Corston was unequivocal regarding penal abolition: 'I do not believe, like some campaigners, that no women should ever be held in custody' (Corston 2007: i). Yet she concluded that, for many women committed to prison, a comprehensive and appropriate programme of alternatives should be established. By enabling smaller prison units adapted to the needs of those women who she considered to require a prison sentence, the logic was that imprisonment would be used sparingly and have the capacity to adapt to the specific needs of those sentenced. Corston proposed the administration of women's custody not by the Prison Service but by 'specialists in working with women' (Corston 2007: 86). This was a key recommendation, immediately dismissed by the government. Prior to Corston, it was well established that prisons were used inappropriately to warehouse women suffering mental illness, who self-harmed and were suicidal.

This included those whose erratic behaviour or impoverished circumstances resulted in repeated low-level offending behaviour, leading to a revolving door of short sentences. Almost three decades ago, Pat Carlen (1990) argued that a reduction in the prison population could be achieved by reducing prison sentences, specifically, by eliminating women's incarceration. This did not happen, and women's imprisonment increased globally, in some jurisdictions, exponentially. In response to penal expansionism, David Scott and Helen Codd (2010: 163) argue for a 'radical rethink of the confinement process itself', coupled with 'profound social change, rooted in a commitment to human rights and social justice'.

In all UK jurisdictions, prison directorates claim adherence to international rights standards in constructing and delivering fair, just and enlightened regimes. Prison inspectorates regularly assess each institution's 'health' using four principles adopted from the World Health Organisation: personal safety, human rights compliance, purposeful activity and preparation for resettlement into the community. Recent prison inspections in England and Northern Ireland have revealed institutionalised, persistent abuses of discretionary powers. As with Corston, however, implementation of the inspectorates' recommendations has been limited. and in some prisons, follow-up inspections have revealed further deterioration in conditions previously assessed as inadequate.

In July 2016, the closure of London's Holloway women's prison had a 'significant impact on the women's estate resulting in more [over]crowding in the remaining women's prisons' (HMCIP 2017: 24). Transfer to other prisons further from home also inhibited family visits. Noting that 'women arriving in custody were more vulnerable' than in previous inspections, the Chief Inspector for England and Wales recorded significantly 'increased levels of reported vulnerability, mental health problems, substance misuse problems and safety concerns, all of which might contribute to self-inflicted deaths in custody' (HMCIP 2017: 55). The expectation of time out-of-cell remains limited to 10 hours per 24-hour period; in some women's prisons, even this restricted period was attained by just 21 per cent of the population.

The inspectorates, however, together with Independent Monitoring Boards and the offices of Prisoner Ombudsmen, continue to operate on the presumption that policy reforms and their implementation can protect rights and deliver sound health within tightly controlled and debilitating regimes. Alternatively, critical research within prisons together with prisoners' testimonies suggest that conceptually, the 'healthy prison' is a contradiction in terms.

McCulloch and Scraton (2009: 11) argue that the premise of contemporary reformism 'facilitates a politics of incorporation in which places of detention become "rights-compliant", their managers and staff gain rights, management and protection diplomas and independent monitors annually report their visits and inspections'. Yet, they argue, 'the violence of incarceration is historically, socially and culturally imprinted on the foundations of the prison'.

It is instructive to return to the earlier Scandinavian work on penal abolition. Mathiesen (1990: 139) specified three core elements that together deny abolitionism political legitimacy. First, the 'widest public sphere', dominated by the 'whole range of modern mass media'. Second, the 'narrower public sphere, consisting of institutions directly engaged in crime prevention such as the police, the courts, the prosecuting authorities and the prisons themselves'. Third, the 'even narrower sphere consisting of particular professional groups' (Mathiesen 1990: 139). The latter includes independent agencies and professionals who claim to represent, monitor and guarantee prisoners' 'best interests'. As Mathiesen (1990: 140) concludes, however, denial of the abject failure of prisons to realise their objectives while breaching prisoners' rights is reflected in the persistent 'pretence' by *all* 'participants' that prisons are 'a success'.

Central to critical analysis of incarceration is the assertion that, within advanced democratic societies, its role and function has to be contextualised and analysed within the ideological, political and economic construction of 'crime', 'criminality' and 'criminal justice'. This requires the rethinking of the proposition that in its commission, 'crime' is 'exceptional', and those who commit criminal acts constitute a 'special category of people' (Hulsman 1986: 63). Challenging mainstream analyses within criminology and criminal justice policy, Louk Hulsman (1986: 67) proposes 'the *abolition* of criminal justice as we know it'. He condemns state-funded criminology for perpetuating the language and discourse of crime, criminality and criminal justice and, therefore, ignoring independent, critical scholarship. 'Crime', he argues, has no intrinsic identity; it is not the *object* but the *product* of criminal policy' (Hulsman 1986: 71). As an institutional process, criminal justice policy and its administration sidelines the relationship between the victim and perpetrator, handing considerable power to 'professionals, whose main interest is not related to the original event, but their daily work in criminal justice' (Hulsman 1986: 72).

Thus, within democratic societies, the abolitionist agenda is not limited to the operational contexts and daily routines of incarceration. It challenges societal definitions of 'crime' and 'criminal justice', interrogating the processes through which criminalising labels are politically constructed and differentially applied. While administrative criminology reflects the traditional linear progression from cause to consequence, critical analyses seek to understand context. By identifying and understanding the political-economic and sociocultural dynamics involved in defining, targeting and regulating 'crime', critical analyses reject pathological explanations – both individual and social – that inform correction and punishment, exposing the limitations of criminalisation in definition, in regulation and in punishment.

Critical analyses propose that the social, political and interpersonal conflicts in and between communities can be identified, understood and addressed only by focusing on the experiential world of everyday life as contextualised within the structural relations of power, authority and legitimacy (see: Scraton 2007). Within these determining contexts, individuals have the limited capacity and opportunity to be active agents in mapping their destinies. They make choices, think differently, act spontaneously, interact responsively and react on impulse or with considered judgement. As 'agents', they also resist the imposition of controls and regulations. They organise, campaign and collectivise their actions in social movements. Yet there are institutional and structural limits to agency. The structural relations on which political economies are built, together with state and private institutions, limit the full potential – agency – of social interaction and personal opportunity. Nowhere is this more evident than in law enforcement, criminal justice and punishment.

Opposition to the powerful punishment lobby underpinning the inexorable expansion of prisons has created a dilemma for abolitionists impelled into arguing for penal reform and prisoners' rights while being well aware that 'frameworks that rely exclusively on reforms help to produce the stultifying idea that nothing lies beyond the prison' (Davis 2003: 103). At the helm of the 'anti-prison movement', Davis remains committed to 'the abolition of the prison as the dominant mode of punishment' while sustaining 'genuine solidarity with the millions of men, women and children who are behind bars'. The challenge for abolitionists is to campaign for 'humane, habitable environments for people in prison without bolstering the permanence of the prison system'. While dismantling prisons, creating alternatives and putting a brake on prison reconstruction remain key objectives, the privations endured by those currently incarcerated require immediate attention.

In the UK, Carol Smart (1976) and Pat Carlen (1983) laid the foundations on which contemporary critical feminist research into the criminalisation, punishment and incarceration of women was built. The consolidation of what has been portrayed as 'second-wave' feminism emphasised the significance of gender-specificity in understanding the relationships between gender, 'crime' and 'deviance'. Central to this understanding is the complexity of relationships contextualised by social, cultural, political and economic determinants that have direct bearing on the marginalisation, regulation and exclusion of women in their communities. These are evident most starkly in the statistics, official and unreported, recording women as 'victims' and/or survivors of male violence – in childhood and adulthood, in the home and on the street, in peace and war.

Alongside these manifestations of direct, oppressive abuse are portrayals of women-as-deviant/as-criminal. It was in this political ideological context that the incarceration of women in prisons and in asylums consolidated. As well as transgressing the law, 'criminal' or 'deviant' women are portrayed as defying the gendered moral code, betraying their womanhood, hence their representation as 'doubly deviant'. While feminist scholarship and activism consolidated their opposition to women's incarceration, successive governments failed to respond. Eventually, the Corston Review at least implicitly acknowledged this body of work. Yet, as the preceding articles in this collection demonstrate, ten years on, Corston's recommendations for meaningful progress towards understanding and responding appropriately to women in conflict with the law remain unaddressed. The institutional denial of her unequivocal yet modest reformism is itself a stark representation of women's societal marginalisation.

Regarding the reformist agenda, Cassandra Shaylor (2009: 148) raises concerns about an unquestioning commitment to 'gender responsiveness'. While this appears to address the needs and experiences of women prisoners, she argues that women's needs are 'complex and changing' rather than consistent and fixed. Improving conditions and programmes for women as a generic, gender-specific category also reinforces notions of respectability and compliance. Shaylor's concern, therefore, is that rather than freeing women prisoners from the expectation of compliance, gender responsiveness affirms the pathology of 'deviant' when applied to women prisoners who refuse to accept the authority imposed on their behaviour, appearance and relationships. In so doing, it neglects the personal, familial and material circumstances that contextualise and individualise their ascribed offending behaviour while failing to understand and respond to their complex physical and mental health needs.

This is a systemic failure rooted in communities riven by poverty and inequality as manifestations of class, race and gender. In advanced capitalist societies founded on the principle of wealth accumulation, it is not by chance that women and men who are politically disenfranchised and economically marginalised are over-represented in prison. To address the inevitability of incarceration within excluded communities, Angela Davis (2003: 107) argues for a 'constellation of alternative strategies and institutions' supported by the 'revitalization of education at all levels, a health system that provides free physical and mental health care to all, and a justice system based on reparation and reconciliation rather than retribution and vengeance'. Within the prison, women's suffering adds significantly to the alienation and objectification already endured in the community. Their suffering cannot wait for abolition. As Corston demonstrates in the UK, starkly reinforced by the 2017 Prisons Inspectorate report, immediate reforms are imperative. Priorities are living conditions and accommodation; gender-appropriate policies, regimes and programmes, including education and training; physical and mental ill health; and where appropriate, supported access to family and children.

For prison abolitionists, commitment to campaigns for improved prison conditions and regimes sensitive to the diversity of incarcerated women is a challenge. Political and media exploitation of the proposition that the prison industrial complex is a logical and necessary consequence of 'crime' and 'criminality' remains central to its maintenance and expansion. In her extensive critiques of Canadian penal reformism, Kelly Hannah-Moffat (2002: 203–204) notes the abject, institutional failure of the 'women-centred ideal' as policies and practices remain 'governed by material structures, cultural sensibilities and mentalities' and limit 'the extent to which the content of a regime can be changed', not least because it remains contextualised by 'punishment, security and discipline'. Further, Pat Carlen and Anne Worrall (2004: 174) note how the 'radical critique' has been partially incorporated into state-initiated penal reformism. This is evident in the adoption of 'key feminist concepts' within the 'official discourse on the reform of women's prisons' amounting to a 'vibrant carceral clawback'.

Yet, as established throughout this collection, the long history of penal abolitionism reveals campaigns that were – and remain – predicated on exposing the inhumanity of locking people away without consideration or understanding of their material circumstances, mental health or social/cultural contexts. Within prison regimes, compliance becomes the only test of prisoners' progress towards release, determining the specific conditions and daily routines imposed. Those in authority, whether managers, guards or associated professionals, present the 'model prisoner' as the woman, man or child who never questions or complains, who trades personal will and social consciousness for an unquestioning obedience to unbending institutional rules and their often arbitrary imposition. The relationship between prisoner and captor is predicated on the constantly proclaimed assumption that incarceration is a rational process realised within rights-compliant facilities, staffed by empathetic guards and associated professionals whose interventions are primarily humanitarian. In exposing the deceit of the rehabilitation agenda, informed arguments for decarceration are crucial in winning public support for well-funded and creative alternatives to prison. Pressing for humanitarian conditions in the short term does not necessarily reinforce, reproduce or perpetuate the compromised history of penal reformism. Neither does it detract from the long-term abolitionist objective.

Acknowledgements

Many thanks to Deena Haydon and Linda Moore, who read and commented on the draft. In memory of Ciara McCulloch.

References

Alexander, M. (2010) *The New Jim Crow: Mass Incarceration in the Age of Colorblindness*, New York: The New Press.

Anthony, T. (2016) 'Deaths in Custody 25 Years After the Royal Commission We've Gone Backwards', *The Conversation*, April. https://theconversation.com/deaths-in-custody-25-years-after-the-royal-commission-weve-gone-backwards-57109.

Baldry, E., Carlton, B. and Cunneen, C. (2015) 'Abolitionism and the Paradox of Penal Reform in Australia: Indigenous Women, Colonial Patriarchy and Co-Option', *Social Justice*, Vol. 41, No. 3, pp. 168–189.

Baldry, E. and Cunneen, C. (2014) 'Imprisoned Indigenous Women and the Shadow of Colonial Patriarchy', *Australian and New Zealand Journal of Criminology*, Vol. 46, No. 3, pp. 276–298.

Birch, T. (2007) 'The Invisible Fire: Indigenous Sovereignty, History and Responsibility,' in Morton-Robinson, A. (ed) *Sovereign Subjects: Indigenous Sovereignty Matters*, Sydney, Australia: Allen & Unwin, pp. 105–117.

Blue, E. (2016) 'Seeing Ms Dhu: Inquest, Conquest, and (In)visibility in Black Women's Deaths in Custody', *Settler Colonial Studies*, Taylor & Francis. doi:10.1080/2201473X.2016.1229294, accessed 27/2/17.

Bosworth, M. (1999) *Engendering Resistance: Agency and Power in Women's Prisons*, Dartmouth: Ashgate.

Carlen, P. (1983) *Women's Imprisonment: A Study in Social Control*, London: Routledge and Kegan Paul.

Carlen, P. (1990) *Alternatives to Women's Imprisonment*, Milton Keynes: Open University.

Carlen, P. and Worrall, A. (2004) *Analysing Women's Imprisonment*, Cullompton: Willan Publishing.

Carlton, B. (2016) 'Penal Reform, Anti-Carceral Campaigns and the Politics of Penal Change in Women's Prisons, Victoria, Australia', *Punishment and Society*, doi:10.1177/1462474516680205.

Carlton, B. and Russell, E. (2015) 'Agenda for Change: Cycles of Women's Penal Reform and Reconfigurations of Anti-Prison Resistance in Victoria, Australia', *Champ Pénal/ Penal Fields*, Vol. XII, pp. 2–21.

Cavadino, M. and Dignan, J. (2007) *The Penal System: An Introduction* (4th edition), London: Sage.

Corston, J. (2007) *The Corston Report: A Review of Women with Particular Vulnerabilities in the Criminal Justice System*, London: Home Office.

Christie, N. (1981) *Limits to Pain*, Oxford: Oxford University Press.

Christie, N. (1994) *Crime Control as Industry* (2nd edition), London: Routledge.

Cole, G. D. H. and Postgate, R. (1961) *The Common People*, London: Methuen and Co.

Crewe, B., Hulley, S. and Wright, S. (2017) 'The Gendered Pains of Life Imprisonment', *British Journal of Criminology*, doi:10.17863/CAM.7437.

Critical Resistance (2005) *Instead of Prisons: A Handbook for Abolitionists*, Oakland, CA: Prison Education Action Project/Critical Resistance.

Critical Resistance (2017) *Toward Liberation: Organizing for Liberation, Defending against Fear: Annual Report*. Oakland, CA: Critical Resistance.

Cunneen, C., Baldry, E., Brown, D., Brown, M., Schwartz, M. and Steel, A. (2013) *Penal Culture and Hyperincarceration: The Revival of the Prison*, Aldershot: Ashgate.

Currie, E. (1998) *Crime and Punishment in America*, New York: Holt.

Davis, A. Y. (2003) *Are Prisons Obsolete?* New York: Seven Stories.

Davis, A. Y. (2016) *Freedom Is a Constant Struggle: Ferguson, Palestine and the Foundations of a Movement*, Chicago, IL: Haymarket Books.

Fleury-Steiner, B. and Longazel, J. (2014) *The Pains of Mass Imprisonment*, New York: Routledge.

Forman, J. (2017) *Locking Up Our Own: Crime and Punishment in Black America*, New York: Farrar, Straus and Giroux.

Foucault, M. (1977) *Discipline and Punish: The Birth of the Modern Prison System*, London: Allen Lane.

Gilmore, R. W. (2007) *Golden Gulag: Prisons, Surplus, Crisis, and Opposition in Globalizing*, Berkeley, CA: University of California Press.

Goffman, E. (1968) *Asylums: Essays on the Social Situation of Mental Patients and Other Inmates*, Harmondsworth: Penguin.

Gordon, A. F. (2009) 'The United States Military Prison', in Scraton, P. and McCulloch, J. (eds) *The Incarceration of Women: Punishing Bodies, Breaking Spirits*, London: Palgrave Macmillan, pp. 164–186.

Hannah-Moffat, K. (2002) 'Creating Choices: Reflecting on Choices', in P. Carlen (ed) *Women and Punishment: The Struggle for Justice*, Cullompton: Willan Publishing.

HMCIP (2017) *HM Chief Inspector of Prisons for England and Wales, Annual Report, 2016–17*, London: HMCIP.

Hulsman, L. (1986) 'Critical Criminology and the Concept of Crime', *Contemporary Crises*, Vol. 10, pp. 63–80.

Ignatieff, M. (1978) *A Just Measure of Pain*, London: Macmillan.

Johnson, E. (1991) *Royal Commission into Aboriginal Deaths in Custody, National Report*, Canberra: Australian Government Publishing Service.

Law, V. (2009) *Resistance behind Bars: The Struggles of Incarcerated Women*, Oakland, CA: PM Press.

Leder, D. (2004) 'Imprisoned Bodies: The Life-World of the Incarcerated', *Social Justice*, Vol. 31, No. 1–2, pp. 51–66.

Mathiesen, T. (1990) *Prison on Trial*, London: Sage.

Mathiesen, T. (2008) 'Response: The Abolitionist Stance', *Journal of Prisoners on Prisons*, Vol. 17, No. 2, pp. 58–63.

McCulloch, J. and George, A. (2009) 'Naked Power: Strip Searching in Women's Prisons', in Scraton, P. and McCulloch, J. (eds) *The Incarceration of Women: Punishing Bodies, Breaking Spirits*, London: Palgrave Macmillan, pp. 107–123.

McCulloch, J. and Scraton, P. (2009) 'The Violence of Incarceration: An Introduction', in Scraton, P. and McCulloch, J. (eds) *The Violence of Incarceration*, London: Routledge, pp. 1–18.

Medlicott, D. (2009) 'Preventing Torture and Casual Cruelty through Independent Monitoring', in Scraton, P. and McCulloch, J. (eds) *The Incarceration of Women: Punishing Bodies, Breaking Spirits*, London: Palgrave Macmillan, pp. 244–260.

Moore, L. and Scraton, P. (2014) *The Incarceration of Women: Punishing Bodies, Breaking Spirits*, London: Palgrave Macmillan.

Quinney, R. (2006) 'The Life Inside: Abolishing the Prison', *Contemporary Justice Review*, Vol. 9, No. 3, pp. 269–275.

Parenti, C. (1999) *Lockdown America: Police and Prisons in the Age of Crisis*, London: Verso.

Porter, A. (2016) 'Why We Should Honour the Humanity of Every Person Who Dies in Custody', *The Conversation*, https://theconversation.com/why-we-should-honour-the-humanity-of-every-person-who-dies-in-custody-57272.

Rodriguez, D. (2009) 'A Reign of Penal Terror: United States Global Statecraft and the Technology of Punishment and Capture', in Scraton, P. and McCulloch, J. (eds) *The Incarceration of Women: Punishing Bodies, Breaking Spirits*, London: Palgrave Macmillan, pp. 187–208.

Ryan, M. and Sim, J. (2016) 'Campaigning for and Campaigning against Prisons: Excavating and Reaffirming the Case for Prison Abolition', in Jewkes, Y., Bennett, J. and Crewe, B. (eds) *Handbook on Prisons*, (2nd ed), London: Routledge. pp. 712–734.

Ryan, M. and Ward, T. (2015) 'Prison Abolition in the UK: They Dare Not Speak Its Name?' *Social Justice*, Vol. 41, No. 3, pp. 107–119.

Scott, D. and Codd, H. (2010) *Controversial Issues in Prisons*, Maidenhead: Open University Press.

Scraton, P. (2007) *Power, Conflict and Criminalisation*, London: Routledge.

Scraton, P. (2016) 'Bearing Witness to the "Pain of Others"': Researching Power, Violence and Resistance in a Women's Prison', *International Journal for Crime, Justice and Social Democracy*, Vol. 5 No. 1, pp. 5–20.

Scraton, P. and Moore, L. (2007) *The Prison within: The Imprisonment of Women and Girls at Hydebank Wood*, Belfast: Northern Ireland Human Rights Commission.

Shaylor, C. (1998) 'It's like Living in a Black Hole: Women of Color and Solitary Confinement in the Prison Industrial Complex', *Criminal and Civil Confinement*, Vol. 24, pp. 385–416.

Shaylor, C. (2009) 'Neither Kind nor Gentle: The Perils of Gender Responsive Justice', in Scraton, P. and McCulloch, J. (eds) *The Incarceration of Women: Punishing Bodies, Breaking Spirits*, London: Palgrave Macmillan, pp. 145–163.

Sim, J. (2009) *Punishment and Prisons: Power and the Carceral State*, London: Sage.

Simon, J. (2007) *Governing through Crime*, Oxford: Oxford University Press.

Smart, C. (1976) *Women, Crime and Criminology*, London: Routledge and Kegan Paul.

Western, B. (2006) *Punishment and Inequality in America*, New York: Russell Sage Foundation.

Whitman, J. Q. (2005) *Harsh Justice: Criminal Justice and the Widening Divide between America and Europe*, Oxford: Oxford University Press.

Wilde, O. (n.d.) *The Ballad of Reading Gaol*, London: Heron Books

Wolfe, P. (2001) 'Land, Labor, and Difference: Elementary Structures of Race', *American Historical Review*, Vol. 106, No. 3, pp. 866–905.

Women in Prison (2017) *Corston+10*, London: Women in Prison.

INDEX

A Better Way 74
abolitionist organisations 182, 184
abolition of prisons 8, 24–6, 33, 71, 84,
    119–22, 184–90; arguments for 24–6, 33;
    in Australia 131; lack of 179; politics of
    172–90; tensions between penal reform
    and 80–1, 132, 136
Aboriginal women: criminalisation
    and incarceration of 7, 115, 182–4;
    discrimination against 137–8; increasing
    rate in prison 138–9; over-representation
    among women prisoners 134, 135; penal
    management in Canada 113; poor prison
    conditions of 140
abortion 8, 151
abuse histories of women prisoners 164–7
Acker, Sandra 63
activism. *see* prison activism
addiction 110
administrative segregation 116
admissions process for prisoners 163
Advisory Board for Female Offenders 21
Africa, Adelene 166
Africa and imprisonment of women
    150–68
African Charter on Human and People's
    Rights 167
African Commission's Special Rapporteur
    on Prisons and Conditions of Detention
    in Africa 151, 168
ageing prison population 22
agency and women prisoners 55–6, 64, 101,
    175–6, 188

Alana House 44
Albertson, Katherine 43
Alexander, Michelle 181
All Party Parliamentary Group on Women
    in the Penal System 20, 45
Angiolini, Elish 76, 77, 80
Annison, Jill 4
anti-carceral activities in Australia 135–7
anti-carceral feminists 131, 183
Anti-Discrimination Board (ADB) 138
Anti-Discrimination Commission
    Queensland (ADCQ) 137
anti-discrimination mechanisms for
    incarcerated women 7, 137–8, 183
Armagh Gaol 89
Article 5 Initiative 153–4
Artz, Lillian 8, 158, 161, 163, 164, 166
Asha Centre 35, 36, 45
Ash House 89, 99, 102
Assessment, Care in Custody and Teamwork
    (ACCT) documents 56–7
Association of Chief Officers of
    Probation 42
austerity policies impacting criminalisation
    of women 57–8
Australia 7–8; current prison environment
    in 138–43; institutionalised racism and
    resistance in prisons in 182–4; Miranda
    Project 129; penal reforms in 183–4;
    prison expansion in 140–4, 183; prison
    reform and activism in 130–2; trying to
    improve women's imprisonment 129–45;
    women's imprisonment rate in 130,

138–9; women's prison action groups 132–5

Aylesbury Convict Prison for Women 12

Bacon, Wendy 132
bail: applications and their delays 96–7; sentencing decisions and 90; support service provision 97
Baker, Anna 1, 10
Baldry, Eileen 7, 131, 139
The Ballad of Reading Gaol 173–4
Bandyup Women's Prison 140
Bar None Winnipeg 120
Bassel, Leah 58
battered women killing intimate partner 132, 158
Belfast Metropolitan College (BMC) 100
Bell, Virginia 133
benefit policies 57–8
Bethlem Hospital (London) 12
Better Outcomes for Women Offenders 44
Better Prisons 142
Beyond Bars Alliance 138
Black and Minority Ethnic (BME) incarcerated women 3, 11, 14, 16, 55, 58, 61–3, 181
Blair, Tony 19, 33
Blue, Ethan 182
Boronia Women's Prison 140
Bosworth, Mary 175–6
Breaking the Cycle 20
bridewells 12
Brighton Women's Centre 39, 41
Brisbane Women's Correctional Centre 139
Broadmoor Criminal Lunatic Asylum 12
Brockhill 54
burglary 35
Burke, Sarah 65
Burman, Michele 75
Bush, George W. 179

Cambridge Women's Resources Centre 36
Cameron, Edwin 160
Campaign for the Prevention of Custodial Death 131
Campbell, Sarah 1, 10
Canada: federal corrections for women in 7, 109–22; gendered violence in prisons 117–19; impact of *Creating Choices* philosophy for women in 109–22; lack of women-centred corrections in 7; segregation of women in prisons 116–17; therapeutic controls for women in prison 111, 114–16
Canadian Association of Elizabeth Fry Societies (CAEFS) 114, 121, 137

Canadian Civil Liberties Association 121
Canadian Human Rights Act 137
Canadian Human Rights Commission (CHRC) 137
carceral clawback 2, 5, 24, 131
carceral Other 53–7, 112–14
Carlen, Pat 2, 4, 5, 14, 15, 24–5, 32–3, 52, 57, 58, 110, 186, 188, 189
Carleton University 120
Carlton, Bree 8, 52, 53, 121, 130–1
'Cat and Mouse' Act 174
Catholicism 91
Cavadino, Michael 22, 24, 174
218 Centre (Scotland) 34, 36, 74–5
Centre for Justice Exchange 121
Chadwick, Kathryn 6, 26, 52, 57, 68
Champion for Women in the Criminal Justice System 18
Changing Lives 44
Chartrand, Vicki 7
children and loss experienced by imprisoned women 2, 14, 16, 36, 79, 94, 154, 165
Children of Prisoners Support Group 133
Christie, Nils 119, 175, 178
Clarke, Becky 26
Clarke, Ken 20
Clarke, Peter 21
Clarke, Rebecca 6
Clinks 44
Clinton, Bill 180
clothes' removal from prisoners symbolic of stripping of rights 176
Coalition Government 18, 42
Codd, Helen 177, 186
Cognitive Behavioural Therapy (CBT) 94, 114–15
Cohen, Stan 73
Commission on Women Offenders 6, 75–9, 81, 83
committal landing 99–100
community-based programmes 6, 15, 21, 37, 80–1, 131, 132, 185
community-based women's centres 6, 32, 74–9, 143, 172
Community Rehabilitation Companies (CRCs) 32, 42–5
Community Restorative Centre 129, 143
community sentences decrease 46
community services for women offenders 38–41, 76
Competition Strategy for Offender Services 42
Conservative Government (UK) 5, 18, 33, 41, 58

Conservative-Liberal Coalition Government (UK) 5, 19
control and surveillance strategies in prison 102–3
Cook, Dee 58
Corbyn, Jeremy 21
Cornton Vale prison (Scotland) 1, 2, 6, 74–5
Corporate Manslaughter and Corporate Homicide Act (2007) 24
Correctional Service Canada (CSC) 82, 110, 137
Correctional Services Act 154
2003 Correctional Services Review 42
Corrective Services NSW 142
Corston, Jean 1, 2–4, 7, 10, 11, 12, 15–22, 25, 32, 35, 37, 51–5, 71, 73–5, 77, 78, 82, 83, 88–90, 93, 96–8, 103, 129–31, 150, 152, 156, 165, 185, 186, 189
Corston Independent Funders Coalition 39
Corston Report 38, 46, 74–6, 109, 129, 131, 134, 143, 144, 151, 162, 167
Corston Review 172, 188
Council For Civil Liberties 132
Craig, Celeste 51
Creating Choices: The Report of the Task Force on Federally Sentenced Women 78, 109–11, 122
'Creating Choices' initiative 7, 54
Creative Interventions Group 120
Crenshaw, Kimberlé 144
Crewe, Ben 25, 177
crime: definitions of 187; industry of crime control 178; seriousness being matched to severity of punishment 174
Crime Trust Fund 180
criminalisation of women 6, 52; Black and Minority Ethnic (BME) women 3, 11, 14, 16, 55, 58, 61–3, 181; disproportionate rates of Foreign National women 61; feminist research into 188; harsher law enforcement and 8, 35, 141–2, 179–83; impacted by political and economic contexts 57–8; of the 'medical' 95; of migration 2, 13; poverty and 2–4, 8, 11, 13–14, 36, 51–5, 58, 60, 72, 80, 89–92, 110–15, 166–7, 176, 179–83; prison-based oppression and 130; race and gender of 60–3; significance of home and family 58–60; social deprivation 80; state's power to punish and 52; of women's survival strategies 13
Criminalization and Punishment Education Project 120
criminal justice, definitions of 187
Criminal Justice Act 1991 33
Criminal Justice Act 2003 34

Criminal Justice Women's Strategy Group 18
Criminal Law Amendment Act 105, 157
criminal personality storyline of women prisoners 115
Critical Resistance 182, 185
Crook, Francis 25
cultural expectations for women and their deviance 91
Cunneen, Chris 139
Currie, Elliott 179
custodial alternatives 76–9, 172
custodial centres 17, 19, 21, 79, 97–8; failure to build 103
custodial remand. *see* remand
custodial sentencing 157; over-utilisation of 152
custody: deaths while in 1, 3, 5, 10, 11, 15, 23–4, 35, 51, 65, 74, 139, 158–9; increased use of for women 35, 46; offering rehabilitation 2; recalled to 46

Davis, Angela 184, 185, 188, 189
DCS Annual Report of 2015/16, 156–7
death of women in prison 1, 3, 5, 10, 11, 15, 23–4, 35, 51, 65, 74, 139, 158–9; Aboriginal women 131, 135, 182–3
decarceration 8, 11, 16–21; politics of 172–90
dehumanisation 176
Department of Correctional Services (DCS) 154
detention, arbitrary 151
deterrence of crime 175
deviant women 91–2, 112, 188; categorised as bad or mad 12
deviation and their causes 95–6
Dignan, James 174
disadvantaged women in prison 4, 51–2, 75, 76, 113, 117
disciplinary segregation 116
discrimination: in decarceration of minorities 62–3; against women in prison 137–40, 151
A Distinct Approach: A Guide for Working with Women Offenders 38
Dobash, Rebecca and Russell 32
2015 Doha Declaration 167
domestic violence leading to incarceration 132
Douglas, Nicola 35
Drake, Deborah 25
drug-related offences and incarceration 181
drug users in prison 74, 94

du Preez, Max 158
Durban Prison 161
duty of care of prisoners 178

Eagle, Maria 18, 19
economically related crimes caused by
women 157
economic marginalisation of incarcerated
women 52, 57–9, 101, 189
Edward, Susan 58
*Effective Interventions for Women Offenders: A
Rapid Evidence Assessment* 44
Emejulu, Awugo 58
empowerment of criminalised women
55–6, 64, 94, 115
End the Prison Industrial Complex 121
enforced isolation 176
England. *see* United Kingdom
Epstein, Rona 59
Equality Act 2006, 36
Equality Duty 38
equality with other public sector duties 36
Equal Opportunity Commission 137

Fairlea Research Group 131, 137
Fairlea Women's Prison Campaign 136
Faith, Karlene 120, 122
family home and criminalisation of women
58–60
family visits 98
Fawcett Society 36, 57
Fell, Liz 132
female gender roles 94
*Female Offenders in the Criminal Justice
System* 75
feminist jurisprudence 33
Feminist Legal Action Group (FLAG) 132
feminist politics 132
feminist research into criminalisation 188
Flat Out Inc. 136, 184
Ford, David 99
Foreign National women 3, 11, 15, 16,
22–3, 61
Forman, James 181
Foucault, Michel 93, 174
Fox, Chris 43
*From Vision to Reality: Transforming Scotland's
Care of Women in Custody* 79
Fry, Elizabeth 4, 12, 17

Gelsthorpe, Loraine 6, 36, 43, 80
gender: differences in offending 2;
discrimination 8; disproportionate
criminalisation rates and 61–3;

incarceration and 2, 14, 52, 58–60,
98–100, 181; inequality 91;
responsiveness to women prisoners 189;
violence in prisons and 94, 111, 117–19
gender duty 36
gendered deviance 92
2007 Gender Equality Duty 20
Gender Equality Schemes 20
Gender Impact Statements (GIAs) 36
gender-related offences 158
gender-specific prison regimes 2, 15, 188
Gender Specific Standards for Women
Prisoners 18, 20
'Gender Specific Strategy' 101
George, Amanda 176
Gilmore, Ruth Wilson 176
Gladstone Committee 24
Gloucester's model prison 12
Goffman, Erving 175
Gordon, Avery 180
Gordon, Mary 63–4
Gove, Michael 21
Government Equalities Office 38
Grafton 142
Grand Valley Institution for Women 118
Grayling, Chris 20

halfway houses 33
Hannah-Moffat, Kelly 54, 110, 115, 189
Hardwick, Nick 20
Hawton, Keith 15
healthcare services of incarcerated women
14, 102, 162–4
Hedderman, Carol 37, 43
Heidensohn, Frances 32
Hjemdal, Kristian 83
HM Inspectorate of Prisons for
Scotland 73
HMP Bronzefield 19, 56
HMP Cornton Vale 14, 52, 72, 76, 78, 80
HMP Doncaster 65
HMP Drake Hall 65
HMP Eastwood Park 21, 56
HMP Holloway 13, 21, 24, 186
HMP Inverclyde 79
HMP Styal 1, 10–11, 21, 35, 65, 74
homelessness 91
House of Commons Justice Committee 18,
21, 44
houses of correction 12
Howard, John 12
Howard League for Penal Reform 32
Hulley, Susie 177
Hulsman, Louk 187

human rights in prison settings 153–4, 177
Hydebank Wood prison 52, 96, 99,
    101, 102
Hydebank Wood Secure College 100–1

Ignatieff, Michael 174
illegal drug use 92
imaginary penalty in prison 101
immigration detention 61
immigration removal centres 22–3
imprisonment: in Africa 150–68;
    alternatives to 6, 15, 36, 76–81, 185; in
    Australia 129–45; of Black and Minority
    Ethic (BME) women 3, 11, 14, 16,
    55, 58, 61–3, 181; contextualisation of
    12–15, 187–8; damaging effects of 3;
    for drug-related offences 181; failure to
    reduce rate of 63–4; healthcare services
    of women in 14, 102, 162–4; industry
    of 178; intensification in USA 179–82;
    for lesser offences 139; in New South
    Wales (NSW) 141–3; overuse for women
    32–3; as a place of safety 166; prisons
    conditions in South Africa 159–61; race
    and 181; rate for Indigenous women
    139, 141–2; rate for women's 1, 13, 22,
    34, 129; rate in New South Wales 134;
    rate in Victoria, Australia 134; for safety
    reasons 96; in Scotland 71–84; in United
    Kingdom 1, 3, 6, 10–24, 32–41; violence
    of 5; for violent crimes 3
incarceration. see imprisonment
Independent Monitoring Board 56
Independent Police Investigative
    Directorate 159
Indigenous women: disadvantaged and
    experiencing force in prisons 117;
    discriminated against in Australian prisons
    137–8; imprisonment in Australia 129,
    139; increase in incarceration of 141–2;
    over-representation in prison 130
indirect discrimination of female prisoners
    in Australia 137–8
individual women's circumstances and
    offending behaviours 4, 6–7, 25–6, 52,
    53, 64, 89, 93
inequality as pathway to offending 5
injustice as pathway to offending 5
INQUEST 17
*Inquiry into Preventing Unnecessary
    Criminalisation of Women* 46
Inquiry into the Increase in Prisoner
    Population 143
Inspector of Custodial Services 140

Inspire Women's Project (Northern Ireland)
    39–41, 103
Institute for Research in Social Services
    (IRISS) 79
Institutional Emergency Response Team
    118
institutional racism 7, 8, 12, 183–4
Interserve 43
interventions, fragmented nature of,
    76–7, 82
Ireland. *see* Northern Ireland
isolation: enforced 176; impacting mental
    health 2, 15, 24–5, 102, 117, 121–2,
    176–7

jails. *see* prisons
Jali Commission 159
Justice Committee 76
Justice Now 182

Kendall, Kathleen 115
Kgosi Mampuru II Prison 161
Kilty, Jennifer 7
Kingston Prison for Women 78, 80

Labour Government (UK) 5, 10, 18,
    33–5, 42
Lammy, David 62
Lansdowne, Robyn 132
Latham, Joanne 11
Law, Victoria 120, 181
Lawrie, Rowena 135
leadership needed for directing female
    penal system 77
Leder, Drew 176
Lemert, Edwin 95
lesbian, gay, bisexual and transgender
    (LGBT) marriage 91–2
lesbians 16
Little, Cath 52, 57, 58
Liverpool Women's Turnaround Project 39
*Luanda Guidelines on the Conditions of Arrest,
    Police Custody and Pre-Trial Detention in
    Africa* 167
Luyt, Louis 158

Maghaberry prison 52, 89
Malloch, Margaret 4, 6
Mama, Amina 58
mandatory minimal sentences 152, 157
Maputo Protocol 167
marginalised women: criminalisation
    trapping 96; economic marginalisation
    impacting criminalisation of women 52,

57–9, 89, 101, 189; nonconformity to heteronormative gender roles and 91; in Northern Ireland 91–3
Mathiesen, Thomas 83, 119, 178, 186–7
Mbkei, Thabo 159
McCulloch, Jude 176, 186
McIvor, Gill 4, 75
McNaull, Gillian 7
medicalisation while incarcerated 12, 95, 98, 115, 162
Medlicott, Diana 177
Melaleuca Remand and Reintegration facility 140
mental healthcare for women in prison 12–13, 75, 91, 162–4; failure to address 101–3
mental ill health 4, 23, 40, 92
mentoring service for women 79, 81
migration, criminalisation of 2, 61
military prison, rise of 180–1
Ministerial Group on Women's Offending 74
Ministry of Justice (MOJ) 21, 38
minority ethnic women. *see* Black and Minority Ethnic (BME) incarcerated women
Miranda Project 129, 143–4
mixed-sex prison 12, 13, 34, 89, 101–2
Montréal Centre les Prisons 121
Moore, Linda 5–6, 52, 117
motherhood while in prison 14, 59
Mourne House Unit at Maghaberry 89
MTC 43
MTCNovo 43
Mulawa Training and Detention Centre 132, 133
Muntingh, Lukas 153

Nacro 43
Nagle Royal Commission 132, 133, 135
National Community Justice and Prison Delivery Board 76
National Institute for Crime Prevention and the Reintegration of Offenders (NICRO) 157
National Offender Management Service (NOMS) 21, 42
National Probation Service (NPS) 6, 42, 47
Native Women's Association of Canada 137
New Economics Foundation 39
New South Wales (NSW) 7, 130, 184; prison activism in 129; women's imprisonment in 134, 141–3
Nicholles, Natalie 39
Nixon, Richard 179

No New Women's Prison Campaign 136
Norma Parker Centre 133
North Coast Correctional Centre 142
Northern Ireland 7; remanded women's experiences in 97–104; women's pathways to offending 90–7, 157
Northern Ireland Department of Justice 90
Northern Ireland Mental Health Order 95
Northern Ireland Prison Rules 100
Northern Ireland Prison Service (NIPS) 99, 102
NSW Aboriginal Justice Advisory Council 135
NSW Women in Prison Advocacy Network 136
NSW Women in Prison Task Force 133–5, 142–3
NSW Women's Correctional Services Advisory Committee 129

observation cell experiences 102–3
Offender Rehabilitation Act 2014, 6, 32; challenges of 41–6
offending: efforts to reduce women's 4, 34–5; gender differences in 2, 158
offending pathways 90–7
Oppler, Sarah 159
oppression in prison and criminalisation 91–2, 94, 130
O'Shane, Pat 133
'othering' criminalised women 53–7
Ouagadougou Declaration and Plan of Action on Accelerating Prison and Penal Reform in Africa 167
Owers, Anne 19

Pankhurst, Sylvia 174
paramilitarism 92
parental responsibility for child's truancy from school 59, 60
Parenti, Christian 180
Pate, Kim 114
pathways to offending 2, 4, 5, 13–14, 25, 90–7, 115
patriarchy: Christian 91; within criminal justice 52; impacting criminalisation of women 57, 139; imprisonment of women and 182–3
payment-by-results 5, 6, 13, 42, 140–1, 144
penal abolition. *see* abolition of prisons
penal expansion 22, 178; in Australia 183; in USA 179–82
penal populism 179

penal reform 4, 6–8, 16–21, 71, 73–4, 119, 172; in Australia 130–2, 183–4; lack of commitment in United Kingdom 173; limitations of 22–4; limited transformative potential of 173–90; tensions between abolition and 80–1, 132, 136; for women in Canada 109–22
personality disorder 95
Peterborough Prison 141
Platform for Gender Justice 182
Player, Elaine 15, 90
Pollack, Shoshana 115
Pollsmoor Prison 160–1
postcolonialism 52
poverty as factor in criminalisation of women 2–3, 8, 11, 13–14, 36, 51–5, 58, 60, 72, 80, 89–92, 110–15, 166–7, 176, 179–83
pregnancy in prison 14
Prevention and Combating of Torture of Persons Act 153
primary deviation 95
prison action groups, women's 132–5
prison activism: in Australia 130–5; in New South Wales (NSW) 129; in Queensland 129; in Victoria 129
prison-associated trauma 15
prison-centricity of government 33
prison deaths 1, 3, 5, 10, 11, 15, 23–4, 35, 51, 65, 74, 139, 158; of Aboriginal women 131, 135, 182–3
Prisoner Education Advocacy Project 185
Prisoner Ombudsman for Northern Ireland (PONI) 102, 186
prisoners: agency of 175–6; characteristics of offending 13–14; as deviant/ as-criminal 188; duty of care of 178; failure to identify and meet needs of 140; gendered discrimination in punishment 118; high rates of victimisation 35; within a male prison 12, 13, 34, 89, 101–2; pathologisation of 12; resistance in prisons 182–3; rights of 167–8; as a social threat in Canada 112; their lives and relationship to offending behaviour 53
1913 Prisoners (Temporary Discharge for Ill-Health) Act 174
Prisoners' Action Group (PAG) 132
Prison Industrial Complex (PIC) 120–1
Prison Justice 121
Prison Moratorium Action Coalition 121
Prison Reform Oversight Committee 99
Prison Reform Trust 20, 32, 77, 78

Prison Review Team Final Report 99
prisons: abolition of for women 8, 24–6, 33, 71, 84, 119–22, 131–2, 172–90; abuses in 186; campaigns against building new ones in Australia 133–8; expansion in Australia 140–4; experiences of women in Ireland 97–103; Gloucester's model 12; ignoring women's needs 16; male-centric design 34, 89, 101–2; mixed-sex 12, 13, 34, 89, 101–2; pregnancy in 14; privatised 42–3, 141; privileges in 175; as profit-making enterprise 5, 6, 13, 42, 140–1, 144; public-private and privatised in Australia 141, 143; punishment in 2–8, 12, 15, 19–20, 54, 59–61, 63–5, 74, 78, 83–4, 93–6, 103–4, 109–11, 116–20, 133, 136, 150–3, 174–9, 181, 183–9; purposeful activity in 100; reduction in the number of 78, 82; regimes being harmful 177–8; in South Africa 156–61; specialty 182; true operation being disguised 175; women population increasing 1, 13, 22, 34, 110, 138, 178
Prisons and Courts Bill 21
Prisons and Probation Ombudsman 1
Prisons Bill 21
prison sentences. *see* sentencing
Prison Service 18
Pritchard, Jeune 132
privatisation of probation caseloads 42–3
probation being privatised 42–3
probation service and the voluntary sector 41–2
probation trusts and their abolishment 42–3
Programme for Government 19
218 project 143
prosecution, alternatives to 75
Protestantism 91
Protocol to the African Charter on Human and People's Rights on the Rights of Women in Africa 167
psychiatry 12
psychologists for prisoners 165
psychopharmaceutical medications 114
psychosocial services in prisons 165–6
psychotropic medications 115
Public Accounts Committee 45
public-private prisons 141, 143
Public Service Commission (PSC) of South Africa 161
Punishment and Reform: Effective Probation Services 42

punishment in prisons 2–8, 12, 15, 19–20,
54, 59–61, 63–5, 74, 78, 83–4, 93–6,
109–11, 116–20, 133, 136, 150–3, 176–9,
181, 183–9; severity being matched to
the seriousness of crime 174–5; tension
with treatment and 103–4
punishment in the community 6
Purple Futures 43

Quakers Fostering Justice/Canadian
Friends Service Committee 121
Queensland 130, 184; prison activism
in 129
Queensland Ombudsman 139
Quinney, Richard 177–8

Race: disproportionate criminalisation rates
and 61–3; incarceration and 181
racial divide in Australian prisons 140
racism 176; in Australian prisons 183–4;
impacting criminalisation of women 57
Ravenhall Prison 141
Reagan, Ronald 179
redress 119
Reducing Re-Offending by Ex-Prisoners 33–4
Reducing Reoffending Change Fund
(RRCF) 81
'Reducing Women Offenders
2013–2016' 90
Reed, Sarah 23
reform: of individual 175; tensions between
abolition and 80–1, 132, 136
reformatory movement 12
reformist reform 120, 122
reformist strategies 131
rehabilitation: challenges of 32, 41–6;
community and women centres 6;
during custody 2; not to be offered by
prisons 178
Reid Howie Associates 79
reintegration into society 175
religion 91–2
remand 7, 17; high number of Australian
women in 134; to process bail
applications 96; rates in Ireland 89,
90; reasons for 90, 96; women's
experiences in Northern Ireland,
88–104
reoffending pathways reduction 37
reoffending rates 40–1
reproductive health needs 14
resettlement by ex-prisoners 15, 36
residential women's centres 103
retributivism 174–5
revolving door syndrome 15

risk paradigm of women 94; public
protection and 93–4
risks 60, 83, 90, 93, 101; criminal risks
linked with social needs 110; in male
prison 101–2; of 'othering' criminalised
women 53–4
Robben Island Guidelines 167
Roberts, Bruce 132
Roberts, Jenny 36
Roberts, Violet 132
Rodriquez, Dyland 181
Royal Commission into Aboriginal Deaths
in Custody (RCIADIC) 131, 135, 182
Ruggiero, Vincenzo 82, 711
Run Ragged 44
Russell, Emma 121
Ryan, Mick 178

same-sex relationship 8, 16, 91–2
'save Fairlea campaign' 135–6
Scotland: imprisonment of women
in 71–84; initiatives in improving
imprisonment of women in 74–80; penal
reform 73–4; use of imprisonment and
noncustodial alternatives 6
Scott, David 25, 177, 186
Scottish Parliament Equal Opportunities
Committee 75
Scottish Prison Commission 75
Scottish Prison System (SPS) 76, 79
Scraton, Phil 8, 52, 103, 117, 186
secondary deviation 95
second-wave feminism 188
sectarianism 89, 91, 92
Section 95 report on women 33
secure college 100–1
security state 93
Segrave, Marie 52, 53
segregation: in Canadian prisons for women
111, 116–17; refusal to
abolish 119
self-harm of women in prison 1, 5, 15, 23,
28, 98, 102, 158; segregation for 117
sentencing 76; arbitrary 152; increase in
157; increasingly severe sentences 75,
179–80; mandatory minimal sentencing
regime in Africa 152
Sentencing Guidelines Council 34
separation from children while in prison 2,
14, 16, 36, 79, 94, 154, 165
severity of crime not related to remanding
reasons 96
sexism 151
sex outside of marriage 8
sexuality and gender models 91

sexual morality 8
sex workers' rights 92
shackling of pregnant women during labour 14
Sharpe, Gilly 36
Shaylor, Cassandra 182, 189
Shine 81
Sim, Joe 175, 178
Sisters Inside 137, 184
Smart, Carol 32, 188
Smith, Ashley 111, 114, 116, 118, 121, 122
Smith, Nissa Ann 1, 10
social disadvantages of women. *see* disadvantaged women in prison
Social Exclusion Report 33–4
Social Exclusion Unit 76
social experiences of women in prison 112
social needs linked with criminal risks 110
social workers for prisoners 165
Social Work Services and Prisons Inspectorates 80
Sodexo Justice Services 43, 140
solitary confinement 116, 176
South Africa: education level 155; HIV prevalence rate 155; imprisonment of women in 8, 150–68; lack of demographics for female prisoners 156–8; population of 155; prisons in 156–61; socio-demographics of 154–6; unemployment rate 155; violent crime in 155
South African Constitution and Bill of Rights 153, 162
SPARS 100, 102–3
Speak Out Speak Strong 135
Stacey, Glenys 45
Standard Guidelines for Corrections in Australia 138
state power 52
Strategic Objectives for Female Offenders 21
'Strategy to Manage Women Offenders and those Vulnerable to Offending Behaviour' 90–1
strip-searching 3, 11, 14, 17–19, 98, 138; symbolic of stripping of rights 176
structural inequalities 4, 6–7, 25–6, 52, 53, 57–8, 83, 93, 95, 134
Structured Supervision Programme 45
Stubbs, Julie 7
Styal prison. *see* HMP Styal
substance addiction 98
suffragettes in prison 174
suicidal ideation 99, 100, 102, 158; segregation for 117
suicide attempts 98, 158

suicide in women's prisons 1, 15, 23
Supporting Prisoners at Risk. *see* SPARS
suspended sentences increase 46
Swift, Jenny 11, 23, 65
Sykes, Gresham 16
systemic discrimination against female prisoners in Australia 137–8

Task Force on Federally Sentenced Women (Canada) 54
television (TV) license convictions for women 59
Termite Collective 121
Thames Valley Community Rehabilitation Company 44
The Conflict (Ireland) 89, 91–2, 94
therapeutic controls in Canadian prisons for women 110–11, 114–16
Thompson, Vicky 11
Thuma, Emily 120
'Together Women' (TW) project 35, 38–41
Tombs, Steve 24
Tomorrow's Women Wirral 143
Torres Strait Islander women: criminisation and incarceration of 7, 182–4; increasing rate in prison 139
torture in prison 153, 159
Transforming Rehabilitation proposals 42
Transgender Case Board 23
transgender women in prison 11, 16, 23, 65
trauma: prison-associated 15; in women's lives 93
Troubled Families Programme 59–60
"troubled" label for criminalised women 55–6
truancy convictions for women 59, 60
Truss, E. 21, 24, 56
Turnaround Project 39
'turning lives around' for criminalised women 56–7, 64

UN Convention against Torture and Other Cruel, Inhuman or Degrading Treatment or Punishment 153
unemployment and incarceration 57, 181
United Kingdom: context of criminalised women in 51–65; failure of reform 10–26; increase in women's imprisonment 1, 13, 22, 34; lack of commitment to penal reform 173; post-Coston developments 32–47
United Nations Rules for the Treatment of Women Prisoners and Non-custodial Measures for Women Offenders (Bangkok Rules) 2, 15, 154, 162, 164, 167

University of Ottawa 120
Unlocking Value 39
USA and mass incarceration 179–82

Vetten, Lisa 150
victimisation 83, 110, 177
victimisation-criminalisation continuum 115
victim/perpetrator dichotomies 93
Victoria (Australia) 7, 184; campaigns against new women's prisons 135–7; prison activism in 129; women's rate of imprisonment 134
Vinson, Tony 131, 133
violence: drugs and 181; against women in prison 2, 5, 38, 164
Violent Crime Control and Law Enforcement Act 180
violent crimes and imprisonment 3
voluntary sector and probation service 41–2
vulnerabilities of imprisoned women 1, 2, 7, 10–11, 13, 15–16, 35, 39, 54, 80, 83–4, 88, 94, 131, 134
vulnerability, gendered 98
vulnerable and controversial use of term 71–2

Wahidin, Azrini 5–6
Wales. *see* United Kingdom
Walsh, Julie 1, 10
Ward, Tony 178
war on drugs 2, 13, 180
war on the poor 13
'welcoming' visitors' centre in prisons 33
Wellington Correctional Centre 142
Western Australia 130
Whitehead, Stephen 39
White Paper on Corrections 162

White Paper on Remand Detention Management 154
Who Cares? Where Next for Women Offender Services?, 44
Wilde, Oscar 173–4
Williams, Hayley 1, 10
Willis, Jolene 1, 10
Willow Project 143
Women Behind Bars (WBB) 132
Women in Prison 24, 173
Women in Prison Advocacy Network 184
Women Offender Model Board 59
Women Offenders: A Safer Way 74, 78
women offender strategy 59
women-only prisons 130
women prisoners. *see* prisoners
Women's Advisory Council of NSW Corrections 143
Women's Breakout 143
women's centres 39; funding of 44–5; referrals to 62–3
Women's Centre Services 40–1
Women's Diversionary Fund 39
Women's Justice Network (WJN) 136–7
Women's Offending Reduction Programme (WORP) 18, 34, 77
Women's Policy Team 34
women's prison action groups in Australia 132–5
Women's Specific Conditional Caution (WSCC) 40
women-wise penology 33
Worrall, Anne 32, 189
Wright, Serena 177
The Wring Outs 136

youth decarceration 62–3
Yúdice, George 114